AFRICA'S LIONS

AFRICA'S LIONS

Growth Traps and Opportunities for Six African Economies

HAROON BHORAT AND FINN TARP

EDITORS

BROOKINGS INSTITUTION PRESS

Washington, D.C.

The Brookings Institution is a private nonprofit organization de-
voted to research, education, and publication on important issues
of domestic and foreign policy. Its principal purpose is to bring the
highest quality independent research and analysis to bear on current and emerging policy problems. Interpretations or conclusions
in Brookings publications should be understood to be solely those
of the authors.

Library of Congress Cataloging-in-Publication data

Names: Bhorat, Haroon, editor. | Tarp, Finn, 1951– editor.
Title: Africa's lions : growth traps and opportunities for six
    African economies / Haroon Bhorat and Finn Tarp, editors.
Description: Washington, D.C. : Brookings Institution Press, 2016. |
    Includes bibliographical references and index.
Identifiers: LCCN 2016031544 (print) | LCCN 2016031765 (ebook) |
    ISBN 9780815729495 (pbk. : alk. paper) | ISBN 9780815729501
    (ebook)
Subjects: LCSH: Africa—Economic conditions—21st century. |
    Economic Development—Africa. | Job creation—Africa.
Classification: LCC HC800 .A57335 2016 (print) | LCC HC800
    (ebook) | DDC 338.96—dc23
LC record available at https://lccn.loc.gov/2016031544

ISBN 978-0-8157-2949-5 (pbk. : alk. paper)
ISBN 978-0-8157-2950-1 (ebook)

9 8 7 6 5 4 3 2 1

Typeset in Electra

Composition by Westchester Publishing Services

Contents

Acknowledgments   vii

1 **The Pursuit of Long-Run Economic
   Growth in Africa**   1
   An Overview of Key Challenges
   HAROON BHORAT *and* FINN TARP

2 **Ethiopia**   37
   An Agrarian Economy in Transition
   YARED SEID, ALEMAYEHU SEYOUM TAFFESSE, *and*
   SEID NURU ALI

3 **Ghana**   77
   A Successful Growth Story
   with Job Creation Concerns
   ERNEST ARYEETEY *and* WILLIAM BAAH-BOATENG

4 **Kenya**   109
   Economic Growth, Labor Market Dynamics, and
   Prospects for a Demographic Dividend
   MWANGI KIMENYI, FRANCIS MWEGA,
   and NJUGUNA NDUNG'U

5 **Mozambique**   145
   Growth Experience through an Employment Lens
   SAM JONES *and* FINN TARP

6 **Nigeria**   181
   The Relationship between Growth and Employment
   OLU AJAKAIYE, AFEIKHENA JEROME, DAVID NABENA,
   and OLUFUNKE ALABA

7 **South Africa**   229
   Demographic, Employment, and Wage Trends
   HAROON BHORAT, KARMEN NAIDOO,
   MORNÉ OOSTHUIZEN, *and* KAVISHA PILLAY

   Contributors   271

   Index   275

Acknowledgments

There can be little doubt that global sentiment around sub-Saharan Africa has changed significantly over the last decade. From being viewed as a continent rife with political and economic uncertainty, together with a tendency toward economic and social collapse, the current dominant view is that sub-Saharan Africa remains the last of the great untapped markets, ripe for rapid growth and development. While research on many of the key themes in African development has increased, there is very little research around trying to understand the relationship between economic growth and employment outcomes at the detailed country level. This book, including its six country case studies of Ethiopia, Ghana, Kenya, Mozambique, Nigeria, and South Africa, together with the editors' introduction, is a successful collaboration of the Brookings Institution, the Development Policy Research Unit of the University of Cape Town, and the United Nations University World Institute for Development Economics Research (UNU-WIDER) to help fill this gap and to stimulate further analytical work in this important area.

The growth of the global working-age population to 2030 will be driven primarily by Africa, so the relationship between population and job growth is best understood within the context of each country's projected demographic challenge and the associated implications for employment growth. Furthermore, a better understanding of the structure of each country's workforce and the implications for human capital development, the vulnerably employed, and the working poor are critical to informing the future development policy agenda. In this sense, outputs from the project that led to this volume can help to inform and guide development policy across these African economies.

We hereby express our sincere appreciation to our collaborating authors who worked with us to implement the African Lions project from its inception in October 2013 to closure in January 2016. They engaged with us in building a quality research team, during which high levels of academic scholarship were maintained, with the results in turn published here for readers to absorb and enjoy.

We wish as well to acknowledge our sincere appreciation for the effective publication support from the Brookings Institution Press and the UNU-WIDER team that helped to publish the working papers. Special thanks go to Sarah Marriott and Toughedah Jacobs for their tireless administrative support to arrange critically important project meetings and to prepare the book manuscript. Thanks are also due to the director of the African Growth Initiative at Brookings Institution, Amadou Sy, for his continued encouragement and assistance.

In addition, Brookings Institution gratefully acknowledges the support provided by the Bill and Melinda Gates Foundation and the William and Flora Hewlett Foundation. Brookings scholars, in conformity with the institution's mission of developing independent, nonpartisan analysis, and recommendations that reflect objective and rigorous scholarship, will make the final determinations regarding the scholarly activities supported by the gift, including the research agenda, content, product, outcomes, use, and distribution of resulting publications, event attendees, and selection of personnel associated with the projects supported by the gift. Brookings scholars and staff will at no time lobby or otherwise promote the interests of any donor.

UNU-WIDER gratefully acknowledges the support and financial contributions to its research program by the governments of Denmark, Finland, Sweden, and the United Kingdom. UNU-WIDER recognizes that the value it provides is in the institution's absolute commitment to quality, independence, and impact. Activities supported by its donors reflect this commitment.

Importantly, the present volume would never have seen the day of light without the stimulating intellectual leadership of the late Professor Mwangi S. Kimenyi, senior fellow and director of the Africa Growth Initiative at Brookings. This book is dedicated in the deepest respect to his memory following his untimely passing in June 2015.

Haroon Bhorat and Finn Tarp

ONE

The Pursuit of Long-Run Economic Growth in Africa

An Overview of Key Challenges

Haroon Bhorat and Finn Tarp

Historically, the African continent has been largely dismissed as a case of regional economic delinquency, with the levels of growth necessary to reduce poverty and inequality deemed to be consistently unattainable. In the last decade, however, significantly higher levels of economic growth have ushered in a new era to the region, suggesting it may, potentially, serve "as the final growth frontier with the last of the great untapped markets, ripe for rapid growth and development" (Bhorat and others 2015a). Data from *The Economist* and the International Monetary Fund (2011) support these assertions, as six of the fastest growing economies globally over the period 2001 to 2010 were in Sub-Saharan Africa (SSA hereafter): Angola, Nigeria, Ethiopia, Chad, Mozambique, and Rwanda. This volume specifically refers to the following six economics as the African Lions: Ethiopia, Ghana, Kenya, Mozambique, Nigeria, and South Africa.

The 1980s is often referred to as the continent's lost decade. The combination of massive external economic shocks; governance failures; under-investment in vital social services; significant macroeconomic imbalances; poor infrastructure; and structural trade deficits (Devarajan and Fengler 2012; Collier and Gunning 1999) undermined the early progress achieved after independence from Africa's colonial masters. Orthodox stabilization and structural adjustment programs dominated the policy agenda (Tarp 1993, 2001) and stagnation continued well into the 1990s. The post-2000 African economic boom, in contrast, has been built around a composite of factors, including improved macroeconomic policy; high commodity prices; significant improvement in the quality of governance and institutions; technology (mobile phones in particular); demographic growth; urbanization and the rise of new, dynamic African cities; and, in some cases, better targeted social policy. In turn, these factors, regularly supported by substantial inflows of foreign aid (Tarp 2015), have enabled the growth momentum on the continent to be maintained.

Not surprising given where African countries found themselves in the mid-1990s, socioeconomic indicators—poverty, inequality, access to social services, institution development, and infrastructure levels—remain weak in Africa (see Arndt, McKay, and Tarp 2016) and typically lag behind developing nations in other regions of the world. There are also concerns related to the sustainability of recent economic performance and socioeconomic advance for various reasons. First, an important part of this growth has been driven by dependence on extractive resources, which are volatile and subject to exogenous factors. Further, being a capital-intensive sector, there remains limited scope to address the rapidly increasing supply of labor through resource-based development. Second, emerging labor trends indicate that agriculture's share of employment is diminishing, with the services sector absorbing a significant share of the labor force (Newman and others 2016a). However, due to low human capital levels, the majority of these workers are employed on the fringes of the economy, working mainly in informal low wage and low productivity jobs. The manufacturing sector in most of these countries is shrinking following a considerable decline in manufacturing value added between 1990 and 2000. Third, while inequality is notoriously difficult to capture, it does appear as if inequality indicators are widening through the continent, driven by wage differentials across sectors, differences in human capital levels, and urban and rural splits. Finally, many African countries are at different stages of demographic transition—shifts from a high fertility, high mortality phase to a low fertility, low mortality state—a state associated with dividends that should, ideally, contribute to economic growth and development, which does not, however, seem to be materializing (Oosthuizen 2015).

A BRIEF MACROECONOMIC OVERVIEW

Africa's postcolonial growth history may be divided into two distinct phases. The first, between 1965 and 1990, was characterized first by progress and then by dismal growth in the 1980s. More recently, growth has surged. This chapter presents a brief overview of key macroeconomic indicators for Africa broadly, and specifically for our sample of six African economies.

Table 1-1 presents an overview of inflation, exchange rates, and current and fiscal accounts, as well as external debt, for the various African subregions. It is evident that macroeconomic performance has significantly improved across SSA, as demonstrated by inflation, which dropped from exceptionally high rates in 1990–94 to single-digit values in the two subsequent periods.

Over this period, these economic regions experienced slight exchange rate depreciation against the US$, but since then, the exchange rates have stabilized closer, possibly, to their equilibrium value. Despite significant currency depreciations, exports have not increased sufficiently to improve the current account balances. For example, Kenya experienced what has been termed a clogged "exports engine" (World Bank 2014) as the exports of goods as a percent of GDP declined in the period between the mid-2000s and 2014, while imports of goods continued to increase. However, over this period, Kimenyi and others (2015) note that Kenyan services exports continued to expand, although not sufficiently to offset the widening gap between exports and imports. Overall, however, current account deficits within the context of a developing

TABLE 1-1. *Macroeconomic Overview for Africa, 1990–2013*

Macroeconomic indicator	Period averages	Central Africa	East Africa[a]	North Africa	Southern Africa[b]	West Africa
Inflation (%)	1990–94	923.05	17.58	11.21	78.5	11.43
	2000–04	28.59	4.43	2.04	21.55	4.77
	2010–13	3.15	4.57	4.94	7.25	5.44
Official exchange rate (LCU	1990–94	284.13	174.13	22.22	3.83	253.35
per US$, period average)[c]	2000–04	596.83	411.55	36.6	22.06	648.79
	2010–13	553.94	552.12	61.17	243.12	933.39
Current account balance	2005–09	22.5	–6.67	7.95	–5.55	–7.21
(% of GDP)[d]	2010–12	–1.55	–7.86	0.78	–9.5	–11
Fiscal balance (% of GDP)	1990–94	–3.82	–3.29	2.78	–3.5	–0.66
	2000–04	1.98	–3.88	5.25	–2.02	–2.66
	2010–12	4.46	–2.55	2.74	–0.7	–2.65
External debt stocks	1990–94	113.36	86.51	92.58	111.12	116.91
(% of GNI)	2000–04	129.74	79.06	67.16	72.69	166.08
	2010–13	24.02	45.75	36.87	32.48	43.51

Source: Bhorat and others (2015a) based on data obtained from World Bank Development Indicators, 2014, and International Money Fund Government Finance Statistics, 2014.

a. Somalia is excluded from East Africa for lack of data.

b. Zimbabwe is excluded from Southern Africa because of episodes of hyperinflation and economic crisis.

c. LCU = Local currency units relative to the US$. Sao Tome and Principe and Madagascar are excluded from the exchange rate data due to rapidly depreciating currencies, which will result in distortions for the Southern Africa results.

d. There is no current account data for Africa before 2005.

nation do not indicate fiscal imprudence, as external funds (that is, especially aid) often supplement domestic resources.

Although the majority of the current fiscal accounts remain negative, they are within a narrow and sustainable range for the different regions. It is also apparent that external debt has been relatively well managed, as debt to Gross National Income (GNI) levels has fallen steadily since 1990 for all regions of the continent. This is in part due to debt relief, but is also partially a result of various African economies diversifying their output, resulting in a significant proportion of these states financing investment through (fast-expanding) domestic credit markets rather than through external debt.

Growth within the African Lion states was often accompanied with significant welfare gains. In South Africa and Ethiopia, significant welfare gains were observed, as measured by increasing access to social services, improved housing and basic infrastructure, and a reduction in poverty levels. Overall, while table 1-1 paints a positive picture of the state of Africa's macroeconomic environment, risks arise from political instability, war and conflict, and external shocks such as changes to commodity prices, as well as the spread of disease (Bhorat and others 2015a).

STRUCTURAL ECONOMIC TRANSFORMATION
AND INCLUSIVE GROWTH

Along with the rapid economic expansion across Africa in the post-2000 period, the continent experienced quickly rising average income levels, as well as shifts in the composition of output of the various economies. Tables 1-2 and 1-3 provide additional insight into these fundamental changes.

Table 1-2 demonstrates that most regions experienced real annual GDP growth exceeding 4 percent over the 2000 to 2014 period, with the exception of Southern Africa, where growth dipped slightly below this threshold. South Africa, the most dominant economy, experienced contractions in overall growth. As already alluded to, growth accelerated relative to the previous decade in all regions, including countries such as Ghana and Mozambique. Lastly, we note an increasing trend in real per capita Gross Domestic Product (GDP), except in the North Africa region, which experienced economic and political turmoil following the social upheaval wrought by the Arab Spring.

While these economic indicators are promising, it is necessary to take a closer look to discuss the overall sustainability of Africa's economic expansion and assess whether this growth translates into the achievement of Africa's development objectives of equitable growth and is also reducing poverty. To understand whether growth is sustainable, it is important to come to grips with the drivers of growth. Economic theory and cross-country evidence suggest that a more diverse economic

TABLE 1-2. *Real GDP and GDP per Capita in Africa for 1990, 2000, and 2014*

Region	Indicator	1990	2000	2014	Annual average % change 1990–2000	2000–14
North Africa	Total GDP (US$million)	180,909	282,313	383,649	4.6	2.2%
	Average GDP per capita (US$)	1,470	2,576	2,588	5.8	0.00
West Africa	Total GDP (US$million)	97,388	123,580	294,148	2.4	6.4
	Average GDP per capita (US$)	481	545	713	1.3	1.9
East Africa	Total GDP (US$million)	34,700	45,860	155,279	2.8	9.1
	Average GDP per capita (US$)	453	367	1,933	−2.1	12.6
Central Africa	Total GDP (US$million)	37,467	39,327	86,648	0.5	5.8
	Average GDP per capita (US$)	1,731	2,070	3,233	1.8	3.2
Southern Africa	Total GDP (US$million)	222,742	271,265	461,063	2.0	3.9
	Average GDP per capita (US$)	2,230	2,653	2,387	1.8	−0.8

Source: Word Development Indicators, 2014, and based on updated figures from Bhorat and others (2015a).

base—achieved through structural transformation—increases the likelihood of sustained economic performance and growth. Such structural transformation involves the reallocation of labor from low- to high-productivity sectors, and the rate of such structural change can encourage growth significantly. Rodrik (2014) posits that rapid industrialization or structural change toward high-productivity sectors can help shift countries into middle or upper income status; this follows the notion that modern manufacturing industries exhibit unconditional convergence to the global productivity frontier.

Table 1-3 presents the contribution of the various sectors to GDP between 1990 and 2012. We see that the agricultural sector remains a dominant contributor to GDP, particularly in West, East, and Central Africa, although there has been an observable downward trend in agriculture in most regions. In the African case, where industrialization has taken place, it has generally been dominated by mining rather than manufacturing activities. In fact, in most regions and periods since the 1990s, manufacturing has declined substantially. This weakness in manufacturing represents a key indicator alluding to the vulnerability of the growth and development trajectory of many of Africa's economies. In contrast, the tertiary services sector has grown to be the largest contributor to GDP for most SSA nations.

Africa's growth dynamic thus far has been characterized, on average, by a move into resource-based production, with small gains spilling over into manufacturing output. Indeed, some of the highest growth has been recorded in low-skilled, low productivity jobs in the urban services sectors of these economies (see Newman and others 2016a). Africa's transition away from primary sector activities toward tertiary sector activities has, in other words, not resulted in a discernable shift toward a more sustainable growth path. Attempting to quantify the effect of this structural change, McMillan and others (2014) estimate that this restructuring made a sizeable negative contribution to overall economic growth between 1990 and 2005, by as much as 1.3 percent per annum on average.[1] In this sense, their estimates show that labor moved in the wrong direction, becoming less productive. In Nigeria, Ajakaiye and others (2015) also find that the manufacturing sector has become more capital-intensive over time, hampering the capacity of this sector to absorb significant volumes of labor. Rodrik (2014) characterizes this phenomenon as premature deindustrialization, where a significant proportion of the population is absorbed into low-productive, informal sector work. This begs the question whether Africa will be able to skip a stage of economic development that all other developing nations have gone through (namely moving from a core, vibrant manufacturing base

TABLE 1-3. *Sectoral Breakdown of Economic Activity in Africa (Regional Averages), 1990, 2000, and 2010–12*

Percent of GDP

Region	Sector	1990	2000	2010	2011	2012	1990–2000 % change	2000–12 % change
North Africa	Agriculture	21.46	18.81	14.18	14.33	14.95	-2.65	-3.87
	Industry[a]	31.83	34.40	35.59	35.65	35.69	2.58	1.29
	Manufacturing	15.17	14.28	13.87	13.93	12.89	0.89	-1.38
	Services	46.71	46.78	50.24	50.02	49.36	0.07	2.58
West Africa	Agriculture	34.97	34.47	31.27	29.54	28.83	-0.50	-5.64
	Industry	21.82	23.41	22.37	24.47	29.18	1.59	5.77
	Manufacturing	9.56	8.91	6.00	5.87	5.99	-0.65	-2.92
	Services	43.21	42.12	47.26	47.12	43.08	-1.10	0.96
East Africa	Agriculture	39.91	32.74	32.63	32.92	35.95	-7.17	3.21
	Industry	16.60	16.58	18.45	18.65	17.06	-0.02	0.49
	Manufacturing	8.82	7.81	8.41	8.26	7.84	-1.01	0.03
	Services	43.49	50.68	48.92	48.43	46.99	7.19	-3.69
Central Africa	Agriculture	30.83	25.01	32.32	32.13	39.73	-5.83	14.72
	Industry	27.26	38.49	36.71	37.90	27.59	11.23	-10.90

Manufacturing[b]	10.97	7.05	4.06	4.13	4.35	-3.91	-2.71
Services	41.91	36.51	30.97	29.97	32.68	-5.40	-3.83
Southern Africa (with South Africa)							
Agriculture	18.44	14.68	12.15	11.78	9.15	-3.76	-5.54
Industry	34.68	33.21	32.84	32.98	31.73	-1.47	-1.49
Manufacturing	17.92	15.39	14.78	14.16	11.44	-2.53	-3.95
Services	46.88	52.40	55.01	55.24	59.13	5.52	6.72
Southern Africa (without South Africa)							
Agriculture	19.59	15.64	14.84	13.02	12.63	9.97	-3.96
Industry	34.23	33.34	31.78	33.11	33.32	32.14	-0.89
Manufacturing	17.44	15.09	14.71	14.83	14.28	-2.35	-0.81
Services	46.18	51.26	53.38	53.86	54.05	57.89	5.08

Source: Bhorat and others (2015a) based on data from the Word Development Indicators, 2014.

a. Industry corresponds to ISIC divisions 10–45 and includes manufacturing (ISIC divisions 15–37). It comprises value added in mining, manufacturing (also reported as a separate subgroup), construction, electricity, water, and gas.

b. Manufacturing and Services are subsets of Industry.

toward growth) and effectively reap the benefits of a mining- and services-
led growth path in the pursuit of long-run growth and employment
creation. On current evidence, it would appear that a "manufacturing-
absent" growth and development path is not a sustainable path to prosperity for the African continent.

Growth, Poverty, and Inequality Interactions in Africa

It is widely acknowledged that economic growth is essential for poverty
reduction. Evidence suggests that the absolute value of the elasticity
of poverty with respect to economic growth ranges between 1 and 5
(Ravallion and Chen 1997), meaning that a 1 percent increase in GDP
will have the effect of lowering poverty by between 1 and 5 percentage
points. This range suggests that economies differ in their ability to translate growth into poverty reduction, implying that economic growth is a
necessary but insufficient condition for rapid poverty alleviation. As will
be shown, African elasticity estimates tend to be lower than globally
comparable averages in line with Arndt and others (2012), who compare
Mozambique and Vietnam and point to the impact of initial structural
characteristics.

Another major contributor to less poverty reduction following rapid
economic growth is the level of inequality. High and increasing inequality weakens the effect of growth on poverty (Ravallion 1997; Fosu
2009). Evidence also suggests that the initial level of income inequality
within an economy is important in predicting the overall impact
of growth on poverty (Ravallion 1997, 2001), where, all else constant,
higher levels of initial income inequality are associated with a lower impact of growth on poverty. Gini coefficients, which measure inequality
and poverty, recorded for the African continent are high relative to the
rest of the world, thus the distribution of income is of particular importance in our context. Finally, the structure and nature of an economy's
growth path will further influence poverty and inequality outcomes.
Evidence suggests, for example, that growth built on labor-intensive
manufacturing is more poverty-reducing and less inequality-inducing
than growth in capital-intensive sectors such as mining and financial
services (Ravallion and Datt 1996; Khan 1999; Ravallion and Chen 2007).

This relationship is a cause for concern for the many African economies where "manufacturing-absent" growth, together with a significant emphasis on the natural resource sector, characterizes their growth trajectories.

The Growth–Poverty–Inequality Nexus in Africa

It follows from the previous section that Africa's improvement in macroeconomic performance has not translated into equally high-impact outcomes in poverty reduction levels. Figure 1-1 shows that, while extreme poverty has fallen in the region since the 1990s, almost 50 percent of SSA's population continues to live below the poverty line. Figure 1-1 also confirms that poverty in Africa is not falling as rapidly as in South and East Asia.

Figure 1-1 indicates that the proportion of the population living in extreme poverty in the African region, except for North Africa, is approximately 39 to 46 percent, which is noticeably higher than the poverty rates of all other developing regions of the world. Further, the depth of poverty in Africa is also more extreme than in other developing regions. For those living below the poverty line in Africa, the average consumption level is just 70 US cents a day, considerably below that of other regions, which are all close to attaining the US$1 a day level (Africa Progress Panel 2014). Hence, excluding North Africa, about two thirds of the population living below the poverty line in Africa are living in extreme poverty.

The estimated growth elasticity of poverty, indicating the percentage change in poverty following a percentage change in growth, provides an indication of the poverty-reducing impact of Africa's growth. Figure 1-2 presents Africa's growth elasticity of poverty for the two decades since 1990. SSA had an elasticity of −0.7, indicating that growth of 1 percent was estimated to have reduced poverty by only 0.7 percent, as compared with an elasticity of approximately −2 in the rest of the world.

Several key factors help explain this difference in elasticity. In addition to higher population growth and the structural features referred to in Arndt and others (2012), three factors can be noted. First, the higher poverty levels and lower incomes in SSA mean that equal absolute changes in both these indicators translate into smaller and larger changes, respectively, which then arithmetically reduces the growth

FIGURE 1-1. *Poverty Headcount Changes from 1981–2008*

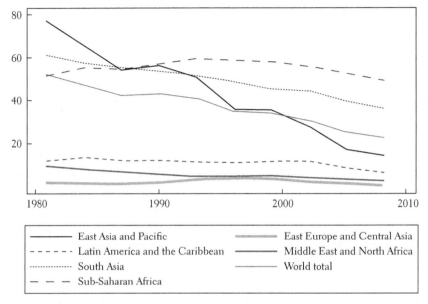

Percent of population in poverty

Source: PovcalNet (World Bank), 2014, based on Bhorat and others (2015a).

elasticity of poverty for SSA (World Bank 2013). Second, it has been shown that higher initial inequality hampers the poverty reducing power of growth. Fosu (2009) calculates the income–growth elasticities for thirty countries in SSA over the 1977 to 2004 period and reveals substantial variation in the estimates, from 0.63 in Namibia to 1.4 in Ethiopia. Many African countries exhibit high and increasing levels of inequality. In addition, aggregate evidence indicates that the average Gini coefficient for the African continent is 0.44, a value that is higher than that of the developing country average of 0.416 (Bhorat and others 2015a). Ultimately, then, the high initial levels of income inequality in many African economies will serve to reduce the estimated growth–poverty elasticities derived for the region.

Last, it is not only growth that matters, but also the pattern and structure of economic growth within individual economies. Cross-country

FIGURE 1-2. *Growth Elasticity of Poverty by Region*[a]

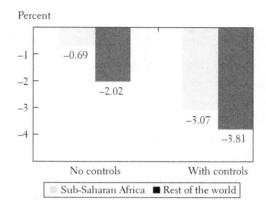

Percent

No controls   With controls

Sub-Saharan Africa   ■ Rest of the world

Source: Bhorat and others (2015a).

a. Controls include initial consumption, inequality, and an indicator for a natural resource share > 5 percent of GDP. Country fixed effects are controlled for in all results.

evidence makes it clear that growth in labor-intensive sectors such as agriculture or manufacturing are typically more poverty-reducing than growth in capital-intensive sectors such as mining (Khan 1999; Ravallion and Chen 2007; Loayza and Raddatz 2010). From the previous data analysis, it is evident that growth for a significant proportion of African economies is centered around capital-intensive sectors and many countries tend to exhibit a pattern of development where the largest contributions to GDP have moved from agriculture to activities in mining, construction, and services, with the notable absence of a manufacturing sector.

Labor Market Characteristics

In examining the inequality–growth relationship, labor demand responses during growth episodes within an economy will often shape and influence the private distributional impacts of growth. An example of this has been the shift toward the demand for highly skilled labor during periods of economic growth. This asymmetric response in occupational demand to growth is critical to understanding how economic growth can have distributional and poverty reduction effects. Bhorat and others (2015a) conclude that, in South Africa, for example, the secondary and tertiary sectors witnessed a rise in the proportion of high-skilled labor force between 2001 and 2012. At the same time, the primary and tertiary sectors saw declining proportions of unskilled labor, overall suggesting that firms in South Africa are investing in capital and skills, causing the shift away from unskilled labor.

The greatest degree of pressure within the labor market is likely to stem from the entry of young workers into the labor market. Figure 1-2 presents the projected increase in the size of the working-age population between 2010 and 2030. The magnitude of the expected growth to 2030 in Africa's youth population (15–24 years of age) is estimated at 2.5 times the growth in the youth population of Latin America, and over three times the growth in Asia. Lam and Leibbrandt (2013) provide an example from Africa's most highly populated country, Nigeria, to illustrate the extent of the youth bulge in Africa. They show that, while growth in the 15–24 age group in Nigeria has fallen from its mid-1990s peak, it is expected to remain above 2 percent until 2030, resulting in Nigerian youth continuing to make up a third of the labor force for the entire period (Bhorat and others 2015a).

The fact that Africa's working-age population is expected to grow so quickly, and particularly the working-age youth, highlights the fact that the continent is not as far along in its demographic transition as many other regions of the world, alluding to the increasing challenge of job creation for the continent (Bhorat and others 2015a).

Regarding the structure of the labor market, table 1-4 summarizes the global labor market, including Sub-Saharan Africa. A key defining feature of the African labor market is that an exceptionally high proportion—approximately 74 percent—of the SSA labor force is self-employed, as opposed to being engaged in wage employment.[2] Income from self-employment, which is directly dependent on the profits of the enterprise/surplus of household activities, is historically more variable than wage employment. Also noteworthy is that the majority of the labor force (56 percent) is engaged in agricultural activities, while 77 percent of the self-employed workers find themselves in the agricultural sector, having a compounding effect on the volatility of household incomes.

Thus, the agricultural sector, as well as the rural labor market, is extremely important for the livelihood of citizens in the SSA region,

TABLE 1-4. *The Global Labor Market at a Glance, 2010*[a]

Millions of people

Region	Wage employment	Self-employment	Self-employed		Employed	Unemployed	Labor force
			Agriculture	Non-agriculture			
SSA	61	236	181	55	297	23	320
	(0.19)	(0.74)	(0.56)	(0.17)	(0.93)	(0.07)	(1.00)
Other non-OECD	1,118	1,068	584	484	2,186	134	2,320
	(0.48)	(0.46)	(0.25)	(0.21)	(0.94)	(0.06)	(1.00)
OECD	333	50	7	43	383	32	415
	(0.80)	(0.12)	(0.02)	(0.10)	(0.92)	(0.08)	(1.00)
Global total	1,512	1,354	772	581	2,866	189	3,055
	(0.50)	(0.44)	(0.25)	(0.19)	(0.94)	(0.06)	(1.00)

Source: Bhorat and others (2015b). The data are based on the World Bank's International Income Distribution Database (I2D2) dataset, which is a harmonized set of household and labor force surveys drawn from a multitude of countries.

a. Estimated percentage of regional labor force is shown in parenthesis.

acting as a potential conduit for poverty reduction and job creation. Working on the land in rural areas is generally low-income work and the sectors potential to help transition workers out of poverty must be developed.

The number of working poor in Africa—defined as those living in households earning less than US$2 a day—currently at 193 million people, constitutes almost two-thirds of the total employed and is approximately eight times the number of unemployed in the region. The pattern of the changes in the number of the ultra-poor (those earning below US$1.25 a day) is consistent and shows a distinct redistribution of the world's working poor from East Asia and South East Asia and the Pacific to South Asia and Africa, with almost a third of the world's working ultra-poor residing in SSA, up from 18 percent in 2000 (Bhorat 2013). Thus, while the proportion of the working poor to total employment in SSA has seen gradual improvement since 2000, the fundamental jobs challenge in the region remains the problem of the working poor.

Ultimately, then, policies targeting the working poor and, in particular, increasing the productivity and competitiveness of the sectors they are located in, remains crucial to reducing the high incidence of poverty in many African economies. As one example, transforming the informal sector to become a more sustainable employer with backward and forward linkages to formal sector firms provides another focus for equitable development. Finally, growing Africa's wage employment base must be a key element of a growth strategy for African policymakers. Expanding the manufacturing sector, as noted, is another element of a job-generating growth strategy, which has worked in the high-success economies of East Asia (Bhorat and others 2015a; Newman and others 2016a, 2016b).

A THREE-PART STORYLINE: EMERGING BARRIERS TO LONG-RUN GROWTH

The detailed country case studies that follow this chapter suggest at least three major common themes that serve, in part, to characterize the nature of the growth challenges and constraints in Africa, which, if unchecked, could reinforce a pattern of low growth accompanied with limited poverty-reducing impact. These themes are a resource-led growth path, an absent manufacturing sector, and the increasing informalization of the work force. In upcoming sections, we discuss each in turn and provide possible policy recommendations.

Resource-Led Growth

Numerous studies highlight the developmental benefit of the diversification of an economy's productive structure. Additionally, these studies also argue that the type of products the economy diversifies toward also matters significantly. One of the most influential studies in reviewing the relationship between resource-rich African countries and overall growth is the well-known cross-country regression finding by Sachs and Warner (2001). This paper finds a negative and statistically significant coefficient for the variable capturing resource dependence (primary product exports as a share of GDP), when controlling for other growth variables such as geography and institutions.

Bhorat, Steenkamp, and Rooney (forthcoming), test for this natural resource curse hypothesis in Figure 1-3 by showing the relationship between natural resource intensity (as measured by the amount of arable land) and the log of GDP per capita for a cohort of high, middle, and low income countries as well as some selected African countries. They observe a weak negative relationship between the two variables (0.11). More specifically, a country that has a high natural resource endowment is more likely to be poorer than those countries with a lower natural resource endowment, *ceterus paribus*. While this negative correlation suggests the potential presence of the natural resource curse, further interrogation remains necessary to better understand the country-specific dynamics as well as the influence of mineral resources on overall growth levels.

Proponents of the resource curse effect argue for a number of channels through which resources adversely impact economic development. First, the terms of trade argument posed by Prebisch (1959) argues that the price of commodities relative to manufactured goods is said to follow a downward trajectory over time and, thus, countries specializing

FIGURE 1-3. *Resource Intensity Relative to per Capita GDP*

Log of revealed natural resource intensity[a]

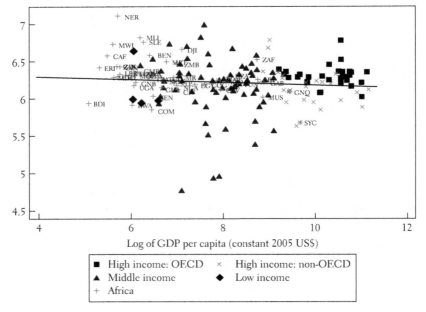

Source: Bhorat, Steenkamp, and Rooney (forthcoming), using the BACI International Trade Database.
  a. The natural resource intensity associated with a country's export basket (2013) is constructed using data from the UNCTAD Revealed Factor Intensity Database developed by Shirotori, Tumurchudur, and Cado (2010). The construction of this measure follows the same technique that is applied by Hausmann, Hwang, and Rodrik (2007) when the use revealed technology content data (known as the PRODY measure) to construct a measure of the productivity level associated with a country's export basket (known as the EXPY measure). In essence, the measure is a weighted average of the revealed natural resource intensity for a country, using each exported product's share of a country's export portfolio as weights.

in resource-intensive activities will experience declining terms of trade over time. Second, Sachs and Warner (1995, 2001) argue that, following a commodity boom, the growth of the resource sector crowds out man-ufacturing activity. Third, a political economy-type argument contends that resource-abundant countries are less likely to develop sound institu-tions because of elites competing over resources rents. It is argued that countries characterized by weak institutions have a higher likelihood of armed conflict. Finally, commodity prices tend to exhibit high levels of volatility that, coupled with export concentration in natural resource–based exports, result in broader macroeconomic volatility.

However, there are, as well, other studies that contest the resource curse hypothesis. First, Mehlum, Moene, and Torvik (2006) propose a "conditional resource curse" whereby the quality of a country's institutions influences whether it is able to successfully exploit its natural resource abundance. They find that resource-rich countries with weak institutions are associated with low growth, whereas resource-rich countries with strong institutions are associated with high growth. Second, Bravo-Ortega and Gregorio (2007) highlight the importance of the country's human capital levels. Specifically, they argue that low levels of human capital and resource abundance are associated with low levels of growth, whereas high levels of human capital and resource abundance are associated with higher levels of economic growth. Finally, Maloney and Lederman (2008) find little evidence for the curse and, instead, propose a "curse of concentration," for countries that are overly dependent upon the exports of just a few natural resource–based products are associated with the negative growth effects.[3]

In summary, an abundance of mineral resources will not automatically limit a nation's economy to low levels of growth and development. Rather, any measurable developmental benefits will arise from the inclusion or the absence of a broader set of requirements for growth, such as the quality of institutions, human capital levels, and a sufficiently diversified economy. And in the final analysis, it is important to keep in mind that, if available resources are spent wisely, then growth is likely to ensue. The country chapters that follow will directly and indirectly attest to the challenges posed to the African growth agenda for African economies that find themselves heavily dependent on resource revenues to fuel fiscal revenue, economic growth, and employment generation.

An Absent African Manufacturing Sector

During the 1970s, manufacturing in Africa thrived due to import-substitution industrialization. However, when economic liberalization and the privatization of state enterprises became rampant under stabilization and structural adjustment in the 1980s, African manufacturing went into secular decline, as the continent could not compete with low-wage Asian countries. Import competition led to the contraction of many domestic industries, resulting in labor moving toward less productive sectors. According to Page (2014), African countries were not

FIGURE 1-4. *Manufacturing as a Proportion of GDP by Subregion, 1994–2013*

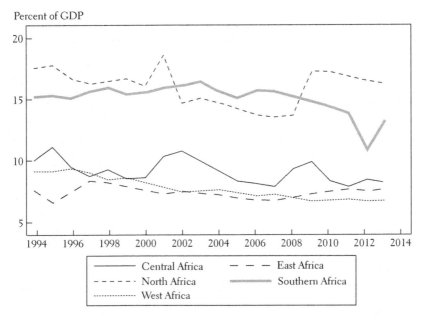

Source: World Development Indicators, 2015.

well prepared for import competition due to state-led import substitution creating high protection and heavy import dependency, but other factors, including bad luck, were also at play. Newman and others (2016b) provide a comprehensive set of comparative studies of industrial development in Africa and Emerging Asia.

Figure 1-4 shows a steady decline or flatlining in the contribution of manufacturing to economic output across five African regions, particularly from 1990. Since 2000, there has been a marginally upward trend for manufacturing in North and East Africa spurred on by the increasing incidence of light manufacturing and medium technology manufacturing, respectively.

An alternative approach to assessing manufacturing performance is to analyze the performance of manufacturing exports, as the ability to export and compete in global markets suggests a level of success and industrial strength. Following the poor performance in manufacturing output across most of Africa, the trends in export performance are equally disappointing. As illustrated in figure 1-4, West Africa's share of manufacturing in exports rose promisingly from 1995 levels to a peak of 24 percent in 2004 before declining back to 1995 levels in 2013, at just under 16 percent of GDP. An encouraging trend is emerging in East Africa, where, on average, manufacturing goods as a proportion of exports has risen from 17.2 percent in 1995 to 20.4 percent currently. Over time, manufacturing exports reached a peak of 27 percent of exports from the East African region in 2006, after which it gradually declined and has now stabilized.[4]

While this proportion varies significantly across the African Lions in focus here, the share of manufacturing as a proportion of GDP is highest in Kenya, Mozambique, and South Africa. Manufacturing in South Africa declined by almost 10 percent between 1994 and 2014. This contraction in South Africa followed the inability to compete in global manufacturing export markets, increased global competition, and volatile real exchange rates. Kenya has failed to capitalize on the manufacturing exports in spite of its location, the presence of a large and skilled labor force, and its market-focused orientation. Additionally, Kenya has significant resource endowment to enable agricultural industries to transform from small-scale downstream industries into expanded upstream manufacturing industries. This would serve a dual purpose of increasing growth and lowering unemployment.

Several trends are observed when focus shifts to the nature of manufacturing exports undertaken by African countries. First, as expected, exports typically consist of primary products. The volume of these exports continues to be high even when compared with developing country counterparts in South Asia, Latin America, and the Caribbean. Second, it is estimated that over half of these manufacturing exports are capital-intensive in nature and heavily resource-based. In Mozambique, for example, the economy remains dominated by agriculture (27 percent) and private and public services (51 percent), while manufacturing has grown more slowly than other sectors and has declined as a share of GDP (18 percent). Growth in the Mozambican manufacturing sector is driven entirely by investments in two aluminum smelters attracted to the country by its preferential tax structure. Smelting is, by nature, a capital-intensive activity, which limits its overall contribution to manufacturing jobs. Finally, manufacturing exports out of Africa have relatively low technology content. Despite the Ethiopian government designating the manufacturing sector as the conduit to achieving middle-income country status by 2025 and establishing various incentives to spur growth, growth remains low (estimated at 5 percent) and employment within this sector is miniscule in relation to the size of the employment challenge.

Positive results from the continent, however, indicate that most economies are in transition, as the share of agriculture relative to GDP has declined while the contribution of services has grown significantly. A closer look at the data reveals that growth in the intermediate sector has principally been driven by expansion of the mining sector, whereas the manufacturing sector has experienced stagnation. Furthermore, the share of manufacturing exports in manufacturing output has remained significantly low historically, which, as alluded to, begs the question of whether service-led growth can deliver a sufficient volume of jobs.

We now turn our attention to examining the possible range of constraints on manufacturing performance in Africa, as well as possible solutions. We briefly analyze the role of skills, capital accumulation, the regulatory environment, and various infrastructure costs.

Low Capital Accumulation

A positive relationship is observed in the relationship between capital accumulation and GDP. This is true for both human capital and physical capital. In general, an increase in wealth is associated with an increase in the use of human capital in exports. Most African countries are not capital abundant when compared to other low-income countries in other regions of the world. Nigeria and South Africa are two exceptions, as they have a similar level of capital stock and wealth compared to other middle-income countries. However, manufacturing in Nigeria has transformed to be more capital intensive amid a large and growing labor force. This is accompanied by a significant reduction in the proportion of workers in this sector, as well as an increasing demand for a more skilled labor force. Overall, however, this lack of both physical and human capital stock, and the intensity of its use in production, suggests that Africa will continue to struggle to industrialize.

FIGURE 1-5. *African Lions' Atlas of Economic Complexity Rankings, 2013*[a]

Ranking

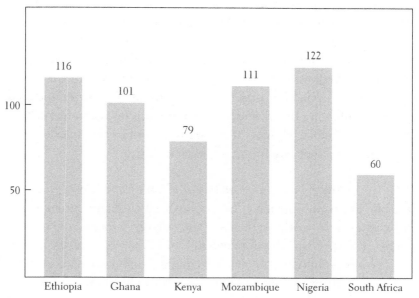

Source: Atlas of Economic Complexity (2013).
a. Total rankings, 124.

Using the Atlas of Economic Complexity toolkit developed by Haus-mann and others (2007), one can explore the link between the sum of knowledge available within an economy to produce goods (the complexity) and connectedness to traded products and what this implies for structural transformation.[5] Countries at lower levels of economic complexity, mainly African countries, have relatively disconnected productive structures and, thus, their ability to diversify and undergo structural transformation is constrained. In essence, the complexity index alludes to the fact that these marginalized countries do not possess the productive knowledge and capabilities needed to shift their production structure to more complex products, particularly manufactured products. The peripheral nature of their product space does not afford them opportunities to diversify and grow in complexity.

Japan and Switzerland are currently ranked first and second, respectively, on the Atlas of Economic Complexity out of 124 states for which

information is available. The higher the ranking, the better the transformation and connectedness of that economy. Figure 1-5 summarizes
the findings for the six African Lion states. The findings are instructive.
They suggest that only South Africa and Kenya have some degree of
economic complexity, as they are ranked somewhere in the middle of
the distribution. The remaining four countries in our sample are ranked
close to the bottom of the distribution in terms of economic complexity. Nigeria is second from last in global distribution of economic complexity, reinforcing the idea of the country's overreliance on crude oil.
It is fair to argue, in addition, that the majority of low complexity economies in this sample are from Sub-Saharan Africa.

Governance, Infrastructure, and Unit Labor Costs

Despite extensive upgrades, Africa's business environment continues
to be plagued by costly inefficiency and onerous bureaucratic requirements. Eifert, Gelb, and Ramachandran (2008) analyze the cost of
doing business in Africa to conclude that the high indirect cost shares
observed in firms in poorer African countries reflect underlying weak
fundamentals, which, in turn, reduces the competitiveness of African firms relative to those in Asian and Latin American developing
countries.

Figure 1-6 plots the World Bank's Ease of Doing Business rank for
Africa, Latin America, and South Asia. The higher the rank, the less
conducive the country is for business. Africa's average rank is 142, compared to Latin America's 98 and South Asia's 137. Elements of the business environment, such as the time it takes to set up a business and get
electricity and access to credit, all remain critical areas that need reform. Finally, weaknesses in the rule of law and regulation mean that
African firms pay higher bribes (as a proportion of sales) and lose a
greater fraction of their sales value to crime and theft than firms in
other developing countries (Eifert and Ramachandran 2004).

All these factors point toward an environment that is not fully conducive to the start up and operation of efficient small, micro, and medium
sized enterprises (SMMEs), as well as a thriving informal sector. This
is, no doubt, one of the contributory factors to the low productivity of
the manufacturing sector in Africa. Furthermore, these business constraints may also limit the entry of formal, foreign manufacturing firms

FIGURE 1-6. *Ease of Doing Business in Africa vs. Latin America and South Asia, 2015*

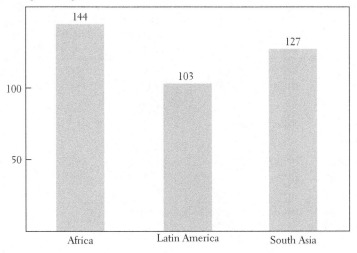

Source: World Bank Doing Business Report, 2015.

into the market given that the business environment is a key cost factor for firms, in addition to the estimated return on investment.

While the Doing Business Indicators have occupied a central place in the dialogue about enterprise development in Africa, it is, as argued in Newman and others (2016a, 2016b), critical to keep the overall context and constraints in mind in developing appropriate policy. Estimates suggest that poor infrastructure hampers economic growth in Africa by at least 2 percent each year and lowers private sector productivity by up to 40 percent (Kaberuka 2013). Poor infrastructure poses a fundamental threat to Africa's potential for growth arising from its manufacturing sector. Table 1-5 indicates that, while infrastructure provision in Africa has grown over the period under examination, current levels remain very low when compared with developing nations in other regions of the world. For example, the road density network as a proportion of land area is estimated at 24.3 in Africa, compared to an average of 54.2 for non-African developing countries. Furthermore, evidence points to the fact that roads in Africa—which are the main means

TABLE 1-5. *Infrastructure Indicators, Africa versus Non-African Developing Countries*

Region	Year	Electricity production (kWh per capita)	Improved sanitation facilities (% population with access)	Improved water source (% of population with access)	Road density (km of road per 100 sq km of land area)
Africa	1990	514.24	41.60	63.66	n.a.
	2010	762.91	49.45	75.06	n.a.
Africa excluding South Africa	1990	457.13	41.23	63.35	n.a.
	2010	705.86	48.93	74.77	24.30
Non-African developing countries	1990	1,515.15	67.57	83.27	n.a.
	2010	1,889.98	78.58	90.48	54.2

Source: World Bank World Development Indicators, 2015.
n.a. = not available.

of transporting freight—are unpaved and in poor condition (PricewaterhouseCoopers 2012). Transport costs are cripplingly high and electricity production remains low and unpredictable.

Inefficient logistics contribute significantly to the cost of doing business in Africa and weaken the ability to leverage a comparative advantage in, say, food processing industries, where perishables require short transit times. Rail infrastructure remains poor and out of date, with few upgrades by most African states. Ports, key to facilitating international trade, are in undersupply and often do not function efficiently, which, in turn, limits their overall ability to handle large volumes of traffic. A case in point is Kenya, which, through the port city of Mombasa, services five landlocked neighboring countries that are fairly resource-rich: Ethiopia, South Sudan, Uganda, Rwanda, and Burundi. To further benefit from this comparative advantage, it is necessary for Kenya to prioritize improvising ports and other transport networks and to develop transport nodes.

High unit labor costs in Africa are also cited as a reason for the poor performance of manufacturing in Africa. Ceglowski and others (2015)

FIGURE 1-7. *Annual Manufacturing Wages as a Percent of GDP per Capita, 2000 and 2010*[a]

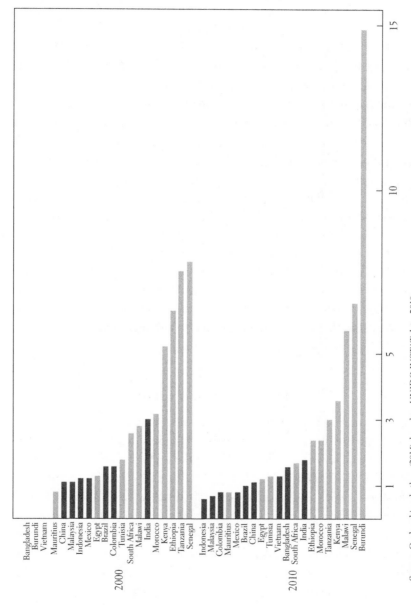

Source: Ceglowski and others (2014), based on UNIDO INSTAT data, 2010.
a. African countries are shown in gray.

find that high unit labor costs are a key explanatory factor as to why African manufactured exports remain globally uncompetitive. Figure 1-7 provides the authors' estimates of formal sector manufacturing wages in Africa. Wages in Sub-Saharan Africa have increased between 2000 and 2010 and are much higher than in Asian countries. In 2010, African countries occupied the highest seven positions with regard to manufacturing wages. Only Tunisia, Egypt, Mauritius, and, to a lesser extent, South Africa can match the Asian countries in terms of costs. However, and to be sure, wages are only one element hampering the progress of the manufacturing sector. The business environment further influences operational costs and, therefore, long-run returns on investment. Investors are willing to pay a wage premium in countries where there is good infrastructure and the population is well educated.

It is worth noting that manufacturing is a heterogeneous sector of an economy and encompasses a variety of industries and products. For instance, manufactured output varies according to the inputs that go into production, such as capital, labor, and natural resources. To capitalize on long-run growth opportunities, it is, thus, crucial for African economies to work on improving the quantity and quality of human capital, to ensure there is an enabling and efficient regulatory environment, and to improve overall infrastructure levels.

Informalization of Labor

The expansion of the African informal economy in the 1990s is often linked to trade liberalization and structural adjustment programs that resulted in civil service employees exiting the sector, as well as global competition that resulted in lowered staffing levels for previously protected industries (Verick 2006; Calvès and Schoumaker 2004). Despite limited data and studies in this area, the general consensus is that the informal sector plays an important role in Sub-Saharan Africa. A 2015 report by the African Development Bank reports that informal economic activities account for approximately 55 percent of GDP across the continent and as much as 70 percent of employment in the Sub-Saharan Africa region. Benjamin and Mbaye (2009) use household level data from the West African Economic and Monetary Union to conclude that in Benin, Burkina

Faso, and Senegal, the informal sector has, on average, contributed 74 percent, 49 percent, and 54 percent, respectively, to GDP since 2000.

In Kenya, in a trend that might apply across the other African economies, weak relationships are observed between economic growth and reduction in unemployment. This might imply that a significant proportion of individuals are employed within the informal sector that is not as responsive to economic growth such that, while growth in wage employment closely tracks GDP, no such relationship is observed for the informal sector. In addition, Gelb and others (2009) observe a strong correlation between rising unemployment and the development of the informal sector, where this sector acts as an employer of last resort for those unable to find wage employment.[6] Moreover, individuals employed in the informal sector have been observed to have, on average, lower levels of education relative to those in the formal sector, which requires a skilled and educated labor force (La Porta and Shleifer 2008).

An International Labor Organization (ILO) report published in 2013 shows that the SSA's working poor not only constitutes almost two-thirds of the total employed but is also approximately eight times the number of unemployed in the region. Unsurprisingly, then, evidence indicates that poverty is significantly higher among individuals employed in the informal sector (Benjamin and Mbaye 2009). Findings from Mozambique indicate the presence of a minority of workers earning a stable wage income, even in urban areas that provide more economic opportunities. Furthermore, wage differentials are prevalent depending on the aggregate economic sector where earnings are obtained. This is particularly true in Kenya, where various barriers exist to limit labor mobility between the informal and the higher-paying formal sector. A wage differential of US$36 is calculated between Ethiopian workers in the formal and informal sectors while, in Ghana, earnings are presumed to be the lowest in the informal sector, with average daily earnings being estimated at 37.5 percent of public sector earnings and 32.1 percent of the average earnings in the private formal sector.

Within the informal economy, certain sectors are clearly dominant across the continent. Domestic work in the private homes of others, home-based work, and street vendors dominate the African informal sector (International Labor Organization 2013).[7] The 2013 ILO report estimates that, in Africa, the number of domestic workers has increased from 4.2 million in 1995 to 5.3 million by 2010, where 73 percent are women. Further research has shown that informal sector firms are significantly less productive than formal firms (Gelb and others 2009; La Porta and Shleifer 2008). There is evidence from selected economies to indicate that retail trade and other non-tradables absorb the majority of informal sector workers (Verick 2006). South Africa, with a relatively smaller informal sector, indicates higher concentration in the retail trade, domestic work in private households, construction, and transport (Wills 2009).

In the case of the African Lions, labor mobility from agriculture to the services sector requires closer interrogation, as it often masks the fact that, despite increases in overall employment share, there is a decline in overall labor productivity. This implies that the bulk of these new workers are mainly located in the informal sector, often have low levels of education, and are undertaking risky or low-paying jobs. The Nigerian services sector is characterized as a low productivity sector, and any inflows of labor will have the effect of lowering overall per capita productivity, which diminishes any inter-sectoral shift effects. (It is similar in Ghana, which has an employment elasticity of 0.47. New jobs are being created in the informal sector generating a significant proportion of the working poor, estimated at 22 percent of the overall working population). The share of employment in Kenya's informal sector was estimated at 83 percent in 2014, following an average increase of 72 percent over a thirty-year period. The widespread growth of the Kenyan informal sector is largely attributable to the fact that the formal sector is not growing rapidly enough to absorb the growing labor force as a result of constraints to capital accumulation within this sector.

A rising informal sector is also significant because workers within this sector are often excluded from contributory social insurance schemes that require an employment relationship. Therefore, raising the productivity of the informal sector becomes an important policy objective. This implies, first, addressing issues surrounding the business regulatory environment that need to be addressed to develop this sector, including improving access to credit and provision of insurance products. Second, investment in basic infrastructure such as electricity, road networks, and information technology is fundamental. Third, wage differentials resulting from the proportion of unskilled labor in the informal sector necessitates the upgrading of skills for individuals within this sector. This has a dual effect, as it may help generate viable firms as well as contributing to overall sectoral productivity. Last, policy strategies and programs should be put in place to make the informal sector more dynamic and formal, to deliver quality employment opportunities.

CONCLUSION

The analysis presented in this chapter suggests that, despite significant advances in terms of macroeconomic stability, it is evident that the structure of the African region's growth remains of concern. The pattern of growth that is resource-dominant and manufacturing-absent would not seem to be the standard economic development path followed by all economies that have successfully transitioned from low- to high-income country status. The dominance of resources in production and exports and services and agriculture in employment would, in turn, not appear to be the most appropriate strategy for long-term and sustained poverty-reducing growth. This lack of complexity in production, underpinned by constraints in infrastructure, a poor regulatory and governance framework, and high unit labor costs serve to reinforce challenges to growth, development, and employment generation strategies of this continent. In the chapters that follow, we hope to elucidate, at the country level, how these challenges are being played out in six African economies.

NOTES

The authors would like to thank Arabo Ewinyo and Kirsten van der Zee for their outstanding and invaluable research assistance.

1. A similar result is observed for Latin America, with Asia being the only one of the three regions where the contribution of structural change to economic growth over this period was positive.

2. According to the International Labor Organization (ILO) (1993), wage employment refers to jobs "where the incumbents hold explicit (written or oral) or implicit employment contracts which give them a basic remuneration" in the form of wages. Self-employment is defined as "jobs where the remuneration

is directly dependent upon the profits (or the potential for profits) derived from the goods and services produced (where consumption is considered to be part of profits)."

3. A case study analysis of Scandinavian countries by Blomstrom and Kokko (2007) argues that the current diverse high-tech manufacturing industries in these countries were developed upon the foundation of knowledge- and technology-intensive natural resource industries. For example, the high-tech telecom company, Nokia, emerged from a forestry company.

4. This aggregate positive trend is driven primarily by increasing growth in Burundi, Tanzania, and Uganda.

5. See this atlas at http://atlas.cid.harvard.edu/media/atlas/pdf/Harvard MIT_AtlasOfEconomicComplexity.pdf.

6. Maloney (2004) is a key proponent for the role that the informal sector could play in advancing better outcomes for entrepreneurs relative to employment within the formal sector. However, he also acknowledges the difficulties faced by workers in this sector, namely restrictive access to formal credit markets and weaker property rights.

7. Home-based work relates to own-account workers and subcontracted workers that carry out remunerated work in or very near their own homes. These types of jobs include the manufacturing of crafts and related trade, the operation of small convenience stores or informal pubs, or brick-makers and construction workers. Street vendors also make up a considerable portion of urban informal work in Africa (12 to 24 percent). Street vendors include those who sell goods at flea markets, street-side hairdressers, and those who sell fruit, vegetables, and other food on city streets (International Labor Organization 2013).

REFERENCES

Addison, Tony, Finn Tarp, and Saurabh Singhal. 2015. "Aid to Africa: The Changing Context." In *The Oxford Handbook of Africa and Economics, Volume II: Policies and Practices*, edited by J. Lin and C. Monga (Oxford University Press), pp. 698–710.

Africa Progress Panel (APP). 2014. "Grain Fish Money: Financing Africa's Green and Blue Revolutions." Africa Progress Report 2014. ISBN 978-2-9700821-4-9 http://app-cdn.acwupload.co.uk/wp-content/uploads/2014/05/APP_APR2014_24june.pdf

Ajakaiye, Olu, Afeikhena T. Jerome, Olufunke A. Alaba, and David Nabena. 2015. *Understanding The Relationship between Growth and Employment in Nigeria* (2015/124. Helsinki: UNU-WIDER).

Arndt, Channing, Andres Garcia, Finn Tarp, and James Thurlow. 2012. "Poverty Reduction and Economic Structure: Comparative Path Analysis for Mozambique and Vietnam." *Review of Income and Wealth* 58, no. 4, pp. 742–63.

Arndt, Channing, Andy McKay, and Finn Tarp, eds. 2016. *Growth and Poverty in Sub-Saharan Africa* (Oxford University Press).

Aryeetey, Ernest, and William Baah-Boateng. 2015. *Understanding Ghana's Growth Success Story and Job Creation Challenges* (2015/140. Helsinki: UNU-WIDER).

Benjamin, Nancy, and Ahmadou Aly Mbaye. 2009. *The Informal Sector in Francophone Africa: Firm Size, Productivity, and Institutions* (Washington, D.C.: World Bank).

Bhorat, Haroon. 2013. *The Challenge of Job Creation: Input to the Post-2015 HLP Agenda* (Unpublished Mimeograph. Cape Town: Development Policy Research Unit, University of Cape Town).

Bhorat, Haroon, Francois Steenkamp, and Christopher Rooney. Forthcoming 2016. *Africa's Manufacturing Malaise* (Unpublished Mimeograph. Cape Town: Development Policy Research Unit, University of Cape Town).

Bhorat, Haroon, Karmen Naidoo, and Kavisha Pillay. 2015a. "Aspiring Africa: Overcoming Development Challenges to Meet Its Long-Term Vision." Mimeograph presented at *Developmental States Conference* (Pretoria).

———. 2015b. "Growth, Poverty, and Inequality Interactions in Africa: An Overview of Key Issues" (Helsinki: Mapping the Future of Development Economics [Anniversary Conference], September 17–19).

Blomstrom, Magnus, and Ari Kokko. 2007. "From Natural Resources to High-Tech Production: The Evolution of Industrial Competitiveness in Sweden and Finland." In *Natural Resources: Neither Curse nor Destiny*, edited by Daniel Lederman and William Maloney (Washington, D.C.: World Bank), pp. 213–46.

Bravo-Ortega, Claudio, and José Gregorio. 2007. "The Relative Richness of the Poor? Natural Resources, Human Capital and Economic Growth," Working Paper (Washington, D.C.: World Bank Group).

Calvès, Anne-Emmanuèle, and Bruno Schoumaker. 2004. "Deteriorating Economic Context and Changing Patterns of Youth Unemployment in Urban Burkina Faso: 1980–2000." *World Development*, Elsevier, vol. 32, Aug., pp. 1341–54.

Ceglowski, Janet, Stephen Golub, Ahmadou Aly Mbaye, and Varun Prasad. 2015. "Can Africa Compete with China in Manufacturing? The Role of Relative Unit Labor Costs," Working Paper 201504 (Cape Town: Development Policy Research Unit).

Collier, Paul, and Jan Willem Gunning. 1999. "The IMF'S Role in Structural Adjustment." *The Economic Journal* 109, no. 459, pp. 634–51.

Devarajan, Shantayanan, and Wolfgang Fengler. 2012. "Is Africa's Recent Economic Growth Sustainable?" (*Institut français des relations internationals (Ifri)*, Notte de l'Ifri, October 2012. Programme Moyen-Orient/Maghreb).

The Economist and IMF. 2011. "Africa's Impressive Growth." Retrieved from The Economist: www.economist.com/blogs/dailychart/2011/01/daily_chart

Eifert, Ben, Alan Gelb, and Vijaya Ramachandran. 2008. "The Cost of Doing Business in Africa: Evidence from Enterprise Survey Data." *World Development* 36, no. 9, pp. 1531–46.

Eifert, Ben, and Vijaya Ramachandran. 2004. "Competitiveness and Private Sector Development in Africa: Crosscountry Evidence from the World Bank's Investment Climate Data," Occasional Paper series (Cornell University: Institute for African Studies).

Fosu, Augustin K. 2009. "Inequality and the Impact of Growth on Poverty: Comparative Evidence for Sub-Saharan Africa." *Journal of Development Studies* 45, no. 5, pp. 726–45.

Gelb, Alan, Taye Mengistae, Vijaya Ramachandran, and Manju KediaShah. 2009. "To Formalize or Not to Formalize? Comparisons of Microenterprise Data from Southern and East Africa," Working Paper 175 (Washington, D.C.: Center for Global Development).

Hausmann, Ricardo, César A. Hidalgo, Sebastián Bustos, Michele Coscia, Sarah Chung, Juan Jimenez, Alexander Simoes, Muhammed A. Yıldırım. 2007. "The Atlas of Economic Complexity: Mappying Paths to Prosperity" (Harvard's Center for International Development (CID)).

Hausmann, Ricardo, Jason Hwang, and Dani Rodrik, 2007. "What You Export Matters," *Journal of Economic Growth*, Springer, vol. 12, pp. 1–25.

International Labor Organization (ILO). 1993. *Fifteenth International Conference of Labour Statisticians, Report of the Conference.* (Geneva: ICLS/15/D.6 (Rev. 1) International Labour Office).

———. 2013. *Women and Men in the Informal Economy: A Statistical Picture*, 2nd ed.

International Monetary Fund (IMF). 2011. *Regional Economic Outlook: Sub-Saharan Africa Recovery and New Risks* (Washington, D.C.: International Monetary Fund).

Kaberuka, Donald. 2013. "Sustaining Africa's Economic Growth: The Challenges of Inclusion and Financing Infrastructure." (Speech by the President of the African Development Bank at the AACB Symposium on Financial Inclusion. AfDB, October). http://www.afdb.org/en/news-and -events/article/sustaining-africas-economic-growth-the-challenges-of -inclusion-and-financing-infrastructure-afdb-president-donald-kaberuka -12215/

Khan, Haider. 1999. "Sectoral Growth and Poverty-Alleviation: A Multiplier Decomposition Technique Applied to South Africa." *World Development* 27, no. 3, pp. 521–30.

Kimenyi, Mwangi S., Francis M. Mwega, and Njuguna S. Ndung'u. 2015. *The African Lions: Kenya Country Case Study* (2015/134. Helsinki: UNU-WIDER).

La Porta, Rafael, and Andrei Shleifer. 2008. "The Unofficial Economy and Economic Development." *Brookings Papers on Economic Activity 2*, (Brookings), pp. 275–364.

Lam, David, and Murray Leibbrandt. 2013. *Global Demographic Trends and Their Implications for Employment.* Paper prepared as background research for the Post-2015 UN MDG Development Agenda on Employment and Employment Growth. http://www.post2015hlp.org/wp-content /uploads/2013/05/Lam-Leibbrandt_Global-Demographic-Trends-and -their-Implications-for-Employment.pdf

Loayza, Norman, and Claudio Raddatz. 2010."The Composition of Growth Matters for Poverty Alleviation." *Journal of Development Economics* 93, no. 1, pp. 137–51.

Maloney, William. 2004. "Informality Revisited." *World Development* 32, no. 7, pp. 1159–78.

Maloney, William F., and Daniel Lederman. 2008. "In Search of the Missing Resource Curse." *Economía: Journal of the Latin American and Caribbean Economic Association*, vol. 9, no. 1.

McMillan, Margaret, Dani Rodrik, and Ignio Verduzco-Gallo. 2014. "Globalization, Structural Change, and Productivity Growth with an Update on Africa." *World Development* 63, pp. 11–32.

Mehlum, Halvor, Karl Moene, and Ragnar Torvik. 2006. "Institutions and the Resource Curse." *Economic Journal*, vol. 116, issue 508, pp. 1–20.

Newman, Carol, John Page, John Rand, Abebe Shimeles, Måns Söderbom, and Finn Tarp. 2016a. *Made in Africa: A New Industrial Strategy* (Brookings).

———, eds. 2016b. *Manufacturing Transformation: Comparative Studies of Industrial Development in Africa and Emerging Asia* (Oxford University Press).

Oosthuizen, Morne. 2015. "Bonus or Mirage? South Africa's Demographic Dividend." *Journal of the Economics of Ageing* 5, April, pp. 14–22.

Page, John. 2014. "Africa's Failure to Industrialize: Bad Luck or Bad Policy?" *Africa in Focus* (Brookings).

Prebisch, Raúl. 1959. "Commercial Policy in the Underdeveloped Countries." *American Economic Review* 49, pp. 251–73.

PricewaterhouseCoopers. 2012. *Africa Gearing Up: Future Prospects in Africa for the Transportation and Logistics Industry* (Johannesburg).

Ravallion, Martin. 1997. "Can High-Inequality Developing Countries Escape Absolute Poverty?" *Economics Letters* 56, pp. 51–57.

———. 2001. "Growth, Inequality, and Poverty: Looking Beyond Averages." *World Development* 29, no. 11, pp. 1803–15.

Ravallion, Martin, and Shaohua Chen. 1997. "What Can New Survey Data Tell Us about Recent Changes in Poverty and Distribution?" *World Bank Economic Review* 11, no. 2, pp. 357–82

———. 2007. "China's (Uneven) Progress Against Poverty." *Journal of Development Economics* 82, pp. 1–42.

Ravallion, Martin, and Gaurav Datt. 1996. "How Important to India's Poor Is the Sectoral Composition of Economic Growth?" *World Bank Economic Review* 10, no. 1, pp. 1–25.

Rodrik, Dani. 2014. *An African Growth Miracle?* (Princeton: NBER Working Paper No. 20188, Institute for Advanced Study).

Sachs, Jeffrey D., and Andrew M. Warner. 1995. *Natural Resource Abundance and Economic Growth* (NBER Working Paper No. 5398, December).

———. 2001. "The Curse of Natural Resources." *Natural Resources and Economic Development* 45, pp. 827–38.

Shirotori, M., Cadot, O., and Tumurchudur, B. 2010. Revealed Factor Intensity Indices at the Product Level (Policy Issues in International Trade and Commodities No. 44). New York: United Nations Conference on Trade and Development.

Tarp, Finn. 1993. *Stabilization and Structural Adjustment: Macroeconomic Frameworks for Analysing the Crisis in Sub-Saharan Africa* (London and New York: Routledge).

———. 2001. " 'Aid and Reform in Africa.' Review of World Bank volume by S. Devarajan, D. R. Dollar and T. Holmgren." *Journal of African Economies* 10, no. 4, pp. 341–53.

———. 2015. *Aid Effectiveness* (United Nations Development Group (UNDG)). https://undg.org/wp-content/uploads/2015/01/Background-Study-on-Aid-Effectiveness.pdf

Verick, Sher D. 2006. *The Impact of Globalization on the Informal Sector in Africa* (Berlin: Economic and Social Policy Division, UNECA, and Institute for the Study of Labor). http://www.iza.org/conference_files/worldb2006/verick_s872.pdf

Wills, Gabrielle. 2009. *South Africa's Informal Economy: A Statistical Profile* (WIEGO Working Paper (Urban Policies), No. 6, April 2009). ISBN 978-92-95095-08-3.

World Bank. 2013. *Africa's Pulse: An Analysis of Issues Shaping Africa's Economic Future* (Washington, D.C.), p. 7.

———. 2014. "Kenya: A Sleeping Lion or Speedy Lioness?" *Country Economic Memorandum* (Washington, D.C.).

TWO

Ethiopia

An Agrarian Economy in Transition

Yared Seid, Alemayehu Seyoum Taffesse, and Seid Nuru Ali

E thiopia has experienced rapid economic growth since 2005, with
gross domestic product (GDP) growing at an average rate of 10.5 percent
per annum in real terms between 2004–05 and 2012–13 (Ministry of
Finance and Economic Development 2013). This makes Ethiopia one of
the fastest growing countries in the world. The rapid economic growth
has a multifaceted effect on a number of social, economic, and political
domains. Considering 2015 is the end of the first Growth and Transformation Plan (GTP), the country's comprehensive five-year development plan
with targets aligned to the aim of achieving middle-income status by the
mid-2020s, it is a good time to explore the pattern of the economic growth
in Ethiopia as well as the relevant growth opportunities and challenges.

Evidence suggests that economic growth in Ethiopia has been accompanied by signs of a structural shift away from traditional and
primary sectors and toward secondary and tertiary ones. For instance,
the pace of output growth has been decreasing in agriculture, whereas
growth rates of industrial and service sectors have been increasing. As

a result, the agriculture share of the GDP is now comparable to that of the service sector, a significant change relative to a couple of decades ago.

Both economic growth and structural shifts have important implications for poverty reduction and income distribution. Labor market outcomes are a potential major avenue through which these influences take place. The high rate of public investment in infrastructure has generated growth in construction and related industries and triggered growth in other sectors through its linkage effects. There are three major channels through which the process is believed to have influenced income distribution in the country. First, the investment on infrastructure and buildings led to higher employment of urban youth and rural migrants in construction and allied subsectors. Second, in part caused by this expansion of employment, the demand for goods and services rose. This is particularly significant to the agricultural sector, leading to improvements in terms of trade, in favor of the sector. Policy responses to these pressures have been aimed to raise productivity in agriculture and included expansion of the agricultural extension system. Structural change formed the third channel.

As a consequence of these changes, the role of agriculture has decreased continuously in the face of an increasing role of the service and construction sectors, and this has led to reallocation of jobs and labor from the low-productive agriculture sector to the high-productive service sector. Historical evidence shows that this type of labor reallocation is vital for more secure employment and higher living standards. The nation's effort is to diversify the shift of economic activities toward the manufacturing sector, to ensure more durable jobs and sustainable growth. This is, in particular, the focus of the second phase of the GTP, which began in the year 2015.

Another aspect of sectoral reallocations is their potential to engender more unequal outcomes. The possibility of this outturn is not small, since the jobs created in the service sector are, on average, relatively more knowledge-intensive and higher paying. The earnings gap between skilled and unskilled workers in Ethiopia can, thus, widen. This is obviously an empirical question. In this study, we, accordingly, attempt to collate and analyze the relevant evidence, such as within- and between-sector employment shifts, to ascertain whether economic growth and structural change in Ethiopia are pro-poor. Moreover, the study explores related social and economic changes that have affected employment of both skilled and unskilled workers in Ethiopia, including population growth and its demographic structure, the expansion of education, returns to education, and the role of the public sector and social protection programs in employment.

BACKGROUND

The following paragraphs consider the pace and sources of economic growth in Ethiopia, which has been observed since the mid-1990s, and the status of structural transformation in the country. The aim is to provide some background to subsequent discussion.

Trends in Economic Growth in Ethiopia

After being stagnant for many decades, Ethiopia's economy has experienced robust and continuous growth in the decade since 2005. Figure 2-1 presents trends in GDP growth in Ethiopia since 1990.[1] As can be seen from the figure, in the 1990s, GDP growth in Ethiopia was not only low on average, it was also highly volatile, with both high positive and negative growth rates throughout the decade. The outcome reflected a combination of factors, including recovery from a lengthy civil war, war with Eritrea (toward the end of the decade), and volatile weather, combined with heavy reliance of Ethiopian agriculture on rainfall and its very large contribution to total GDP. Since the mid-2000s, on the contrary, Ethiopia has enjoyed accelerated and sustained economic growth, with growth rates exceeding global averages. Indeed, it has become one of the fastest growing countries in the world, along with some Asian countries. Even during the global economic recession that began around 2008, Ethiopia continued to grow steadily.

In addition to favorable weather conditions for agriculture, a set of factors has contributed to the growth in Ethiopia. Conducive government policies, including large market reforms in the 1990s, are a vital and defining element of this set. Improvements in access to basic

FIGURE 2-1. *Gross Domestic Product (GDP) Growth in Ethiopia,*
1990–2014

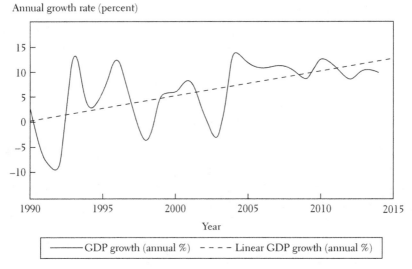

Annual growth rate (percent)

Year

———— GDP growth (annual %)   – – – – Linear GDP growth (annual %)

Source: Authors' computation using data from the World Development Indicators (WDI) database
(World Bank 2015b).

services (such as health and education) and heavy investment in infrastructure (such as roads and telecommunications) have significantly helped, also, by addressing critical bottlenecks. More broadly,
overall growth has been symbiotically accompanied by greater commercialization of agriculture and private sector development.

An important attribute of this high growth episode is that it has
been resilient to various shocks, such as drought and international economic crises, contrary to the nation's historical susceptibility to such
shocks. It can be shown that war in the 1990s and very early 2000s and
drought in 1975, 1985, 1997, and 2003 have had adverse effects on the
Ethiopian economy (see figure 2-2).

Sources of Growth

This section explores the sources of aggregate and sectoral growth
using Solow decomposition analysis. Such growth decomposition has a
long history, stretching back to Solow (1957).[2]

FIGURE 2-2. *Sustained Growth in per Capita GDP in Ethiopia (Hodrick– Prescott Decomposition)*

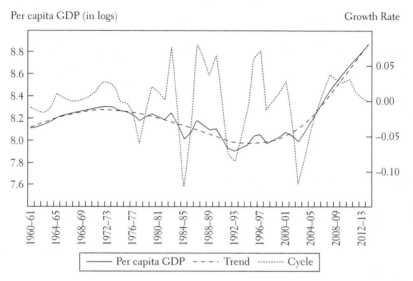

Source: Authors' calculations using data from Ministry of Finance and Economic Development (MoFED).

Table 2-1 reports half-decade averages for GDP growth and the part of that growth that originated in increased use of labor and capital as well as changes in total factor productivity (TFP).[3] The acceleration of GDP growth after 2004 is clear. Perhaps not surprisingly, the contribution of all factors rose in later years. Labor (employment expansion) continues to be an important source of growth. Interestingly, the role of labor quality improvements (particularly changes in labor composition) has edged upward again, albeit from a very low base and remaining still small. This is most likely linked to expansion in education and elements of structural change to be outlined later. The importance of capital as a source of growth is also going up with aggregate capital– labor and capital–output ratios increasing (figure 2-3). There is some corresponding micro-evidence suggesting capital intensity is rising and, more specifically, generating discernible productivity differentials in industry. Finally, consistent with Ethiopia's significant exposure to economic shocks in the past, changes in TFP were negative or weak as

TABLE 2-1. *Aggregate Growth Accounting for Ethiopia*

Percent

Period	GDP growth	Employment growth in GDP growth	Labor composition growth in GDP growth	Non-ICT capital services growth in GDP growth	Total factor productivity growth
1990–94	−1.23	0.96	0.03	1.01	−3.23
1995–99	4.37	1.49	0.02	2.42	0.43
2000–04	4.00	1.39	0.01	1.88	0.72
2005–09	9.80	2.01	0.00	3.10	4.69
2010–14	9.51	2.07	0.06	3.42	3.96

Source: Authors' computation using country details data from the Total Economy Database (TCB 2015b).
GDP = gross domestic product.
ICT = information and communication technologies.

a source of growth up to 2004. In contrast, they have been the largest contributor during the decade up to 2014. Nevertheless, TFP growth and its share in GDP growth appear to diminish slightly in the last half-decade (2010–14), perhaps indicative of things to come.

Finally, a comparison across the African Lions—the six large and rapidly growing African economies—reveals broad similarity among them regarding the role of employment expansion as a source of growth over the two and half decades since 1990. Whereas Ethiopia and Mozambique show comparable contributions from non-ICT (information and communication technologies) capital and TFP growth, South Africa, not surprisingly, is a clear outlier.

STATUS OF STRUCTURAL TRANSFORMATION IN ETHIOPIA

Studies on structural transformation (Chenery 1960, 1986; Syrquin 1988) have documented that capital accumulation (both physical and human), high rate of growth in per capita income, and a shift in economic activities from sectors of low productivity to sectors of high productivity are key signs of structural transformation. Ethiopia has been laying foundations to transform its economy since the mid-1990s. The most noticeable

FIGURE 2-3. *Signs of Capital Deepening in Ethiopia—Increasing Capital–Labor and Capital–Output Ratios*

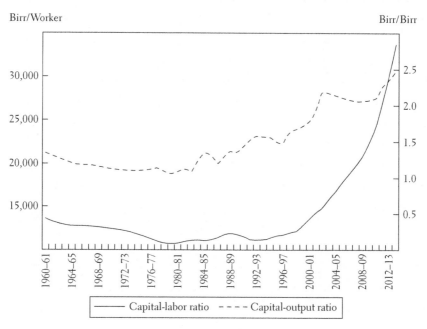

Source: Authors' computations using data from MoFED.

endeavors to be rewarded with high rates of economic growth took place under the country's Plan for Accelerated and Sustained Development to End Poverty (PASDEP), spanning the period from 2005–06 to 2009–10, and the GTP, which has been in place since 2010–11 (see figures 2-1 and 2-2 for trends in economic growth in Ethiopia).

The country's public investment in the economic and social infrastructure and its intervention in the rural economy have been paying off, both in terms of accumulations and in the form of high economic growth. For instance, the rate of gross capital formation expanded from 27.5 percent in 2010 to 40.3 percent in 2014. Efforts in domestic resource mobilization resulted in a significant increase in the rate of gross domestic saving, from 7.6 percent in 2010 to 22.5 percent in 2014.

The process of accumulation seems to have succeeded on two counts. First, the country has developed a relatively better capability in

FIGURE 2-4. *Sectoral Shares of GDP in Ethiopia, 1990–2014*

GDP shares (percent)

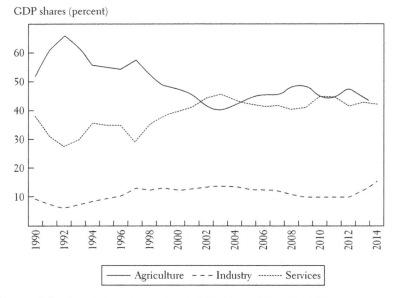

Source: Authors' calculations using data from the WDI database (World Bank 2015b).

terms of physical infrastructure and human capital. Second, the process of accumulation in the infrastructure sector has generated high growth in per capita income. The Ethiopian economy has grown at an average rate of 11 percent from 2005 to 2014.

Nevertheless, there are challenges to be tackled to ensure that such changes are accompanied by shifts in sectoral proportions in terms of factor use and contribution to GDP. The share of agricultural value added in GDP declined by about 10 percentage points between 1990 and 2014 (from 52 to 42 percent; see figure 2-4).

Moreover, measures of sectoral contributions to GDP growth reveal that the role of agriculture, which jointly led the growth momentum with the service sector during the period of PASDEP, has declined during the period of the first phase of the GTP. The industrial sector, which had a declining contribution to growth during PASDEP, reversed its momentum and doubled its contribution to growth during the first phase of the GTP. Changes in the growth contributions of subsectors also corroborate the fact that changes in the structure of the economy are occurring across sectors, from agriculture to service and construction sectors. Crop production, traditionally a dominant contributor, has been overtaken by construction and wholesale and retail trade subsectors. The increase in the industrial sector's contribution to growth has largely originated in the construction subsector.[4]

If the process of structural transformation in the Ethiopian economy is judged by the historical patterns of industrialization, there is still a lot to be done. The process that earned the nation an 11 percent growth in GDP and a 40 percent rate of gross capital accumulation was not accompanied by a substantial change in the share of the manufacturing sector in the economy. About 70 percent of the decline in the GDP share of agriculture was accounted for by the service sector, with the remaining 30 percent going to the construction sector. In contrast, the share of the manufacturing sector in GDP hovered around 4.4 percent in 2013–14, only 0.2 percentage points higher than its share in 2005.

Many studies (Bigsten and Gebreeyesus 2007; Siba 2010; Sutton and Kellow 2010; Söderbom and others 2006) identify limited access to credit, declining returns to capital, and limited backward and forward linkages as important constraints facing manufacturing in Ethiopia. Söderbom and others (2006) also hint at the limits to saving and reinvestment due to consumption needs of owners' households as another growth-restricting possibility.

Manufacturing firms also rely heavily on imported raw materials, which, generally, does not play to their advantage given the limited availability of foreign exchange and lack of access to adequate credit, particularly for small and medium-size firms. There is also a lack of appropriately skilled labor to support the production of high-quality manufacturing goods.[5]

The Ethiopian government has made the growth of manufacturing a major focus of its second and subsequent five-year development plans. It actively encourages the private sector to diversify activities from localized services to manufacturing by addressing some of the key bottlenecks already identified. In this regard, the considerable public investments in infrastructural capabilities are likely to support industrial expansion. Perhaps reflecting this collection of positive factors, the manufacturing sector had an encouraging performance, with its value added growing at an annual average rate of 17.2 percent between 2010 and 2014.

HUMAN CAPITAL DEVELOPMENT IN ETHIOPIA

Investment in human capital, in particular in education and health, has been one of the important pillars of intervention by the Ethiopian government to foster the long-term capabilities of the country and to deal with rampant poverty. Policies and social mobilization in these sectors have paid off in the form of improvements in the stock of human capital, better livelihoods, and reduced poverty. Key outcomes of social sector endeavors, including child and maternal care as well as family planning, are reductions in mortality and fertility rates. If effectively used, these are expected to result in yet another opportunity for Ethiopia's economic growth in the form of the demographic dividend.

Population Growth and the Demographic Dividend

With a population close to 100 million, Ethiopia is the second most populous country in Africa; only Nigeria has a larger population. The country is also characterized by a high, albeit falling, fertility rate. As a result, Ethiopia's population is expected to grow at a high rate in the coming few decades. The link between this population dynamic and economic growth is complicated. It depends on the size of the population, its age structure, the speed with which both are changing, and the policy response of governments to these changes (Bloom, Canning, and Sevilla 2003; Drummond, Thakoor, and Yu 2014). The demographic transition in the form of declining mortality and fertility rates leads to longer life expectancy and a bigger working-age population. The former encourages investment in education and health in general, particularly focused on children. The change in the age structure in favor of the working-age segment promotes savings, higher female labor force participation, and even lower fertility rates (Bloom, Canning, and Sevilla

2003). Moreover, the rise in share of the working-age population can lead to increased labor supply, lower dependency ratio, higher savings and investment, and larger output (Bloom, Canning, and Sevilla 2003; Gribble and Bremner 2012; Drummond, Thakoor, and Yu 2014). This potential for higher growth constitutes the demographic dividend. Appropriate government policies are required to realize this potential and avoid the possible negative effects of rapid population changes.

Data from the 2012 Inter-Censal Population Survey show that the national average fertility rate has decreased from 6.2 in 2007 to 4.6 in 2012, a 26 percent fall (Central Statistical Agency of Ethiopia 2013). The onset of the decline in fertility rate, the second phase of demographic transition, has followed the decline in overall mortality rates, the first stage of demographic transition. This implies that Ethiopia is on the right track to start enjoying the demographic dividend, in part through a growing labor force.

There are some indications that this may have started, albeit slowly. Fertility rates in Ethiopia are likely to remain high and, as a result, the country's population is expected to grow at a fast pace in the coming few decades. However, the age structure of the population will continue to change, as the fertility rate is projected to continue declining. The Ethiopian Central Statistical Agency (CSA), for instance, has projected that the percentage of children aged fourteen years or younger will decrease to 27 percent in 2037, from 44 percent in 2007, while the share of the working-age population will rise from 53 percent to 68 percent during the same period (CSA 2013). This is a good outcome because it implies a decrease in dependency ratio, which, indeed, is expected to fall from 0.89 in 2007 to 0.52 by 2037.[6]

Data from the 2015 revision of the "World Population Prospects" (United Nations 2015) reaffirms the decline in dependency ratio in Ethiopia, as depicted in figure 2-5. The figure shows that the dependency ratio has been declining continuously since the turn of the century, and although the dependency ratio for Ethiopia started to decline a bit later than the Sub-Saharan Africa (SSA) average, it did so at a faster rate. Hence, the dependency ratio for the country is currently below the SSA average. The change in Ethiopia's demographic structure is in the right direction but needs to go much further before the country can start

FIGURE 2-5. *Ratio of Working Age to Dependent Population in Ethiopia*

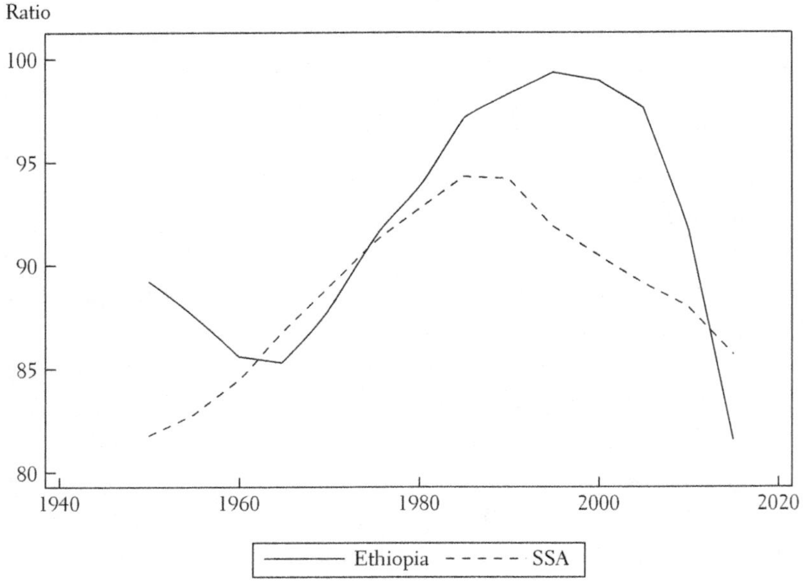

Ratio

Source: Authors' calculations using the "World Population Prospects" (United Nations 2015).

enjoying its demographic dividend (Gribble and Bremner 2012). Ethiopia has gone a long way in improving its stock of human capital. Nevertheless, more needs to be done in the spheres of education, health, family planning, and policies promoting savings and investment. All these are required to further increase its stock of human capital and boost job creation before Ethiopia starts to fully enjoy the demographic dividend.

Reforms in the Education Sector

One of the preconditions for exploiting any potential demographic dividend is a government's commitment and ability to provide basic health and education services. In this regard, the government of Ethiopia has been more efficient than other governments of similarly poor countries. Through a series of five-year education development programs, called Education Sector Development Programs (ESDPs), the government of Ethiopia has built a large number of primary and secondary schools throughout the country, with the prime objective of achieving universal primary education. This effort has been largely successful, as most of the regional states of Ethiopia have achieved universal primary education.

The government of Ethiopia also has aggressively introduced the Technical and Vocational Education and Training (TVET) program with the aim to increase the supply of semi-skilled and relatively well-suited workers to the growing manufacturing and construction sectors. These types of complementary investments have the potential to pay off in the long run by increasing labor productivity in these specific sectors as well as in the entire economy.

The government's effort in expanding TVET institutes is commendable and has led to substantial increases in the number of graduates from the institutes. Since the inception of the program, for instance, a large number of TVET institutes have been built. As a result, according to data from the Ministry of Education (1999–2015), the number of students enrolled in TVET institutes increased from 5,264 in academic year 1999–2000 to 271,389 in 2014–15. This, in turn, has led to a large increase in the number and range of available skills in the Ethiopian labor market.[7]

However, there appears to be a mismatch between the types of skills students acquire at TVET institutes and the skill sets most manufacturing firms are looking for. Besides that, research findings indicate that the quality of TVET graduates does not meet the quality standards of manufacturing firms, and the TVET program does not seem to be driven by demand (Shaorshadze and Krishnan 2013). Thus, careful assessment of the sector to understand the current skill gaps and the trajectory of skill needs is crucial for tailoring the TVET program to the requirements of manufacturing firms.

In this regard, the federal TVET agency has taken steps to improve the quality and relevance of the TVET program. In line with this, the agency has adopted and expanded cooperative training programs by bringing an increasing number of public and private enterprises into the training process. In cooperative training, theory is taught in TVET institutes and practical skills are acquired through student apprenticeship in the enterprises. As trainees must be supervised and may operate expensive equipment, offering training is costly to enterprises. Also, increasing the number of enterprises that participate in cooperative training programs is a serious obstacle. The challenge, thus, is convincing enterprises that participating in the apprenticeship scheme is profitable.

At the same time, there have been ongoing debates and attempts to define occupational standards, assess occupational standards, and, subsequently, certify TVET trainees. Certification of occupational qualification has, thus, been introduced into the TVET system. The certificates are awarded to students upon passing the occupational assessments. Unlike previous practice, access to occupational qualifications does not depend on attending a formal TVET program. This means graduates from any formal or nonformal TVET program now have access to occupational assessment and certification, including those who have learned informally and those who have acquired the skills through traditional apprenticeship.

Similarly, higher education has also gone through restructuring since the mid-1990s. The rapid expansion of both private and public colleges has been one of the major changes in higher education. As a result, the number of public colleges in Ethiopia has increased from eleven in academic year 1999–2000 to thirty-four in 2013–14, according to data from the Ministry of Education (1999–2015). Hence, college enrollment has increased from a little more than 10,000 in 1990 to more than 360,000 in 2015. This number is expected to grow further with the planned inauguration of more than ten new public universities as well as possible private colleges.

The expansion of college education availability and the high population growth rate have put tremendous pressure on the Ethiopian labor market. Approximately 600,000 individuals enter the labor force every year (World Bank 2007). The economy, however, does not seem to create enough jobs to match this influx. The imbalance between the increase in the supply of and demand for workers in Ethiopia has resulted in a high unemployment rate and long unemployment duration, particularly among the youth.

Unemployment is a new phenomenon in Ethiopia's skilled labor market. Anecdotal evidence suggests that the large increase in the number of college graduates following the expansion of tertiary education in recent years partly explains the high unemployment rate and long unemployment duration among new college graduates. In academic year 2009–10, for instance, 66,999 students graduated from college (Ministry of Education 1999–2015) and entered the skilled labor market, whereas a total of 46,304 vacancies were reported during the same year, of which only 13 percent (about 6,020) were opened for skilled workers (Ministry of Labour and Social Affairs 2009–10). As a result, mean unemployment duration among new college graduates seems to be rising. In fact, one recent estimate puts it as high as forty-five months (Serneels 2007).

Restricted/costly information flow between employers and job seekers can lead to longer spells of job search and unemployment for new college graduates. Understanding how the labor market functions, particularly the job search process, is crucial to addressing this issue. In Ethiopia, the majority of employers advertise job openings in newspapers and/or on small boards installed on the busiest street corners and squares of cities in which the employers are located. It is not likely that these types of advertisements will reach the large number of new college graduates throughout the country. Also, there is no communication among employers to coordinate their job advertisements and post them at a specific period of the year, say, around the months during which college students graduate. Rather, job openings are advertised randomly throughout the year, which may negatively affect the intensity of the job search and, hence, increase the unemployment duration.

On the other hand, senior college students do not generally start looking for jobs before they graduate. Starting the job search early (that is, while they are still in college) may help reduce the unemployment duration among new college graduates. That most universities do not have career placement offices to assist graduating seniors in their job search means it is difficult for students to initiate such searches. Moreover, in most cases, employers require job applicants to have their degree certificates in hand when they apply for jobs.

Considering the Ethiopian skilled labor market is not well organized, it is worth exploring the role information plays in unemployment duration among new college graduates. Better flow of information may improve the functioning of the labor market by increasing both the intensity of the job search and the quality of the job match. Job fairs may be one mechanism to nurture and exploit in this regard.

Educational Expansion and Returns to Education

As discussed earlier, the Ethiopian education sector has undergone a series of changes since the mid-1990s. As a result, both enrollment and graduation from primary, secondary, and tertiary schools have increased significantly. Overall, Ethiopia has achieved universal primary school enrollment and the average years of schooling in the country have increased. However, the same cannot be said for improvement in quality. In fact, some commentators argue that the quality of education has been compromised during the period of rapid school expansion (Kahsay 2012).

Although there is no rigorous research on the effect of this school expansion program on the returns to education in Ethiopia, it is plausible that the increase in years of schooling for an average worker led to higher earnings. It is also likely that negative changes in the quality of education dampened the effect of the education expansion on returns to education.

Human capital has been emphasized as a critical determinant of economic progress. Better educational attainment implies more skilled and productive workers who, in turn, increase an economy's output of goods and services. Given the importance of educational achievement, we first assess whether (non-agricultural) wageworkers in Ethiopia have become more educated over time. Using data from the 2005 and 2013 National Labour Force Surveys (CSA 2006, 2014), we present the education profile of workers in Ethiopia in 2005 and 2013 in figure 2-6.

As expected, a large proportion of workers in Ethiopia (40 percent) had completed only primary education in 2005, followed by workers with secondary (34 percent) and tertiary (25 percent) education. Only a very small proportion of workers (less than 1 percent) had completed more than a college education. In contrast, in 2013, about 46 percent of workers have completed secondary education, a 12 percentage points increase from the level in 2005. Similarly, the proportion of workers with above college education increased from 0.8 percent in 2005 to

FIGURE 2-6. *Workers' Education Level in Ethiopia*

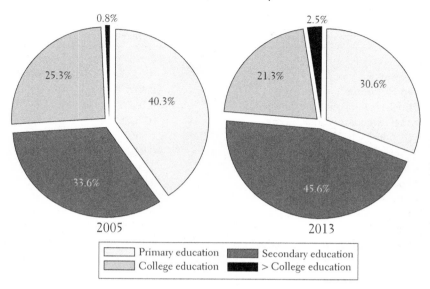

Source: Authors' computation based on data from the 2005 and 2013 National Labour Force Survey (CSA 2006, 2014).

2.5 percent in 2013, but the proportion of workers with primary and college education decreased.

There is extensive empirical work on returns to education, both in developed and developing countries. In Ethiopia, however, there are limited studies on the topic, particularly those that attempt to mitigate biases from potential endogeneity of ability in the returns to education equation.[8] Perhaps an exception to this is the study by Girma and Kedir (2005) that has attempted to deal with the potential endogeneity of ability by using instrumental variable quantile regression. The authors found a positive and significant effect of education on earnings and that the returns to education are higher for people at the lower end of the income distribution. For instance, the impact of schooling at the 25th quantile is more than 10 percentage points higher than the returns to education at the 90th quantile.

Given the data we have (that is, pooled cross-sectional data from the 2005 and 2013 National Labour Force Survey (see CSA 2006, 2014)), it is

TABLE 2-2. *Ordinary Least Squares Regression of the Returns to Education in Ethiopia*

	Coefficient	SE
Age	0.070***	0.004
Age squared	−0.001***	0.000
Female dummy	−0.426***	0.014
Primary school graduate dummy	0.141***	0.030
Some secondary school dummy	0.281***	0.025
Secondary school graduate dummy	0.566***	0.025
Some college education dummy	0.842***	0.025
College graduate dummy	1.204***	0.031
Above college education dummy	1.454***	0.038
Father's years of schooling	−0.029***	0.003
Mother's years of schooling	0.013***	0.002
Married dummy	0.274***	0.023
Divorced/widowed/separated dummy	−0.151**	0.070
Constant	4.606***	0.164
Observations	19,104	
R^2	0.528	

Source: Authors' calculations using data from the 2005 and 2013 National Labour Force Survey of Ethiopia, Ethiopian Central Statistical Agency, 2006 and 2014.

Notes: The dependent variable is log(wage). Robust standard error (SE) is clustered by enumeration area, a primary sampling unit. The regression also controls for district and year fixed effects.

*$p < 0.10$, **$p < 0.05$, ***$p < 0.01$.

difficult to control for endogeneity of ability in the returns to education equation. However, as a complementary analysis to prior studies conducted on the returns to education in Ethiopia, and in the interest of presenting more current results, we estimated the returns to education equation using ordinary least squares regression and uncovered positive correlation between earnings and education level (see table 2-2 for regression results).

In table 2-2, the coefficient estimates of education level dummies are positive and statistically significant, implying reasonably high returns to education. For instance, workers who completed primary education earn 14.1 percent higher wages relative to workers with below primary level education (the omitted group). The table also shows that returns to education increase with years of schooling, where workers with above college education earn the highest.

THE EFFECT OF ECONOMIC GROWTH ON THE LABOR MARKET

As indicated, there are important changes in the Ethiopian economy, including huge investment in infrastructure, interventions in the agriculture sector, and rapid economic growth. These changes are expected to alter the structure of the labor market, which, in itself, is one of the indicators of intensity of structural transformation in an economy. Changes in labor force participation, unemployment rate, sectoral share of employment, productivity, and wage rates are some of the indicators of changes in the structure of the labor market. In this part of the analysis, we consider trends and patterns of labor force participation, employment-to-population ratios, sectoral distribution of workers, unemployment rates, and labor engagement in the informal sector to make a preliminary judgment on the impact of the change in the economic momentum on the structure of the labor force over the last fifteen years. The analysis uses data from the 1999, 2005, and 2013 National Labour Force Survey (CSA 1999, 2006, 2014) and the Groningen Growth and Development Centre (GGDC) 10-Sector Database of the University of Groningen (Timmer and others 2014).

The general observation is that the nationwide activity rate of the labor force increased between the years 1999 and 2013, and the change is predominantly attributed to the increase in female labor force participation in rural areas. This pattern has been corroborated by the rise in the employment-to-population ratio over the same period. The rise in employment-to-population ratio is dominated by the increase in female labor force participation in rural as well as urban areas of the country.

A decline is recorded in the share of labor force in the agriculture sector by 7.5 percentage points between 2005 and 2013. This rate is paralleled by an increase in the share of labor force in the service and construction sectors. The subsectors in the service sector in which net labor flow has increased vary significantly by geography and gender. Consistent with productivity measures, there is no net shift of labor force to the manufacturing sector during the period between 2005 and 2013.

Other important developments during the period under consideration include a decline in unemployment rate in both rural and urban

TABLE 2-3. *Rates of Labor Force Participation in Ethiopia*

Percent

	Rates of participation		
	1999	2005	2013
Ethiopia			
Male + Female	80.5	84.5	83.6
Male	89.7	90.7	89.6
Female	71.9	78.8	77.8
Rural areas			
Male + Female	81.5	87.2	86.2
Male	91.2	93.7	91.7
Female	72.3	81.2	80.8
Urban Centers			
Male + Female	75.0	71.4	74.1
Male	81.5	75.8	81.6
Female	69.8	67.7	67.5

Source: National Labour Force Surveys, Ethiopian Central Statistical Agency, 1999, 2006, and 2014.

areas and a decline in the share of labor force operating in the informal sector in urban centers.

Changes in Labor Force Participation

There is an overall rise in labor force participation rate between 1999 and 2013 (see table 2-3). The change in participation rate is solely accounted for by the rise in participation of female workers. Between 1999 and 2013, labor force participation rates increased by about 6 percentage points for female workers. This change is the result of the upsurge in activity rate among rural women. The rise was robust enough to more than offset the decline in participation rate of female workers in urban centers (see table 2-3).[9]

Changes in the Employment-to-Population Ratio

The employment-to-population ratio is found to have increased by about 7 percentage points between 1999 and 2013 (see table 2-4). Consistent

TABLE 2-4. *Trends in Employment-to-Population Ratio by Gender in Ethiopia*

Percent

	Employment-to-population ratio		
	1999	*2005*	*2013*
Ethiopia			
Male + female	69.1	76.6	76.2
Male	80.2	84.7	82.7
Female	58.5	69.0	69.8
Rural areas			
Male + female	73.0	82.0	81.6
Male	84.0	89.8	86.9
Female	62.1	74.4	76.3
Urban centers			
Male + female	48.2	50.2	55.5
Male	57.4	57.7	65.6
Female	40.5	43.7	46.6

Source: National Labour Force Surveys, Ethiopian Central Statistical Agency, 2000, 2006, and 2014.

with the trend in labor force participation rate, the significant increase in the employment-to-population ratio is accounted for by the increase in employment of female workers. Unlike in the case of labor force participation rate, the rise in employment-to-population ratio was also an urban phenomenon, though the change in rural areas is by far greater.

Between- and Within-Sector Employment Shift

In this part of the analysis, we consider sectoral contributions of labor to the Ethiopian economy using time series data from the GGDC 10-Sector Database (Timmer and others 2014). Figure 2-7 shows the interaction between GDP and employment growth by sector. Each of the bubbles in the figure represents a sector. The vertical axis measures average annual employment growth, whereas the horizontal axis shows the annual growth in gross value added, both in percentages. Thus, the coordinates for the center of each of the bubbles are the relevant sector's

FIGURE 2-7. *Mean Value Added and Employment Growth by Sector in
Ethiopia, 1990–2011*

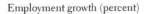

Employment growth (percent)

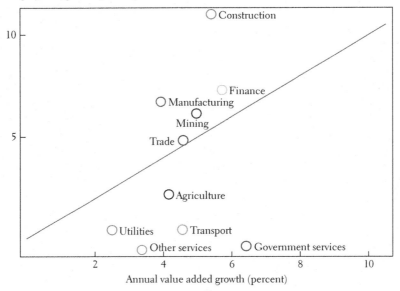

Annual value added growth (percent)

Source: Authors' computation based on data from the GGDC 10-Sector Database (Timmer and others 2014).

employment and gross value added growth rates for the period. The 45°
line divides the figure into two sections. Bubbles below the line represent sectors in which employment growth was lower than gross value
added growth, whereas bubbles above the line represent sectors in which
employment growth exceeded output growth.

Figure 2-7 shows that all sectors in Ethiopia did well in the period
between 1990 and 2011, where each sector experienced positive output
growth. Regarding employment growth during the same period, however,
"government services" and "other services" (that is, community, social,
and personal services) performed particularly poorly, with negative
employment growth, suggesting employment in these two sectors
shrank during the period of analysis. Note that these are the only two
sectors that experienced contractions in employment in the period of
analysis, with employment growth in government services and other

services contracting by 0.4 and 0.6 percent, respectively. One potential factor contributing to the contraction of employment in the government services sector could be the privatization of a number of government-owned enterprises, particularly in the 1990s.

The construction sector experienced a disproportionately high level of employment expansion in the period between 1990 and 2011, where the employment growth (11 percent) was almost twice as high as output growth (5.6 percent) in the sector. This is not surprising considering the construction boom in Ethiopia since the early 2000s, which is driven by, among other factors, large public investment in infrastructure development, including the construction of large dams such as the Grand Ethiopian Renaissance Dam.

Financial services, mining, and manufacturing sectors also experienced higher employment growth than growth in output. Specifically, employment growth for the finance, mining, and manufacturing sectors was 7.3, 6.1, and 6.5 percent, respectively, for the period of analysis. In contrast, the corresponding output growth rate for these sectors was 5.9, 5.1, and 4.1 percent, respectively. Trade, on the other hand, experienced labor-neutral growth, where both employment and output grew by about 5 percent. The agriculture sector experienced growth in both output and employment, the latter at a slower pace. Finally, the utilities and transport subsectors recorded employment growth rates of 0.41 and 0.44 percent, respectively.

When we look at the patterns of within-sector employment shift between 2005 and 2013 using a different dataset, a similar pattern emerges. As discussed, changes in sectoral shares in employment of factors of production, in particular labor, are both important outcomes of critical changes in the economy and also key indicators of intensity of structural transformation within an economy.

Data from the 2005 and 2013 National Labour Force Survey (CSA 2006, 2014) reveal that the share of labor in the agriculture sector declined by 7.5 percentage points between 2005 and 2013.[10] This is paralleled by the increase in the share of labor in the service sector by 5.8 percentage points and in other industries (typically, the construction subsector) by 1.1 percentage points. In contrast, the manufacturing sector's share of the labor force declined marginally (0.4 percent).

A major focus of the development effort in Ethiopia has been on laying foundations for industrialization in the form of infrastructure such as roads, railways, power, telecommunications, and human capital formation. This focus had two implications for the manufacturing sector. First, initially limited infrastructure meant the country was less ready for manufacturing development. Power shortage is a case in point. Second, the service sector has enjoyed better linkages with high rates of return to the relatively large public investments on social and economic infrastructure, thus attracting investors away from the relatively risky manufacturing sector. In the face of quick and high rates of returns in the service sector, the manufacturing sector is believed to have encountered a number of deterrents. Banks tend to extend loans to short-term businesses in the service sector rather than to the manufacturing sector. The backward linkage of the manufacturing sector within itself and with the agriculture sector is weak, thus compelling investors to rely on imported raw materials and face the corresponding constraints.

A closer look at the patterns of changes in the sectoral share at disaggregated (that is, subsector) level (in table 2-5), on the other hand, reveals that the 7.5 percentage points decline in the share of labor in agriculture and allied activities is paralleled by a 6.7 percentage points increase in the share of labor in the subsectors of services such as social, cultural, personal household activities, and activities by private households with employed persons. The balance is distributed to other subsectors, the maximum being a 1 percentage point rise in education and health sectors.

The patterns of change in the distribution of the labor force by rural and urban centers of economic activities are different among sectors. In the case of urban centers, the share of labor in the wholesale and retail trade, hotels and restaurants, public administration and defense, and other household services has declined. This decline is largely dominated by the decline in female labor. The other side of the change is that the share of labor in other subsectors (that is, construction, transport, storage, communication, real estate and business activities, and health and education sectors) has increased. Female labor has dominated the increase in the share of labor in the health, education, and social work subsector, whereas male labor has dominated the increase in the labor force in the other subsectors.

Changes in Unemployment Rate

In general, there is a decline in the national rate of unemployment among people age fifteen years and above, from 8.2 percent in 1999 to 5.4 percent in 2013. Unemployment in Ethiopia has been an urban phenomenon. Over the same period, urban unemployment dropped from 26.1 to 21.0 percent (see figure 2-8).

A Transition of Labor from the Informal to the Formal Sector

One of the important developments in the structure of the Ethiopian labor force is the significant decline in the share of the labor force operating in the informal sector. Between 1999 and 2013, the share of labor force in the informal sector declined from 50.6 to 25.8 percent. The usually high rate of female labor force in the informal sector declined from 64.8 percent in 1999 to 36.5 percent in 2013, and the share of male labor force more than halved, dropping from 38.9 to 18.1 percent (see figure 2-9).

Differential Effects of Economic Growth on Skilled and Unskilled Workers

In recent years, Ethiopia has seen patterns of economic transformation that have directly affected its labor market, particularly the salaried urban sector. Real wages have shown strong increases across the distribution, where the increase in wages is relatively higher for skilled workers.

The Blinder–Oaxaca wage decomposition between skilled and unskilled workers reveals that unskilled and skilled workers, on average, earn about 1,021 and 1,782 Ethiopian birr (ETB) per month, respectively. This is a wage differential of 761 ETB per month in favor of skilled workers. Our regression analysis suggests that changes in demographic and labor market characteristics explain a large portion (i.e., 55 percent)

TABLE 2-5. *Change in the Composition of Labor Force by Subsectors, 2005–13*

Percentage points

Major industrial divisions	Country total			Urban			Rural		
	Total	Male	Female	Total	Male	Female	Total	Male	Female
Agriculture, hunting, forestry, and fishing	-7.5	-4.8	-10.8	0.5	0.2	0.7	-5.3	-1.6	-9.6
Mining and quarrying	0.1	0.2	0.1	0.3	0.5	0.0	0.2	0.1	0.1
Manufacturing	-0.4	0.6	-1.5	0.1	0.1	0.3	-1.0	0.1	-2.2
Electricity, gas, and water supply	0.4	0.2	0.8	0.6	0.5	0.7	0.4	0.1	0.7
Construction	0.5	0.7	0.2	2.1	2.6	1.2	0.1	0.1	0.0
Wholesale and retail trade, repair of vehicles, personal and household goods	0.2	-0.1	0.6	-1.8	-3.9	1.0	-0.3	-0.4	-0.2
Hotels and restaurants	-1.4	0.0	-2.8	-5.7	-0.5	-11.3	-1.0	0.0	-2.1
Transport, storage, and communication	0.5	0.7	0.2	1.9	2.6	0.8	0.1	0.1	-2.7
Financial intermediation	0.2	0.3	0.2	0.9	1.1	0.6	0.0	0.0	0.0

Real estate, renting, and business activities	0.5	0.6	0.4	2.5	2.9	2.1	0.1	0.0	0.1
Public administration and defense, compulsory social security	-0.5	-0.5	-0.5	-3.5	-4.8	-2.1	-0.2	-0.2	-0.4
Education, health, and social work	1.0	1.0	1.1	3.1	2.0	4.3	0.4	0.5	0.3
Other social, cultural, personal, and household activities	-0.3	-0.6	0.0	-2.5	-4.7	-0.1	-0.2	-0.4	-0.2
Private households with employed persons	6.5	1.8	12.0	1.1	1.2	1.6	7.1	1.8	13.4
Extraterritorial organization and bodies	-0.1	-0.2	-0.2	-0.4	-0.5	-0.2	-0.2	-0.2	-0.1

Source: National Labour Force Surveys, Ethiopian Central Statistical Agency, 2006 and 2014.

FIGURE 2-8. *Changes in Unemployment Rate in Ethiopia, 1999–2013*

Percent

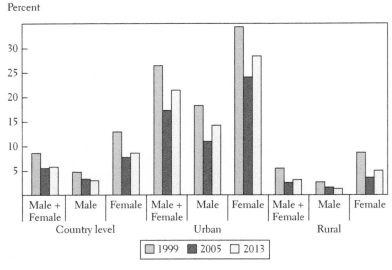

Source: National Labour Force Surveys, Central Statistical Agency, 2000, 2006, and 2014.

FIGURE 2-9. *Trends in the Proportion of Labor Force in the Informal Sector in Ethiopia, 1999–2013*

Percent

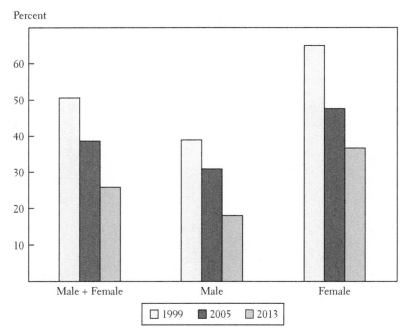

Source: National Labour Force Surveys, Central Statistical Agency, 2000, 2006, and 2014.

of the observed increase in wage among skilled workers.[11] The results from our analysis also indicate that the increase in wages is driven by faster wage growth for high-skilled jobs.

Although it is difficult to be conclusive, the results from our Blinder–Oaxaca decomposition analysis seem to suggest that Ethiopia is in some sort of skill-biased labor demand trajectory. This, too, is implied by the discussion above, where data from the National Labour Force Surveys of 2005 and 2013 (CSA 2006, 2014) show that the employment share of agriculture has decreased by 7.5 percentage points, whereas that of the service sector has increased by 5.8 percentage points. This is particularly true since the average number of years of schooling among workers in the industrial sector is higher than that of workers in the agriculture sector.

The Role of Public Sector in Employment

Given the extensive history of Ethiopia, public administration has long been at the center of different regimes in the country. However, the inception of modern public administration and the emergence of civil servants and public enterprises are believed to have become prominent since the beginning of the twentieth century.

The public sector has gone through a number of reforms since the current government came to power in 1991. In particular, the government put in place a number of political and economic measures that influenced the role and the relative importance of the public sector in the economy. Following the country's change in economic ideology from a mixed/command economy to a market-based economy and the subsequent adoption of the World Bank's Structural Adjustment Program in the 1990s, a number of government-owned enterprises have been privatized. Another major reform during the 1990s was the issuance of a retrenchment policy, resulting in the cutback of civil servants and employees of public enterprises who were said to be redundant. Among other things, these changes have decreased the relative role the public sector plays in the economy as well as in job creation.

These changes and the subsequent policy choices made by the government are based on the assumption that the private sector is the

TABLE 2-6. *Public Sector Employment Share in Urban Ethiopia by Gender and Year*

Percent

	2003	2006	2009
Male	24	22	14
Female	16	14	13
Male + female	20	19	13

Source: Authors' calculation based on data from the Urban Employment Unemployment Survey (Ethiopian Central Statistical Agency 2000–09).

engine of growth. As a result, the relative size of the public sector (in total GDP and employment) has been decreasing continuously since the 1990s.

Although lack of data prevents us from presenting the effects of the policy changes (which favored the private sector) on the role of the public sector in employment in the 1990s, table 2-6 shows the change in the employment share in the public sector in the 2000s.

As can be seen in table 2-6, the relative share of the public sector in total employment has been continuously decreasing in the 2000s. In 2003, for instance, about 20 percent of workers in urban areas in Ethiopia were employed by the public sector. This figure fell to 13 percent in 2009, a 35 percent decrease from its 2003 level. Table 2-6 also shows that the decrease in the employment share of the public sector was nearly, but not quite gender neutral; the decrease was a bit higher among male workers.

The Role of Social Protection in Growth and Employment

Most of the social protection programs in Ethiopia target people in rural areas, with the Productive Safety Net Programme (PSNP) being the largest social protection program in the country and the second largest in SSA, next only to South Africa (Gilligan and others 2009). PSNP is a government program that attempts to offer temporary public works employment as well as food or cash transfer to eligible households.

Attempts have been made to assess the effects of PSNP on a number of growth-related outcome variables. For instance, it has been documented that PSNP increases the likelihood that households will use improved agricultural technologies and be more food secure (Gilligan and others 2009), increases the number of trees that households plant (Andersson and others 2011), and improves child nutrition (Debela and others 2014).

Evidence for the effects of PSNP on employment is, however, limited, except the findings by Gilligan and others (2009) that there are no short-term disincentive effects of PSNP on labor supply. The scarcity of evidence for the effect of PSNP on employment is surprising considering the program is also designed to provide employment (that is, public works) to vulnerable households during the agricultural slack season.

Although Ethiopia's PSNP is one of the largest social protection programs ever, a parallel government-sponsored social protection program is not yet available to vulnerable urban households in Ethiopia despite the tremendous pressure faced by the Ethiopian urban labor market in recent years.

As mentioned, Ethiopia is the second most populous country in Africa and has one of the highest fertility rates in the continent. The fast growing population puts tremendous pressure on the Ethiopian labor market. Approximately 600,000 individuals enter the labor force every year (World Bank 2007). The economy, however, does not create enough jobs to match the influx of workers into the labor market. The imbalance between available jobs and the increase in the supply of workers results in high unemployment rates and long unemployment duration, particularly among the youth. These issues suggest a need to introduce government-sponsored urban safety net programs. The government's effort to do so is at a well-advanced design stage. More broadly, studies on the design of urban social protection programs in other typical developing countries have strong potential to inform policy makers in Ethiopia.

CONCLUSIONS

Since the mid-1990s, there have been significant public investments in Ethiopia. The nation has invested significantly in social and economic infrastructure such as roads, schools, health facilities, and, more recently, railways and energy. These investments are a vital ingredient to enhancing the nation's long-term capabilities. Considerable effort has also been exerted to transform the agriculture sector, reduce vulnerability of rural livelihood to adverse shocks, and transform the rural areas, more broadly. More specifically, agricultural extension programs have been extended, schools have become considerably more widely available and accessible in rural areas, preventive rural health facilities have been expanded, and rural road networks have been enlarged. Recent interventions in urban development in the form of urban infrastructure and major housing schemes have not only contributed to the modernization of urban spaces but also created jobs for many urban youth.

Such investments spearheaded by the Ethiopian government have generated fast economic growth, on average 11 percent real GDP growth between 2005 and 2014. This growth has translated into rising incomes, with per capita GDP doubling between 2000 and 2014 (WDI database, World Bank 2015b). Indeed, growth has led to reductions in poverty from a 45.5 percent head count rate to 29.6 percent between 1995 and 2012. Combined with successes in the health sector, income growth has also contributed to the rise of life expectancy to sixty-three years in 2013, up from forty-three to forty-six years in the early 1990s.

Following the investments and other policy interventions, economic activities have shown signs of shifting from the agriculture sector to the services and construction sectors. The contribution of the traditionally dominant crop subsector to the growth of GDP has been overtaken by the construction sector, followed by the wholesale and retail trade sector. The change in the share of the labor force has also been in line with changes in productivity. Changes in the labor force participation rate and employment-to-population ratio, in particular among the female labor force, the reduction in unemployment rate, and the movement of labor outside the agriculture sector (up to 7.5 percentage points) are indicative of some level of change in the structure of the economy. Still, the country has to continue to deepen its focus on long-term capabilities toward industrialization.

Although investments in the manufacturing sector show encouraging trends with fairly high growth in value added in the sector (17 percent between 2010 and 2014), overall contribution to overall output and employment growth has been overwhelmed by the sheer rate of expansion of value added growth in the construction sector. This trend can be deemed positive because of the nature of investment in the construction sector; most of the investments are targeted toward curbing infrastructural and energy constraints for the much-anticipated expansion of the manufacturing sector.

The next primary focus for the country is to ensure ways of redirecting the already accumulated capabilities toward delivering sustainable growth and development. This, in particular, calls for changing gears toward the more productive sectors, such as new niches in the agriculture sector and targeted manufacturing industries.

Cognizant of such a need for transforming the Ethiopian economy toward a vibrant manufacturing industry, beginning in 2014–15, the second phase of the GTP—Ethiopia's major policy and planning framework—has duly emphasized the indispensable role of the private sector in this process. The correct stress on domestic resource mobilization needs to include widening the set of saving and investment instruments available to citizens of the country.

APPENDIX TABLE 2A-1. *GDP Growth Decomposition in Ethiopia*

Percent

Country	Years	GDP growth	Employment	Labor composition	ICT capital services	Non-ICT capital services	Total factor productivity
					GDP growth due to growth/change in:		
Ethiopia	1990–94	-1.23	0.96	0.03	n.a.	1.01	-3.23
	1995–99	4.37	1.49	0.02	n.a.	2.42	0.43
	2000–04	4.00	1.39	0.01	n.a.	1.88	0.72
	2005–09	9.80	2.01	0.00	n.a.	3.10	4.69
	2010–14	9.51	2.07	0.06	n.a.	3.42	3.96
	1990–2014	5.29	1.58	0.02	n.a.	2.36	1.31
Ghana	1990–94	4.04	0.27	0.01	n.a.	-0.45	4.20
	1995–99	4.29	1.03	0.01	n.a.	0.27	2.98
	2000–04	4.71	1.04	0.00	n.a.	0.29	3.38
	2005–09	5.87	1.77	0.00	n.a.	2.77	1.34
	2010–14	7.88	2.21	0.08	n.a.	1.61	3.98
	1990–2014	5.36	1.26	0.02	n.a.	0.90	3.18
Kenya	1990–94	1.56	2.60	0.05	0.21	0.53	-1.83
	1995–99	2.81	3.16	0.07	0.30	0.41	-1.14
	2000–04	2.66	2.12	0.05	0.36	0.34	-0.22
	2005–09	4.13	1.84	0.04	0.75	1.27	0.23
	2010–14	5.69	1.88	0.14	1.15	1.35	1.17
	1990–2014	3.37	2.32	0.07	0.55	0.78	-0.36

Country	Period						
Mozambique	1990–94	3.05	1.52	0.01	n.a.	1.42	0.10
	1995–99	11.01	1.62	0.00	n.a.	3.98	5.40
	2000–04	7.18	0.95	0.00	n.a.	4.77	1.46
	2005–09	7.36	0.72	0.00	n.a.	3.78	2.86
	2010–14	7.04	0.91	0.04	n.a.	6.30	-0.21
	1990–2014	7.13	1.15	0.01	n.a.	4.05	1.92
Nigeria	1990–94	2.00	0.90	0.07	0.11	-0.08	0.99
	1995–99	2.45	1.19	0.07	0.28	0.72	0.19
	2000–04	9.71	0.89	0.07	0.76	0.77	7.23
	2005–09	6.24	1.12	0.06	3.18	3.09	-1.21
	2010–14	5.61	0.88	0.10	5.02	2.39	-2.78
	1990–2014	5.20	1.00	0.07	1.87	1.38	0.89
South Africa	1990–94	0.06	1.51	0.30	0.42	0.20	-2.37
	1995–99	2.55	0.91	0.43	0.73	0.88	-0.40
	2000–04	3.55	0.29	0.41	0.71	1.09	1.04
	2005–09	3.60	0.71	0.41	1.67	2.11	-1.30
	2010–14	2.49	0.83	0.20	1.61	1.81	-1.96
	1990–2014	2.45	0.85	0.35	1.03	1.22	-1.00
Tanzania	1990–94	3.92	1.40	0.01	n.a.	2.94	-0.42
	1995–99	3.96	1.17	0.01	n.a.	0.97	1.81
	2000–04	6.35	1.40	0.01	n.a.	0.09	4.85
	2005–09	6.15	1.75	0.01	n.a.	2.25	2.15
	2010–14	6.90	1.32	0.04	n.a.	3.62	1.91
	1990–2014	5.46	1.41	0.01	n.a.	1.98	2.06

Source: Authors' computation using country details data from the Total Economy Database™ (TCB 2015b).
GDP = gross domestic product.
ICT = information and communication technologies.
n.a. = data not available.

APPENDIX 2

APPENDIX TABLE 2A-2. *Students in Public and Private TVET Institutes in Ethiopia by Sector, 2015*

Number

	Public institutes			Private institutes			Public + private institutes		
	Levels 1 + 2	Levels 3 + 4	Level 5	Levels 1 + 2	Levels 3 + 4	Level 5	Levels 1 + 2	Levels 3 + 4	Level 5
Agriculture	8,083	4,554	96	1,972	1,356	147	10,055	5,910	243
Industry	43,088	11,051	2,183	4,618	1,484	889	47,706	12,535	3,072
Mining	96	0	0	0	0	0	96	0	0
Utilities	80,716	54,578	1,829	18,208	7,160	5,391	98,924	61,738	7,220
Trade	60	218	0	74	445	0	134	663	0
Health	1,070	4,214	236	1,430	2,947	1,812	2,500	7,161	2,048
Tourism	6,244	952	159	886	480	60	7,130	1,432	219
Social Affairs	2,015	40	0	478	70	0	2,493	110	0
Total	141,372	75,607	4,503	27,666	13,942	8,299	169,038	89,549	12,802

NOTES

1. Analogous patterns emerge from the data of the Ministry of Finance and Economic Development (MoFED) from various years.

2. For further details, see Barro (1998), among others. Also see World Bank (2015c) for a more detailed examination of the growth performance of the Ethiopian economy covering 2004–14. Bachewe and others (2015) do the same specifically for the agricultural sector.

3. This analysis uses the Total Economy Database™ to enhance cross-country comparisons (see The Conference Board 2015a). Analogous results were obtained using data from Ethiopia's Ministry of Finance and Economic Development (MoFED). See appendix table 2-A1 for complete data.

4. These are authors' calculations using data from Ministry of Finance and Economic Development (2013). The tables and charts summarizing the details of these trends can be obtained from the authors upon request.

5. World Bank (2015a, 2015c) provides detailed exploration of the prospects and challenges of manufacturing sector development in Ethiopia.

6. These figures refer to the medium variant of CSA's projections. See CSA (2013).

7. See Appendix table 2-A2 for the number of students enrolled in TVET institutes in Ethiopia in 2015.

8. Earning equations are the workhorse of estimating the returns to education. The specific challenge is effectively controlling for endogeneity of ability to earnings. For instance, more able individuals may be inherently different and earn more regardless of their education level. For this reason, it is important to control for differences in ability in the returns to education equation.

9. On the other hand, labor force participation rate by age group shows a slight decrease in activity rate among the young in urban areas, whereas a slight increase in activity rate is observed in rural areas for the similar age group. In general, the usual (inverted-U shaped) pattern of relationship between age and activity rate is maintained during the period of analysis.

10. The figures in this paragraph are computed from data collected by the National Labour Force Surveys of 2005 and 2013 (CSA 2006 and 2014).

11. The figures in this paragraph are computed using data from the National Labour Force Surveys of 2005 and 2013 (CSA 2006 and 2014). The complete regression results from Blinder–Oaxaca decomposition analysis are available upon request.

REFERENCES

Andersson, C., A. Mekonnen, and J. Stage. 2011. "Impacts of the Productive Safety Net Program in Ethiopia on Livestock and Tree Holdings of Rural Households." *Journal of Development Economics* 94 no. 1, pp. 119–26.

Bachewe, Fantu Nisrane, Guush Berhane, Bart Minten, and Alemayehu Seyoum Taffesse. 2015. "Agricultural Growth in Ethiopia (2004–2014): Evidence and Drivers." Working Paper 81 (Addis Ababa, Ethiopia: International Food Policy Research Institute/Ethiopia Strategy Support Program).

Barro, R. 1998. "Notes on Growth Accounting." (Harvard University). (http://scholar.harvard.edu/files/barro/files/notes_growth_accounting_1998.pdf).

Bigsten, A., and M. Gebreeyesus. 2007. "The Small, the Young, and the Productive: Determinants of Manufacturing Firm Growth in Ethiopia." *Economic Development and Cultural Change* 55, no. 4, pp. 813–40.

Bloom, David E., David Canning, and Jaypee Sevilla. 2003. *The Demographic Dividend—A New Perspective on the Economic Consequences of Population Change* (RAND).

Central Statistical Agency (CSA) of Ethiopia. 1999. "Statistical Report on the 1999 National Labour Force Survey (Statistical Bulletin 225)." (Addis Ababa: CSA). (http://www.csa.gov.et/images/documents/surveys/Labour_Force_Survey/Labour_Force_Survey_1999/survey0/data/docs/Pdf/Report/labour%20force%2019990001.pdf).

———. 2006. "Statistical Report on the 2005 National Labour Force Survey Statistical Bulletin 365." (Addis Ababa: CSA). (http://www.csa.gov.et/images/documents/surveys/Labour_Force_Survey/Labour_Force_Survey_2004/survey0/data/docs/Pdf/Report/Labour_force_survey_Final_Report_2005.pdf).

———. 2000–09. "Ethiopia: Urban Employment Unemployment Survey, (2009, 2006, 2010, 2011)." (Addis Ababa: CSA).

———. 2013. *Inter-Censal Population Survey 2012* (Addis Ababa: CSA).

———. 2014. *Statistical Report on the 2013 National Labour Force Survey* (Addis Ababa: CSA). (www.csa.gov.et/images/general/news/nlfs_statstical_report_2013).

Chenery, H. B. 1960. "Patterns of Industrial Growth." *American Economic Review* 50, no. 4, pp. 624–54.

———. 1986. "Growth and Transformation," in *Industrialization and Growth: A Comparative Study*, edited by H. Chenery, S. Robinson, and M. Syrquin (Oxford University Press).

Debela, B. L., G. Shively, and S. T. Holden. 2014. "Does Ethiopia's Productive Safety Net Program Improve Child Nutrition?" Working Paper 01/14 (Norwegian University of Life Sciences). (www.umb.no/statisk/clts/papers/clts_wp_01_14.pdf).

Drummond, Paulo, Vimal Thakoor, and Shu Yu. 2014. "Africa Rising: Harnessing the Demographic Dividend." Working Paper 14/143 (International Monetary Fund).

Gilligan, D. O., J. Hoddinott, and A. S. Taffesse. 2009. "The Impact of Ethiopia's Productive Safety Net Programme and Its Linkages." *Journal of Development Studies* 45, no. 10, pp. 1684–706.

Girma, S., and A. Kedir. 2005. "Heterogeneity in Returns to Schooling: Econometric Evidence from Ethiopia." *Journal of Development Studies* 41, no. 8, pp. 1405–16.

Gribble, James N., and Jason Bremner. 2012. "Achieving a Demographic Dividend." *Population Bulletin* 67, no. 2.

Kahsay, M. N. 2012. "Quality and Quality Assurance in Ethiopian Higher Education: Critical Issues and Practical Implications." Ph.D. Thesis. Universiteit Twente. (www.utwente.nl/bms/cheps/phdportal/CHEPS%20Alumni%20and%20Their%20Theses/thesis%20Kahsay%20final.pdf).

Ministry of Education. 1999–2015. "Education Statistics Annual Abstracts 1992-2005E.C (1999/2000-2014/15G.C." (Addis Ababa: Federal Democratic Republic of Ethiopia). http://www.moe.gov.et/web/Pages/edustat).

Ministry of Finance and Economic Development (MoFED). 2013. "Brief Note on the 2012/13 GDP Estimates Series." (Addis Ababa: Federal Democratic Republic of Ethiopia).

Ministry of Labour and Social Affairs. 2009–10. "Labour Market Information Bulletin 2009/10." (Addis Ababa: Federal Democratic Republic of Ethiopia). (www.molsa.gov.et/English/Resources/Documents/LMI%20Bulletin%202009%20-%2010.pdf).

Serneels, P. 2007. "The Nature of Unemployment among Young Men in Urban Ethiopia." *Review of Development Economics*, 11(1), pp. 170–86.

Shaorshadze, I., and P. Krishnan. 2013. "Technical and Vocational Education and Training in Ethiopia." Working Paper (London: International Growth Centre). (www.theigc.org/wp-content/uploads/2014/09/Krishnan-Shaorshadze-2013-Working-Paper.pdf).

Siba, E. 2010. "Returns to Capital and Informality." (University of Gothenburg).

Söderbom, M., F. Teal, and A. Harding. 2006. "The Determinants of Survival among African Manufacturing Firms." *Economic Development and Cultural Change*, 54(3), pp. 533–55.

Solow, R. 1957. "Technical Change and the Aggregate Production Function." *Review of Economics and Statistics*, 39(3), pp. 312–20.

Sutton, J., and N. Kellow. 2010. *An Enterprise Map of Ethiopia* (London: International Growth Centre). (www.theigc.org/project/the-enterprise-map-series/#outputs).

Syrquin, M. 1988. "Patterns of Structural Change," in *Handbook of Development Economics, vol. 1*, edited by H. Chenery and T.N. Srinivasan (Amsterdam: North-Holland), pp. 203–73.

The Conference Board (TCB). 2015a. "Total Economy Database™: Key Findings." (www.conference-board.org/data/economydatabase).

———. 2015b. "Growth Accounting and Total Factor Productivity, 1990–2014." (www.conference-board.org/data/economydatabase/index.cfm?id=27762).

Timmer, M., G. de Vries, and K. de Vries. 2014. "Patterns of Structural Change in Developing Countries." Research Memorandum 149 (Netherlands: Groningen Growth and Development Centre, University of Groningen).

United Nations. 2015. "World Population Prospects: The 2015 Revision, Key Findings and Advance Tables." Working Paper ESA/P/WP.241 (New York: United Nations). (http://esa.un.org/unpd/wpp/; http://esa.un.org/unpd/wpp/publications/files/key_findings_wpp_2015.pdf).

World Bank. 2007. *Urban Labour Markets in Ethiopia: Challenges and Prospects, Volume I: Synthesis Report.* Report 38665-ET (Washington, D.C.). (https://schoklandtvet.pbworks.com/f/Labour+market+vol+1+Feb+23.07.pdf).

———. 2015a. "4th Ethiopia Economic Update: Overcoming Constraints in the Manufacturing Sector, the World Bank." (Washington, D.C.).

———. 2015b. "World Development Indicators." (Washington, D.C.). (http://data.worldbank.org/data-catalog/world-development-indicators).

———. 2015c. "Ethiopia's Great Run: The Growth Acceleration and How to Pace It." (Washington, D.C.).

THREE

Ghana

A Successful Growth Story with Job Creation Concerns

Ernest Aryeetey and William Baah-Boateng

G hana attained a middle-income
status in 2007 after rebasing its
national accounts in 2006. After recovering from economic recession
in 1984 thanks to Bretton Wood's sponsored economic reform introduced at the time, Ghana's growth has been remarkably strong, with
the lowest economic growth rate of 3.3 percent recorded in 1994. The
country's growth rate reached its peak of 14 percent in 2011 on the back
of the commencement of commercial oil production, making it one of
the fastest growing economies globally during that year. The concern,
however, has been the ability of the country to sustain this growth momentum given the low level and quality of education and skills in the
population. In addition, this strong growth performance has not been
reflected in the creation of productive and decent jobs toward improved
incomes and livelihood.

The structure of the economy remains highly informal, with a shift
in the country's national output composition from agriculture to low
value service activities in the informal sector. The commencement of

77

the commercial production of oil raised the share of the industrial sector in national output, but the continuous decline in manufacturing activities has undermined the country's economic transformation effort. Essentially, structural change toward higher value added sectors and upgrading of technologies in existing sectors allow for better conditions of work, better jobs, and higher wages.

Evidence of low level and quality of human resources, however, not only diverts the economy from its structural transformation path of development but also makes it difficult for the benefits of the growth to be spread widely through the creation of gainful and productive employment. Indeed, a highly skilled, innovative, and knowledgeable workforce constitutes a key ingredient in the process of structural economic transformation. Additionally, an expansion of productive sectors applying more complex production technologies and research and development activities implies increased demand for education and skills. However, the weak human capital base does not provide a strong base for the structural economic transformation of Ghana.

There is also a widespread concern about the quality of the country's growth in terms of employment and inequality, as well as general improvement in the livelihood of the people (see Alagidede and others 2013; Baah-Boateng 2013). A key indicator for measuring the extent to which growth results in gains in the welfare of the citizenry is the quality of jobs that the economy generates. Ghana's employment growth lags behind economic growth due to weak employment response to economic growth, with every 1 percent annual economic growth implying 0.47 percent employment growth (see Baah-Boateng 2013). In addition to the slow rate of job creation is the pervasiveness of vulnerable employment and working poverty. In 2010, seven of every ten jobs were estimated to be vulnerable, with low incomes and precarious working conditions (Baah-Boateng and Ewusi 2013), while, in 2013, one of every five persons employed belonged to a poor household.

GHANA'S ECONOMIC GROWTH PERFORMANCE

Ghana's current status on the global income ranking as a lower middle-income country is an outcome of rapid economic growth performance, particularly after the rebase of the national accounts in 2006. This section overviews the trend and pattern of economic growth and the changing structure of national output.

Growth Trends

After a decade of unstable growth performance in the 1990s, the eight years of continuous rising growth from the beginning of the new millennium came to a halt in 2009 at the height of the global economic crisis, with the lowest growth, 4.0 percent, in nine years (figure 3-1). Economic growth bounced back to hit a peak of 14 percent because of commercial production and the export of oil for the first time in the country's history, before subsequently nose-diving in 2013 to record the lowest annual growth, 7.6 percent, in four years.

Ghana's economy has experienced generally faster growth relative to Sub-Saharan Africa (SSA), particularly after 2007. On average, the Ghanaian economy grew annually by 5.8 percent, compared to 3.7 percent in SSA in thirteen years from 1991. The strong growth performance pushed the country to the rank of lower middle-income after recording per capita GDP of US$1,099 in 2007. Per capita GDP, which stood at about US$439 in 1991, increased to US$502 in 2005, and after rebasing of the national accounts, it surged to US$930 in 2006 and rose further to reach US$1,858 in 2013 (figure 3-1).

Drivers of Growth

An analysis of the drivers of growth from the demand side confirms the significance of oil rents in the strong economic growth recorded upon the commencement of the country's commercial production of oil in 2011. Export of goods and services surged from 29.5 percent in 2010 to 44.1 percent in 2011, and further up to 48.1 percent in 2012 (table 3-1) largely as a result of the export of crude oil. The increase in exports is

FIGURE 3-1. *Real GDP Growth and per Capita GDP, Ghana, 1991–2013*

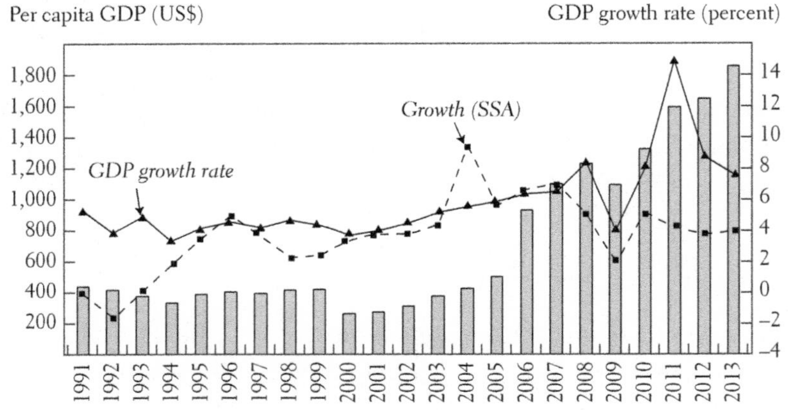

Source: World Bank (2014).

deemed a positive development and makes a large contribution to Ghana's economy through its effect on economic growth and export earnings, but the concern is the concentration of export in only a few primary commodities. Indeed, available data from the Bank of Ghana suggests that gold, cocoa, and oil accounted for approximately 80 percent of total exports in 2013.

In contrast, imports do not seem to exhibit a clear tendency, but has consistently trended above exports, culminating in the country's chronic trade deficits. Private consumption, which has been a major source of demand in the economy, has lost over 20 percent of its share in the GDP since 1990, reducing its dominance in favor of other demand sources. Public consumption reached new heights during the period of 2011 through 2013, while gross capital formation peaked in 2012 before falling by about 9 percent in 2013 as a result of a decrease in oil exploration, transport, and machinery (Ghana Statistical Service 2014a).

In terms of sectoral composition, economic growth has largely been driven by stronger growth in mining and construction in the industrial sector and financial intermediation in the services sector, particularly since the rebasing of the national accounts in 2006. These sectors are known to create a limited number of direct jobs. Between 1993 and 2013, mining and oil recorded the highest growth rate of 15.9 percent,

TABLE 3-1. *Demand Side Drivers of Growth, Ghana, 1990–2013*
Percent

Demand source	1990	1993	1995	2000	2005	2010	2011	2012	2013
Private Consumption	85.2	80.2	77.8	84.3	81.0	80.4	59.3	51.0	64.2
Gross Capital Formation	14.4	24.2	21.6	24.0	29.0	25.7	29.6	32.9	24.2
Public Consumption	9.3	15.0	12.3	10.2	15.3	10.4	16.6	21.0	16.7
Exports	16.9	18.2	25.0	48.8	36.4	29.5	44.1	48.1	42.3
Imports[a]	(25.9)	(34.2)	(33.5)	(67.2)	(61.7)	(45.9)	(49.7)	(53.1)	(47.4)

Source: National Accounts of GSS and World Development Indicators (World Bank, 2014).
a. Numbers in parentheses are negative numbers.

followed by 9.9 percent in construction and 9.1 percent in financial intermediation (table 3-2). On the other hand, growth has been slower in the high labor absorption sectors of agriculture and manufacturing. Indeed, agriculture recorded the lowest annual growth rate, of 3.9 percent on average, in the two decades after 1993, followed by manufacturing, with annual average growth rate of 4.2 percent over the same period (table 3-2).

The slower growth in manufacturing and agriculture has culminated in the dwindling share of these sectors in GDP, while mining and oil, construction, and finance recorded gains in terms of their contribution to GDP. Agriculture lost its dominance in national output, from 41.4 percent in 1993 to only 22.0 percent in 2013. Similarly, manufacturing also saw its share in GDP drop, from 10.5 percent to a low of 6.3 percent, over the same period, relegating it from its dominant position in the industrial sector to the third largest contributor to industrial output. On the other hand, the share of mining and oil in GDP, which declined by 1.1 percent between 1993 and 2005, improved considerably, from 5.0 percent in 2005 to 8.8 percent in 2012, largely as a result of the commercial production of oil, which commenced in 2011. The share of construction in GDP also appreciated substantially, from 8.3 percent to a new high of 12.6 percent in 2013, while the share of financial and business services in GDP rose from 4.4 percent in 2011 to 5.2 percent in 2013.

Essentially, the performance of Ghana's economy in terms of growth has been robust. The major concern, however, is that the growth has

TABLE 3-2. *Growth Rate and Sectoral Distribution of Real GDP, Ghana*

Percent

Sector	Annual average growth rate				Sectoral shares of GDP						
	1993–99	2000–06	2007–13	1993–2013	1993	2000	2005	2011	2012	2013
Agriculture	3.8	4.6	3.4	3.9	41.4	39.4	40.9	25.3	23.0	22.0
Industry	4.4	5.5	12.9	7.6	27.8	28.4	27.5	25.6	28.6	28.6
Mining, Quarrying and Oil	5.5	4.5	37.7	15.9	6.1	5.6	5.0	8.4	8.8	7.9
Manufacturing	3.6	4.4	4.8	4.2	10.5	10.1	9.5	6.9	6.9	6.3
Construction	7.3	6.6	15.8	9.9	8.3	9.7	10.0	8.9	10.5	12.6
Service	5.5	5.5	8.6	6.5	30.8	32.2	31.6	49.1	48.4	49.4
Trade	7.2	6.2	7.4	6.9	6.5	7.5	7.8	5.9	5.6	5.4
Finance	7.0	5.9	14.3	9.1	4.6	4.8	4.8	4.4	5.0	5.2

Source: Computed from National Accounts, Ghana Statistical Service (GSS) (2014a).

been driven largely by the extractive subsector, which is known to have limited job-creation impact, while manufacturing and agriculture, with relatively better employment generation effect, continue to record slower growth. The loss of agriculture dominance to services in terms of contribution to national output after rebasing of the national accounts tends to be misconstrued as a structural transformation of the economy. However, productivity in both agriculture and services is still low and, coupled with the weak growth performance and the declining size of manufacturing termed as the "missing middle," makes it difficult to equate the sectoral shift in national output to economic transformation.

EMPLOYMENT AND UNEMPLOYMENT IN GHANA

The relevance of economic growth is measured by its effect on the quality of life of the citizenry through the creation of jobs in sufficient numbers and of sufficient quality. What has been the labor market performance in terms of quantity and quality of jobs created in response to high economic growth performance over the last three decades? What is the pattern of change in unemployment in Ghana over the period?

High Level of Employment Dominated by Low-Quality Jobs

The availability of jobs and the quality of them, as well as poverty and income inequality, constitute key indicators of the health of an economy. Employment growth in Ghana has generally been slower than economic growth, raising concerns about the quality of Ghana's growth overall. Some concerns have been raised about the failure of SSA's solid growth for more than a decade to translate into a significant improvement in labor market outcomes, especially the generation of sufficient decent jobs (Sparreboom and Gomis 2015).

Overall employment levels in Ghana are marginally higher than the SSA average, based on a higher employment-to-population ratio in Ghana than in SSA (table 3-3). This ratio measures the ability of an economy to create employment. Developed economies tend to have lower ratios than developing economies, and an excessively high ratio

TABLE 3-3. *Quantity and Quality of Employment, Ghana*

Percent

Economic sector	1984	1992	1999	2000	2006	2010	2013
Employment-to-population ratio, SSA	n.a.	64.3	64.1	64.1	64.9	65.2	65.5
Employment-to-population ratio	80.2	72.9	73.9	66.9	67.7	67.4	75.4
Total employment (million)	5.42	5.77	7.22	7.43	9.14	10.24	12.03
Economic Sector							
Agriculture	61.1	62.2	55.0	53.1	54.9	41.6	44.7
Industry	13.7	10.0	14.0	15.5	14.2	15.4	14.6
Manufacturing[a]	10.9	8.2	11.7	10.7	11.4	10.7	9.1
Service	25.2	27.8	31.0	31.5	30.9	43.0	40.9
Institutional Sector							
Public	10.2	8.4	6.2	7.2	5.7	6.4	5.9
Private	6.0	6.1	7.5	8.9	7.0	7.4	6.1
Informal	83.8	85.5	86.1	83.9	87.3	86.2	88.0
Type of Employment							
Paid employees	16.2	16.8	13.8	16.0	17.5	18.2	22.5
Self-employment	69.6	71.3	68.7	73.4	59.5	60.8	52.6
Contributing family worker	12.5	11.9	17.2	6.8	20.4	11.6	22.3
Other	1.7	n.a.	0.3	3.8	2.6	9.4	2.6
Quality of Employment							
Gainful/productive employment[b]	20.9	n.a.	n.a.	21.2	22.0	23.1	28.7
Vulnerable employment[c]	77.4	82.5	80.8	74.9	75.4	67.5	68.7
Working poverty	n.a.	48.7	80.8	n.a.	25.6	n.a.	22.3

Source: Computed from Ghana Living Standards Survey (GLSS) III of 1991/92, IV of 1998/99, V of 2015/06, and VI of 2012/13; 1984, 2000, and 2010 population census.

a. Manufacturing is a subset of Industry.

b. Gainful/productive employment comprises paid employment and self-employed with employees.

c. Vulnerable employment comprises own account and contribution family work.

associated with developing countries is an indication of an abundance of low productive and low quality employment. Employment levels in Ghana rose from 5.77 million in 1992 to 12.03 million in 2013, representing a 3.7 percent average annual employment growth, compared to 3.0 percent in SSA (table 3-3).

Agriculture still constitutes the leading source of employment in Ghana, even though its share has been in steady decline. The sector now accounts for 44.7 percent of total employment, compared to 61.1 percent in 1984 (table 3-3). In contrast, employment in the services sector has seen remarkable improvement, from 25.2 percent to 40.9 percent, over a period of three decades since 1984, with industry experiencing a marginal increase of about 1 percent over the period. The shift in employment from agriculture to services may not reflect structural and productive transformation, however, since the rising services activities mostly occur in the informal sector. This is evident in the increasing share of informal sector employment, from 83.8 percent to 88.0 percent, and declining formal sector employment between 1984 and 2013. The decline in formal sector employment, particularly in the 1980s and early 1990s, largely emanated from public sector retrenchment as part of the Structural Adjustment Program (SAP) implemented in the 1980s. Most of the job losses in the public sector seem to have been absorbed by the informal sector, considering the slower expansion of the private formal sector in terms of employment generation.

Despite the widespread concern about the high level of employment, there are few decent jobs in terms of returns and type of employment in Ghana. Even though the working poverty rate has seen a continuous decline since 1992 (table 3-3), it remains high, at 22.3 percent, indicating that at least one-fifth of working people live in households considered to be poor. The problem of working poverty is linked to the high rate of vulnerable employment in the labor market. Vulnerable employment is a defined measure of persons employed under relatively precarious circumstances as indicated by the status in employment. It consists of own account and contributing family work less likely to have formal work arrangements or access to benefit or social protection programs, and are more "at risk" to economic cycles (International Labor Organization 2009).

As reported in table 3-3, two of every three jobs in 2013 are considered to be vulnerable, with gainful or productive employment accounting for 28.7 percent, suggesting a high decent work deficit in the country. The rate of vulnerable employment has seen a decline, with a corresponding increase in productive and gainful jobs since 1984, but the pace of improvement has been very slow. The low income associated with vulnerable employment implies high working poverty in such jobs compared to productive and gainful jobs.

Unemployment

Unemployment does not seem to be a major labor market challenge in Ghana even though the rates have generally increased over three decades. Like most SSA countries, unemployment is generally low in Ghana, partly on account of a high degree of informality and vulnerable employment. As Baah-Boateng (2015) notes, the high degree of informality tends to mask the problem of unemployment, considering the large number of discouraged workers who are jobless and available for work but fail to make the effort to seek work for various reasons. In 2006, the unemployment rate more than doubled, from 3.1 percent to 6.5 percent after accounting for discouraged workers (Baah-Boateng 2015), pointing to the extent to which the discouraged-worker effect undermines the unemployment rate in Ghana.

It is estimated that about 5 percent of the labor force was unemployed in 2013. The rate of unemployment rose consistently from 2.8 percent in 1984 to 10.4 percent in 2000, and slowed down subsequently, to 7.3 percent and 3.1 percent in 2003 and 2006, respectively (table 3-4). The rate went up again in 2010 to 5.8 percent and dropped by 0.6 percentage-point three years later, to 5.2 percent in 2013.

Unemployment is a bigger challenge to the youth than adults, with youth unemployment rates estimated to be twice as high as the overall unemployment rate. The gender dimension of unemployment shows lower rates among females than males in 1984, and the reverse emerging thereafter. Baah-Boateng (2012) attributes the gender reversal of the relative unemployment rates since 1984 to the increasing desire of women to participate in market work against the backdrop of fewer employment

TABLE 3-4. *Unemployment Rates, by Age, Sex, and Locality, Ghana*

Percent

Demographic group	1992[a]	1999[a]	2000	2003[a]	2006[a]	2010	2013
All (15+)	3.3	7.5	10.4	7.3	3.1	5.8	5.2
Youth (15–24)	8.6	15.9	16.7	16.3	6.6	12.9	10.9
Sex							
Male	3.4	7.9	10.1	6.9	3.0	5.4	4.8
Female	3.2	7.2	10.7	7.7	3.2	6.3	5.5
Locality							
Urban	8.2	13.2	12.8	10.7	6.1	8.0	6.5
Rural	1.7	4.9	8.6	4.8	1.3	3.5	3.9
Level of education[a]							
No education	0.7	n.a.	9.6	n.a.	2.4	3.1	2.7
Basic education	3.6	n.a.	10.6	n.a.	4.6	6.0	3.3
Secondary or more	4.3	n.a.	12.7	n.a.	10.9	8.3	6.6
Tertiary	8.0	n.a.	11.0	n.a.	7.8	18.4	6.0

Source: Ghana Living Standards Survey (GLSS) III of 1991/92, IV of 1998/99, V of 2005/06; Core Welfare Indicators Questionnaire (CWIQ) 2003; and 1984, 2000, and 2010 population census.

a. Computed by authors.

opportunities available to them. The labor force participation rate of women improved faster than that of men between 1984 and 2010 (Baah-Boateng 2012).

The unemployment rate is also higher among the highly educated than the less educated. The rate was highest among tertiary graduates, followed by secondary school leavers in 1992 and 2010, with the reverse being the case in 2000, 2006, and 2013 (table 3-4). The rate is lowest among those with no formal education, followed by those with basic education, on the grounds that the less educated comfortably take refuge in the informal sector since they have limited access to formal sector jobs (Baah-Boateng 2013, 2015). In contrast, the highly educated labor force would always focus on the formal sector as the source of employment and see the informal sector as an unattractive employment destination. Hence, limited job opportunities in the formal sector relative to the number coming out of secondary schools and tertiary institutions creates a larger army of educated unemployed.

POVERTY AND INEQUALITY

The extent of poverty and inequality is a function of the labor market. The level and distribution of employment, as well as unemployment, which relate to the rate and structure of economic growth, has implications for the earning power and the poverty status of individuals and households.

Ghana has made considerable progress toward poverty reduction since the mid-1980s and managed to achieve the first goal of the Millennium Development Goals (MDG) of halving extreme poverty ahead of the target date of 2015 (NDPC 2015). After an initial rise from 56 percent in 1987–88 to 61 percent in 1988–89, poverty incidence declined consistently to 24 percent in 2012–13 (figure 3-2). Similarly, extreme poverty also declined from 42 percent to 8 percent over the same period, suggesting that Ghana's strong growth performance has reflected positively on the poverty situation in the country. There are, however, concerns about worsening inequality in the country, implying that the benefits of the high growth performance that pushed the country to a middle-income level have not been distributed evenly among Ghanaians. The extent of inequality, measured by the Gini coefficient, increased continuously from 35.4 percent in 1987–88 to 42.3 percent in 2012–13 (figure 3-2).

Clearly, Ghana prides itself for having managed to reduce poverty substantially since 1991 to the extent of meeting the Millennium Development Goal (MDG) target ahead of time, but it has not been able to win the battle against inequality. Poverty is still endemic in three regions in the north, and the depth of poverty also remains a challenge even in urban areas (Osei-Assibey and Baah-Boateng 2015). The poverty reducing strategy of giving cash transfer to extremely poor households under the Livelihood Empowerment against Poverty (LEAP) since 2008 has yet to make the hoped-for impact of averting increasing inequality and depth of poverty. This requires a re-examination of Ghana's growth performance, to make it more inclusive by ensuring that the benefits of the growth are evenly spread out through the generations of productive employment across all segments of the country.

FIGURE 3-2. *Incidence of Poverty and Inequality, 1987–2013*

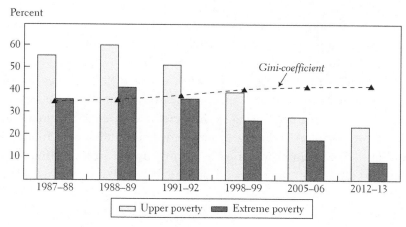

Source: Ghana Living Standards Surveys I–IV, Ghana Statistical Service.

EARNINGS DIFFERENTIALS BY EMPLOYMENT

Related to the issue of inequality is earnings diversity according to status of employment and demographic groups, as well as the application of minimum wage in a labor market dominated by self-employment. Earnings differentials across employment type and sectors have implications for inequality among different groups in the labor market. An estimate by Baah-Boateng and others (2013) indicate that, across economic sectors, average daily earnings were highest in services in 2006, followed closely by industry, with the least average daily earnings reported in agriculture, with 46.1 percent and 46.3 percent of average daily earnings in services and industry, respectively.

In 2013, agriculture reported the lowest average basic hourly earnings of GH¢0.69, compared with a range of between GH¢1.07 (in manufacturing) and GH¢2.56 (in energy) in industry, and between GH¢0.98 (in domestic work) and GH¢3.40 (in public administration) in the services sector (Ghana Statistical Service 2014b). Earnings are also estimated to be the lowest in the informal sector, with average daily earnings of that sector estimated at 37.5 percent of the earnings in the public sector and 32.1 percent of the average earnings in the private formal sector in 2006 (Baah-Boateng and others 2013). Employers were estimated to earn the highest in 2006, on average, followed by paid jobholders with average daily earnings of about 49 percent of employers' earnings. Own account work on average earns about 26 percent of employers' average earnings and 54 percent of earnings in paid jobs.

To capture the earnings differentials among different types of employment, a standard semi-logarithmic earnings function (see appendix 3A-1) was estimated using an instrumental variable technique to avoid any potential endogeneity problem. Each individual's mother's and father's education was used as an instrument in the estimation. Data for estimation were drawn from the fifth and sixth rounds of the Ghana Living Standards Survey of 2005–06 (GLSS V) and 2012–13 (GLSS VI). Table 3-5 presents the estimated results to confirm highest average earnings among employers, followed by paid jobs, with own-account workers being the lowest earners. Relative to agriculture, earnings are also found to be higher in industry than services in 2005–06, while services jobs are estimated to earn better than jobs in the industrial sector in 2012–13.

Earnings are observed to increase with age from fifteen years. Beyond forty years, earnings begin to increase at a declining rate with age. Gender earnings differentials favor men, with females earning significantly lower than their male counterparts. The differentials worsened in 2012–13, with females earning about 49 percent less than men, from about 9 percent in 2005–06, which has implications for increasing gender inequality. The results also confirm higher earnings in urban over rural areas, while married workforce members earn more than unmarried ones. Education, work experience, and effort at work have significantly increasing effects on earnings, and with a lower share of educated workforce in total employment, this implies that a smaller proportion would benefit from higher earnings, with many uneducated workers working to earn a subsistence wage.

The lower earnings among people in vulnerable employment, mostly in the informal sector relative to paid employment, can largely be linked to the exclusion of that type of employment from the benefits of labor regulations.[1] Indeed, a shift in employment from agriculture to service and from public to informal implies changing earnings in the

TABLE 3-5. *Results of Earnings Function by IV Technique, 2005–06 and 2012–13, Ghana*[a]

Explanatory variable	2005–06	2012–13
Age	0.0169	0.0479***
Age squared	−0.0002	−0.0006***
Female dummy	−0.0853*	−0.4938***
Married dummy	0.0174	0.0639***
Urban dummy	0.1842*	0.1573***
Years of education	0.1481***	0.0541***
Work experience (years)	0.0132***	0.0108***
Effort (hours worked weekly)	0.0023***	0.0033***
Employment status (contributing family worker and others as reference dummy)		
Paid employment	1.5908***	0.2958***
Employer	1.7629***	0.6097***
Own account work	1.4058***	0.0974**
Industry of employment (agriculture as reference dummy)		
Industry	1.4376***	0.6635***
Service	1.3480***	0.7617***
Constant	8.7204***	3.1142***
R^2	0.1684	0.2568
F-statistic	127.34***	313.44***
Number of observations	10,456	15,843

Source: Estimated by Authors using Ghana Living Standards Survey (GLSS) V and VI Datasets (2014b).

a. Dependent variable is lnE, which denotes log of monthly earnings.

* $p < 0.1$, ** $p < 0.05$, *** $p < 0.01$.

labor market. Since ratifying the Minimum Wage-Fixing Machinery Convention, 1928 (Convention 26) in 1959, Ghana has been fixing minimum wage and expecting employers to abide by it. Essentially, the benefit of minimum legislation accrues to wage earners whose employment contract is anchored on an employer–employee relationship. Over the past three decades, the National Daily Minimum Wage (NDMW) has witnessed substantial improvement in real terms. The determination of the NDMW is anchored on the cost of living. The growth of minimum wage has largely been above the rate of inflation, suggesting rising real minimum wage over time (figure 3-3).

FIGURE 3-3. *Minimum Wage Growth and Inflation Rate*

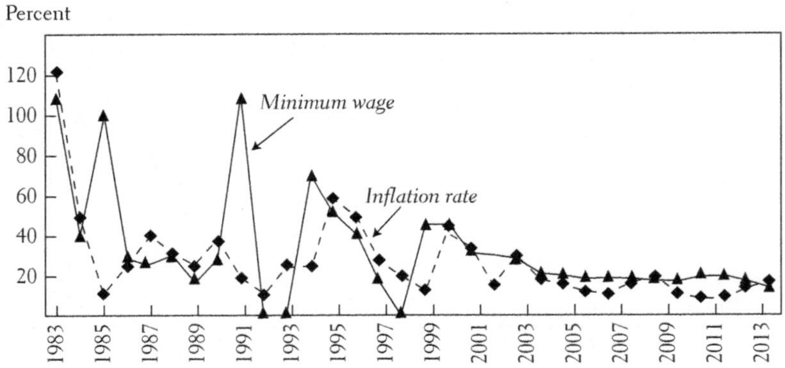

Percent

Source: Computed from government budget statements, Statistical News Letter of GSS.

The beneficiaries of the improvement in the minimum wage are mostly wage earners in the formal sector whose employers largely adhere to the minimum wage legislations. Indeed, the base pay of the government's Single Spine Pay Structure (SSPS) for workers in the public service is directly linked with the NDMW and cannot fall below it. Consequently, all public service workers on the SSPS enjoy upward salary review when the nominal minimum wage is upwardly adjusted. This could explain the highest average basic hourly earnings of GH¢3.40 among workers in public administration and defense in 2013 (Ghana Statistical Service 2014b). However, a vast majority of the workforce engaged in the informal sector dominated by own account and contributing family workers, where enforcement of labor regulation is a challenge, do not enjoy such benefits associated with upward review of nominal minimum wage in Ghana. This has implications for widening the earnings gap among different employment groups and, thus, exacerbating income inequality.

GROWTH OF LABOR PRODUCTIVITY

Economic growth and an increase in the size of the workforce, as well as the shift in the sectoral distribution of national output and employment, have implications for the growth of labor productivity. Labor productivity is crudely measured by output per worker and, based on employment data of the GLSS III, IV, V, and VI, we can compute annual growth of labor productivity over 1991–99, 1999–2006, and 2006–13 at the aggregate and sectoral levels.

To identify the principal sources of change in aggregate labor productivity over time, a formal decomposition into two sector specific effects—within sector effect and between sector effects—is carried out. "Within sector" effect captures the growth of productivity within given sectors, while the "between sector" component measures the contribution to productivity growth of changes in the pattern of employment across sectors. The formula for the computation of annualized growth rate and the sources of changes in aggregate productivity are reported in appendix 3-2 and the results are presented in table 3-6.

The Ghanaian economy recorded improvement in the aggregate annualized productivity growth rate from 1.3 percent in the 1990s to 2.4 percent over 1999–2006 and, further, up to 4 percent over 2006–13. The source of the improved productivity growth varies across sectors and periods. The substantial productivity growth in 2006–13 was mostly driven by growth of output per worker in industry, at about 8 percent annually, on the back of the commercial production of oil from 2011. Growth of output per worker in services was the key underlying factor behind the labor productivity growth, of 2.4 percent, in 1999–2006. An annual labor productivity growth of 2.1 percent in agriculture was the driving force behind the moderate economy-wide productivity growth of 1.3 percent over 1991–99, with output per worker in industry declining annually by 3.0 percent.

In terms of sector-specific decomposition effects, a strong contribution of services to aggregate productivity gains in the 1990s emanated from both productivity gains within the sector and labor reallocation gains from other sectors. Productivity gain within agriculture was highest as a result of sectoral output growth as against a declining share of the sector in employment over 1991–99. Productivity loss in agriculture as a result of the shift in agriculture labor to other sectors undermined the productivity gains within the sector and, thus, reduced the sector's net contribution to aggregate productivity to only 0.3 percent.

TABLE 3-6. *Contribution to Annual Aggregate Productivity Growth by Broad Sectors, Ghana*

Year	Broad economic sector	Annual productivity growth (%)	Contribution to productivity		
			Within effect	Between effect	Net contribution
	Agriculture	2.1	1.7	-1.4	0.3
1991–99	Industry	-3.0	-3.4	5.0	1.6
	Service	1.5	1.5	1.4	2.9
	All	1.3	. . . .	. . . .	. . . .
	Agriculture	1.9	2.0	-0.03	2.0
1999–2006	Industry	2.5	2.7	0.2	2.9
	Service	2.8	3.0	-0.05	3.0
	All	2.4	. . . .	. . . .	. . . .
	Agriculture	2.7	2.4	-2.7	-0.2
2006–13	Industry	7.8	10.0	0.2	10.2
	Service	0.3	0.4	4.6	5.0
	All	4.0	. . . .	. . . .	. . . .

Source: Constructed from Ghana Living Standards Survey (GLSS) III of 1991/92, IV of 1998/99, V of 2005/06, and VI of 2012/13 for employment and national accounts for value added.

Note: Based on rebased figures.

In spite of the average annual output growth of about 4 percent in industry during 1993–99 (see table 3-2), the flow of labor into the sector, accounting for a 4 percent increase in the sector's share of total employment over 1991–99, largely explains the productivity loss recorded within the sector. The productivity loss within the industrial sector emanated largely from the manufacturing subsector. Indeed, the subsector that, during the period, was the dominant subsector in industry in terms of output and employment, grew by only 3.6 percent (see table 3-2) as against the 3.5 percent gain in its employment share (see table 3-3). Nonetheless, productivity gains resulting from the flow of labor into the industrial sector outweighed the productivity loss recorded within the sector, to yield a net contribution of the sector to aggregate productivity of 1.6 percent.

In 1999–2006, aggregate productivity growth was driven largely by productivity gains within the sectors. Services and industry recorded 3.0 percent and 2.7 percent annual productivity gains, respectively, with agriculture recording the least productivity gain within the sector. This is reflected in the higher average output growth of 5.5 percent in services and industry sectors, compared with 4.6 percent recorded by agriculture over the 2000–06 period (table 3-2). Shifts in employment across sectors during the period were quite minimal, resulting in very small productivity gains or losses between sectors. The drop in the share of agriculture and services in total employment by only 0.1 percentage-point each in favor of industry (table 3-3) accounted for the marginal productivity loss for agriculture and services against marginal productivity gains for industry across sectors during the period.

The strong contribution of industry to aggregate productivity growth in 2006–13 is traced mainly to productivity gains within the sector as a result of the high output growth of the sector upon the commencement of commercial oil production in 2011. Productivity gains from labor reallocation were, however, weak in industry. The shift of employment from agriculture largely to services is evident in the productivity loss from the labor reallocation effect, which overshadowed the productivity gains within the agricultural sector, resulting in overall negative net contribution to aggregate productivity. The contribution of services to aggregate productivity growth is exclusively due to the reallocation of employment into the sector with very limited productivity gains within the sector. The small productivity gains recorded within the services sector could be explained by the large amount of informal employment of low skilled workers that were relocated largely from agriculture to the sector.

Essentially, workers with a low level of skills who moved mainly from agriculture to services largely accounted for the low "between effect" productivity gains in the sector. For Ghana to reap high productivity gains in all sectors of the economy requires large investment in human capital development to promote high and quality education and improve the skills of the country's workforce.

Growth–Employment–Poverty Linkage

The relevance of economic growth is measured by its effect on the livelihood of the people through the generation of productive and gainful employment. As Baah-Boateng (2008) remarked, whereas the link between economic growth and job creation depends on the extent to which growth generates employment, the impact of employment creation on poverty reduction depends on the extent to which poor workers benefit from their labor. Thus, the poverty-reducing effect of economic growth is a function of quantity and quality of jobs created from the growth.

Generally, the pattern and distribution of employment growth mirrors activities in the real sector of the economy since demand for labor is a derived demand. Evidence, however, shows that employment growth has not kept pace with the speed of economic growth over the last two-and-half decades. Between 1991 and 2013, total employment increased from about 5.77 million to 12.03 million, representing 3.39 percent annual employment growth on average, compared to annual real GDP growth of 5.83 percent. Baah-Boateng (2013) estimates employment elasticity of national output of 0.47 between 1984 and 2010, suggesting that every 1 percent economic growth produces job growth of 0.47 percent.

Using the arithmetic computation of elasticity (see appendix 3-3), we present employment response to growth and poverty-reducing response to employment creation based on employment figures of GLSS III, IV, V, and VI in table 3-7. The results in column 1 show declining elasticity values from 0.76 in 1991–99 to 0.68 in 1999–2006, suggesting a marginal slowdown in job creation response to economic growth over the two periods. The subsequent seven years (2006–13) saw a substantial drop in employment elasticity, to 0.5, largely as a result of high economic growth driven by mining and commercial oil production, which commenced in 2011. Thus, in 2006–13, every 1 percent growth of real GDP implies a 0.5 percent growth in employment, compared to 0.68 percent in 1999–2006 and 0.76 percent in the 1990s. The declining employment elasticity since 1991 confirms the observation by the International Labor Organization (2009) of a decline in employment elasticity from 0.64 over 1992–2000 to 0.52 in 2000–04 and further down to 0.4 in 2004–08.

Columns 2 and 3 of table 3-7 present the results of the arithmetic poverty elasticity of employment to suggest a strong poverty reduction response to employment growth. Indeed, between 1991 and 2013, every 1 percent employment growth is accompanied by more than 1 percent

TABLE 3-7. *Growth–Employment–Poverty Relationship by Elasticity, Ghana*

Year	Employment elasticity of output	Poverty elasticity of employment	Poverty elasticity of productive employment
	1	2	3
1991–99	0.760	−1.199	−2.16
1999–2006	0.679	−1.387	−4.62
2006–13	0.505	−1.006	−1.04
1991–2013[a]	0.598	−1.033	−1.65

Source: Authors' own calculation from national accounts and GLSS III, IV, V, and VI.
a. Based on gross domestic product (GDP) at 2006 constant prices.

reduction in poverty incidence. The poverty reducing response to job creation was strongest in 1999–2006, with about 1.4 percent drop in poverty incidence in response to 1 percent rise in total number of jobs. The extent of poverty-reducing response to job creation also depends on the quality of job. As shown in column 3 of table 3-7, a 1 percent increase in the share of productive employment over 1991–2013 is associated with a 1.65 percent drop in poverty. This observation clearly supports the view that a poverty reduction strategy would be most effective if it is directed at promoting the creation of productive and better-paid jobs.

Employment response based on estimation from an annual time series multivariate regression model (see appendix 3-3) is reported in table 3-8. Over a thirteen-year period between 1991 and 2013, a 1 percent economic growth induced a 0.6 percent growth in employment (based on employment elasticity of 0.632) without accounting for other relevant variables that influence employment growth. The elasticity drops to 0.216, suggesting a weak employment response to economic growth over the last two decades, when wages and population are controlled for in the employment model. Thus, a 1 percent growth of real GDP is able to produce only 0.2 percent growth of employment. The statistically significant coefficient of the rebase dummy clearly shows that employment response to growth was lower during 2006–13 than during 1991–2005, confirming the declining employment elasticity in table 3-8.

6update98 Aryeetey and Baah-Boateng

TABLE 3-8. *Linear Regression Results, Ghana, 1991–2013*[a]

Variable	Base	Base + controls
lnYt (log of real gross domestic product)	0.632***	0.216***
lnRMWt (log of Real Minimum Wage)	....	−0.009
lnPt (log of population size)	....	0.839***
D (dummy for rebasing of national accounts in 2006)	−2.107***	−0.717***
Constant	−1.943**	13.351***
R2	0.9836	0.9965
F-stats	628.57***	1368.17***
Breusch–Godfrey LM test for autocorrelation Chi2	11.81***	0.446
Breusch–Pagan test for Heterskedasticity Chi2	3.64**	2.19*
Ramsey RESET test for omitted variable F (3, 15)	28.95***	1.71
N	23	23

Source: Estimated by authors.
a. Dependent variable is log of employment.
* $p < 0.10$, ** $p < 0.05$, *** $p < 0.01$.

CONSTRAINTS TO GROWTH AND JOB CREATION

The weak job creation effect of Ghana's strong economic growth performance requires investigation into the reasons underlying such an outcome. Giving the abundance of natural and human resources, the country's growth would have been higher than what has been recorded if constraints particularly related to skills development were addressed.

Quantity and Quality of Labor Force

Economic growth and job creation depend on the size and quality of the labor force. Indeed, the availability of human resources in the right quantity and quality form the foundation of growth and development. Ghana's population has been growing at an annual average of 2.5 percent over the last three decades, with an estimated population of 26.3 million in 2013 with the working-age population accounting for 60.7 percent.[2] The size of Ghana's labor force in 2013 stood at 12.31 million, increasing from 6.04 million in 1992, translating into 3.4 percent annual growth on average (see table 3-9). Thus, the economically active population, of

47 percent of the total population, is responsible for feeding the entire population.

Faster economic growth relative to the labor force suggests that the size and growth of the labor force has not reached a level that could be inimical to growth. The economy grew, on average, by 5.3 percent annually between 1991 and 2013, compared with a growth of the labor force of 3.4 percent. The challenge, however, is that the quality of the labor force has a constraining effect on long-term growth, the genera-tion of quality employment, and poverty reduction. Historically, Ghana's economic growth performance, measured by per capita income growth, seems to be largely attributed to productivity rather than production in-puts (Aryeetey and Fosu 2002). Bosworth's growth accounting decom-position of Ghana between 1994 and 2000 attributes Ghana's per capita growth of 1.77 percent largely to growth in factor accumulation as mea-sured by physical capital per worker (1.17%), with education per worker and total factor productivity constituting 0.15 percent and 0.44 percent, respectively (Ndulu and O'Connell 2003).

The strong growth effect of physical capital after 2000 is attributed to the strong contribution of capital-intensive sectors of mining and oil, as well as finance, to growth. This is reflected in the improved contri-bution of gross capital formation to GDP, which peaked at 33 percent in 2012 from a low of 14 percent in 1990 (table 3-1). The lowest contri-bution of education to growth, as measured by education per worker, in the growth accounting raises a question about the quality of Ghana's labor force. The level of education and skills of the Ghanaian labor force is generally low, with eight of ten having less than secondary educa-tion (table 3-9). This does not seem to be enough to propel the country for a sustainable long-term growth and economic transformation.

The pace of improvement in the level of education of the labor force has also been slow. In 1992, only 2 percent of the labor force had ter-tiary education, and this improved to 5.4 percent in 2013. Even though the proportion of the labor force with no formal education has im-proved substantially, dropping from 44 percent to 26 percent over a pe-riod of two decades, an improvement in the proportion of the labor force with post-basic education has been very slow, rising by about 10 percentage points from 7.7 percent in 1992 (table 3-9). Essentially,

TABLE 3-9. *Trends in Size and Education Level of the Ghana Labor Force*

Indicator	1992	1999	2000	2006	2010	2013
Total labor force (million)	6.04	8.21	8.29	9.42	10.88	12.31
Level of education (percent)						
None	44.1	40.1	38.7	34.5	32.1	25.6
Basic or less	48.2	49.1	44.7	53.1	48.0	55.8
Secondary / vocational / technical / commercial	5.7	7.9	11.0	8.2	13.0	12.1
Post-secondary and tertiary	2.0	2.9	5.7	4.2	7.0	5.4

Source: Constructed from Ghana Living Standards Surveys and population censuses.

the implementation of the Free Compulsory Universal Basic Education (FCUBE) largely explains this rise in the proportion of labor force with basic education from 48 percent to 56 percent over two decades. However, limited access to secondary education due to a combination of factors, including an insufficient number of secondary schools and a lower pass rate at the basic level, leave a large number of people ending their education at that level.

With a high proportion of low skilled labor force, the informal sector is expected to be the main source of employment, culminating in a high degree of informality and a high vulnerable employment rate in the country. Indeed, job openings in the formal sector generally require at least secondary school certificates and, therefore, a chunk of the labor force with at most basic education would find it difficult to secure employment in the formal sector. In effect, they are left with no option than to settle for jobs in the informal sector, where formal education is not an entry requirement.

Skills Gap as Constraint to Growth

Ghana is constrained by an insufficient number of high skilled labor force relative to demand, especially in the areas of medicine, engineering, science, and mathematics. Boateng and Ofori-Sarpong (2002) estimated supply deficits in medical and health, engineering and technical, and business administration graduates, and an oversupply of graduates in arts/social sciences and agriculture in 1999–2000. Anecdotal evidence suggests that when Ghana started commercial production of oil in late 2010, there were some specific skills, such as engineers, drillers, and production and operation workers that were difficult to obtain on the domestic labor market. Oil companies had to rely on skills from Cote d'Ivoire and Nigeria to fill those vacancies. This observation is generally linked to the fact that Ghana's education system tends to produce a large number of graduates in humanities, in excess of what the economy requires, while scientists, engineers, and technologists needed for sectors such as manufacturing, construction, mining, and oil extraction are produced in limited numbers. Even though enrollment in science in public universities and polytechnics has been rising in recent times, the improvement is very slow.

Over the last two decades, most of the newly established universities and polytechnics in the country have focused largely on training graduates in business at the bachelor's and graduate levels, while the existing ones continued to step up their enrollment in business and humanities. In addition, while most of the newly established universities train students largely in the humanities, which the labor market does not need in such large quantities, existing science and technology universities are shifting from their core mandate to train more students in humanities. Some have attributed this development to the high cost of training graduates in the science and technology areas relative to costs of training graduates in the humanities (Baah-Boateng and Baffour-Awuah 2015).

Besides the shortage of specific skills in terms of area of qualification, the issue of quality becomes a problem due, largely, to the method of training that is not fundamentally linked to the world of work. Lack of practical training and internships and the limited use of case study in teaching and training at the secondary and tertiary level leads to a situation where, after graduation, the trainees are unable to cope effectively with the world of work. This type of skill mismatch tends to create a high degree of joblessness among the educated labor force while, at the same time, firms are looking for specific skills in new employees. Essentially, while the decision by the industry to resort to external labor at a higher cost has the effect of boosting economic growth, the benefits to be accrued to the domestic labor force is limited. Enterprises that find it difficult to fill the skill gap from abroad are compelled to fall on local sources, which may not necessarily match the vacancy, and this may have adverse productivity implications and contribute to reduced growth.

CONCLUSION AND POLICY SUGGESTIONS

Ghana's growth performance has been robust over the last three decades, accompanied by a shift from agriculture dominance to services, creating a missing middle, on account of dwindling manufacturing activity. Manufacturing, which until about 2005 was the highest contributor to industrial output, is now the third largest subsector after construction and extractive (mining and oil) in the industrial sector. Consequently, employment response to growth has remained low, with declining employment elasticity of output. Essentially, Ghana's economic growth has largely been driven by the low employment-generating sectors of mining and oil extraction, with high labor absorption sectors of agriculture and manufacturing experiencing slower growth.

The labor market has also experienced a structural shift in employment, from agriculture to services, a situation that largely mirrors the structural change in output. Employment in manufacturing (particularly wage manufacturing jobs) as a share of total employment has also suffered a decline. In contrast, most of the jobs that have emerged in the services sector are mainly informal, culminating in low productivity growth in the sector. Thus, apart from the low and declining response of employment to economic growth, most of the job creation has occurred in the informal sector. On the supply side, the low level of education has translated into low quality of labor, and this underlies the rising informality. That chunk of the labor force is constrained from accessing productive and/or formal sector jobs, which are characterized by better remuneration and working conditions with the implication for widening earnings differentials and inequality in the midst of declining poverty incidence.

It is obvious that these observations are indications of the urgent need for a rethink of Ghana's growth strategy. The starting point is for policymakers to acknowledge the adverse consequences of the strong obsession with economic growth regardless of the source of the growth and its job creation effect. Indeed, growth is a necessary condition but can only pass the sufficient condition test if it translates into the generation of productive and high-earning jobs for all. A redirection of growth strategy toward the promotion of manufacturing activities that are strongly linked with agriculture is key to making economic growth better and more inclusive. Thus, fixing the problem of the missing middle (that is, the declining manufacturing subsector) and raising productivity in agriculture should be the priority of policy toward growth inclusiveness. This calls for investment in areas that would promote manufacturing and agricultural activities, where job creation potentials are high. Thus, investment in the energy sector to ensure a consistent power supply within a stable macroeconomic environment would be a major step to reducing constraints to private sector–led growth. The business environment could also be improved if the country's institutional arrangements and regulatory framework are properly streamlined in line with best practices.

On the supply side, low quality of labor, measured by a reduced number of workers with at least secondary education, requires urgent policy attention. The link between education and productivity is quite clear and, thus, a comprehensive review of the current education system is needed to assess the medium and long-term relevance of education and skills development to promote high productivity and facilitate the creation of productive and more formal sector jobs.

The declining importance of agriculture relative to industry and service activities is ample evidence of weak policy attention to the sector considered to be a major source of employment and livelihood for Ghanaians. Agriculture research support through improvement in agriculture extension services, development of irrigation schemes to promote uninterrupted farming activities, provision of guaranteed price, and buffer stock facility are key policy interventions that would improve agriculture productivity. Finally, Ghana could also leverage on the strong growth performance of the low labor absorption sectors of mining and oil extraction to boost growth in other sectors by channelling the returns from these sectors into infrastructure to support growth agriculture and manufacturing.

APPENDIX 3A-1. EARNINGS FUNCTION

A function to capture earnings differential in a Mincerian form is specified as:

$$\ln E = \alpha_0 + X'\beta + Y'\phi + W'\delta + \varepsilon$$

Equation (1)

Where:

$\ln E$ = log of monthly earnings

ε = the random error term

X = a vector of demographic characteristics of the employed person (that is, age and age squared measured in years); female dummy (female 1, male 0); married dummy (married 1, single 0); urban dummy (urban 1, rural 0)

Y = a vector of productive characteristics of the employed, that is, education and work experience (measured in years) and effort at work (measured by the number of hours worked per week)

W = vector of dummies of employment type (paid employment, employer, and own account work with contributing family work, domestic worker, and other as reference dummy); and dummies of industry of employment (that is, industry and services with agriculture as the reference dummy)

Instrumental variable estimation technique is applied to avoid potential endogeneity problem with the level of educational attainment of mothers and fathers used as instruments.

APPENDIX 3A-2. LABOR PRODUCTIVITY

Aggregate labor productivity measured by GDP per worker at time t is given as:

$$P_t = \frac{Y_t}{E_t}$$

Equation (2)

Where:

P_t = aggregate labor productivity

Y_t = total real gross value added

E_t = total employment

In terms of sectors, equation (1) could be expressed as:

$$P_{it} = \frac{Y_{it}}{E_{it}}$$

Equation (2a)

Where:

subscript i = sector

t = period of time

Following Sparreboom and Gomis (2015), equation (1) could be expressed in terms of aggregate sectors as:

$$P_t = \Sigma \frac{Y_{it}}{E_t} = \Sigma \frac{Y_{it}}{E_{it}} \frac{E_{it}}{E_t}$$

Equation (3)

The growth rate of aggregate productivity can, therefore, be decomposed based on the relationship:

$$\frac{P_t - P_0}{P_0} = \frac{\Sigma \left(\frac{Y_{i,t} E_{i,t}}{E_{i,t} E_t} \right) - \Sigma \left(\frac{Y_{i,0} E_{i,0}}{E_{i,0} E_0} \right)}{\Sigma \left(\frac{Y_{i,0} E_{i,0}}{E_{i,0} E_0} \right)}$$

$$\Rightarrow \frac{P_t - P_0}{P_0} = \frac{\Sigma \left(\frac{Y_{i,t}}{E_{i,t}} - \frac{Y_{i,0}}{E_{i,0}} \right) \frac{E_{i,t}}{E_t}}{\Sigma \left(\frac{Y_{i,0} E_{i,0}}{E_{i,0} E_0} \right)} + \frac{\Sigma \left(\frac{E_{i,t}}{E_t} - \frac{E_{i,0}}{E_0} \right) \frac{Y_{i,0}}{E_{i,0}}}{\Sigma \left(\frac{Y_{i,0} E_{i,0}}{E_{i,0} E_0} \right)}$$

Equation (4)

Where the first term in (3) measures the "within sector effect" and the second term accounts for the "between effect." The "within sector effect" is due to the sectoral productivity growth (measured by the difference between sectoral value added growth and employment growth) weighted by the employment share of the sector (which is held constant). The "between effect" is due to changes in sectoral employment shares, weighted by a constant sectoral productivity. A positive "between effect" arises when sectoral employment shares increases and vice versa.

APPENDIX 3A-3. ELASTICITY

The arithmetic formulae for computing employment elasticity of output is given as:

$$\sigma_{E,Y} = \frac{\frac{E_t - E_{t-1}}{E_t}}{\frac{Y_i - Y_{t-1}}{Y_1}} = \frac{\frac{\Delta E_t}{E_t}}{\frac{\Delta Y_t}{Y_t}} = \frac{\partial \ln E_t}{\partial \ln Y_t}$$

Equation (5)

Where:

E = employment

Y = real GDP

t and $t - 1$ = current and previous periods, respectively

The arithmetic formula for computing poverty elasticity of employment is:

$$\sigma_{P,E} = \frac{\frac{P_t - P_{t-1}}{P_t}}{\frac{E_t - E_{t-1}}{E_t}} = \frac{\frac{\Delta P_t}{P_t}}{\frac{\Delta E_t}{E_t}} = \frac{\partial \ln P_t}{\partial \ln E_t}$$

Equation (6)

Where:

P = poverty incidence

E = employment

t and $t -1$ = current and previous periods, respectively

A log linear regression of employment–output relationship to be estimated using annual times series data over 1991–2013 is specified as:

$$\ln E_t = \beta_0 + \beta_1 \ln Y_t + \beta_2 \ln W_t + \beta_3 \ln P_t + \beta_4 D_t + \varepsilon_t$$

Equation (7)

Where:

$\ln E$ = log total employment

$\ln Y$ = log of real GDP

$\ln W$ = log of real minimum wage

$lnP = \log$ of total population

D = rebase dummy $(D = 0: 1990–2005; D = 1: 2006–13)$

ε = random error term

$lnE\ \beta_1$ = employment elasticity of output

NOTES

1. Vulnerable employment is the sum of own account and contributing family work.

2. The working-age population includes people age fifteen years and above.

REFERENCES

Alagidede, P., W. Baah-Boateng, and E. Nketiah-Amponsah. 2013. "The Ghanaian Economy: An Overview." *Ghanaian Journal of Economics* 1, no. 1, December, pp. 1–33.

Aryeetey, E., and A. Fosu. 2002. "African Economic Growth Performance: The Case of Ghana." Working Paper 7 (African Economic Research Consortium Growth Research Project).

Baah-Boateng, W. 2008. "Employment Generation for Poverty Alleviation," in *Poverty Reduction Strategies in Action: Perspectives and Lessons from Ghana*, edited by J. Amoako-Tuffour and B. Armah (Lexington Books, Roman & Littlefield Publishers, Plymouth).

———. 2012. "Labour Market Discrimination in Ghana: A Gender Dimension." (LAMBERT Academic Publishing, Germany).

———. 2013. "Determinants of Unemployment in Ghana." *African Development Review* 21, issue 4, December, pp. 385–99.

———. 2015. "Unemployment in Africa: How Appropriate Is the Global Definition and Measurement for Policy Purpose?" *International Journal of Manpower* 36, no. 5, pp. 650–67.

Baah-Boateng, W., Y. Ansu, and J. Amoako-Tuffour. 2013. "Mapping of Country Information on Employment, Unemployment, and Policy Initiatives." Report submitted to African Centre for Economic Transformation (ACET), for Knowledge Platform Development Policies.

Baah-Boateng, W., and D. Baffour-Awuah. 2015. "Skills Development for Economic Transformation in Ghana." Research Report submitted to

African Centre for Economic Transformation (ACET) and presented at a forum held in Accra, 7–8 February 2015.

Baah-Boateng, W., and K. Ewusi. 2013. "Employment: Policies and Options," in *Policies and Options for Ghana's Economic Development*, 3rd ed., edited by K. Ewusi (Institute of Statistical Social and Economic Research, University of Ghana, Legon Publication), pp. 190–221.

Boateng, K., and E. Ofori-Sarpong. 2002. *Analytical Study of the Labor Market for Tertiary Graduates in Ghana* (World Bank/National Council for Tertiary Education and National Accreditation Board Project).

Ghana Statistical Service. 2014a. *Gross Domestic Product 2014* (Accra: Ghana Statistical Service).

———. 2014b. "Ghana Living Standards Survey 6, Main Report." (Accra: Ghana Statistical Service).

International Labor Organization (ILO). 2009. "Key Indicators of the Labor Market." (www.ilo.org).

Ndulu, J. B., and A. S. O'Connell. 2003. "Revised Collins/Bosworth Growth Accounting Decomposition." AERC Explaining African Economic Growth Project, African Economic Research Consortium (AERC), Nairobi.

Osei-Assibey, E., and W. Baah-Boateng. 2015. "Determinants of Incidence and Depth of Poverty in Ghana: Does Development Benefit the Extreme Poor?" in *Globalisation and Development, vol. 3, In Search of a New Development Paradigm*, edited by S. T. Otsubo (Routledge, Oxon, U.K.), pp. 194–213.

Sparreboom, T., and R. Gomis. 2015. *Structural Change, Employment, and Education in Ghana* (Geneva: International Labor Office).

World Bank. 2014. "World Development Indicators." (Washington, D.C).

FOUR

Kenya

Economic Growth, Labor Market Dynamics,
and Prospects for a Demographic Dividend

Mwangi Kimenyi, Francis Mwega,
and Njuguna Ndung'u

Following recent rebasing of its economy, Kenya is now classified as a lower middle-income country. With a 2013 GDP of US$53.4 billion and a per capita income of US$1,246, the country is ranked the ninth largest economy in Africa and the fourth in Sub-Sahara Africa (SSA). As it stands now, the Kenyan economy is the dominant economy in the East African Community (EAC) and the primary source of foreign direct investment (FDI) for some of the countries of the region. The country has a youthful population and is well positioned to reap the population dividend.

In addition, the country has recently discovered oil and it is likely to be an oil exporter in the near future, joining Uganda and South Sudan. Even without the oil discovery, the Kenya economy stands at a strategic location in the Eastern Africa region. It serves five landlocked countries that are relatively resource-rich (Ethiopia, South Sudan, Uganda,

Rwanda, and Burundi). So its relative comparative and locational advantages lie in improving port facilities, road and railway networks, and transit airports as trade routes for these five countries. Even more significant has been the strengthening of the institutions of governance through the 2010 enactment of a progressive constitution that has radically altered the previous dominance of the executive. At the core of the new constitutional dispensation is devolution of decision-making powers to forty-seven county governments. All these factors augur well for continued strong economic performance.

This study seeks to analyze the drivers of economic growth both in the past and the more recent period and to evaluate the impact of economic growth on labor market prospects, the population structure, and growth. We also review opportunities and pitfalls that are likely to influence the country's growth trajectory. Initially, we start with a background of Kenya's economy and some important policy and political developments that have a bearing on economic performance. Next, the study presents a discussion of the country's population growth, structure, transition, and demographic dividend prospects. The interest here is primarily on those aspects of the population that have a bearing on economic performance and, specifically, on the labor markets.

We also look at Kenya's labor market, with a focus on the structure of employment and the growth–employment dynamics. We discuss the distribution of employment by industry and, also, by formal and informal sectors. We then discuss some aspects of labor supply side, including wage earnings, labor productivity, and returns on human capital. We conclude that examination with some evidence of the growth–employment nexus. Following that, we discuss some of the emerging challenges and opportunities to growth and employment and, finally, provide conclusions that tie the study together to show why Kenya qualifies to be an African Lion, but with immense challenges to overcome.

KENYA'S GROWTH PROFILE

This section explains Kenya's economic growth performance since 2000, updating an earlier study that covered the period from the 1960s to the 1990s (Mwega and Ndung'u 2008). This earlier study showed that the good economic performance in the 1960s and early 1970s was not sustained in the 1980s and 1990s. The latter period was characterized by persistently low growth and limited economic transformation, despite the fact that the country maintained a large measure of political stability and pursued a fairly consistent development strategy. In the 1960s, growth averaged 5.7 percent, accelerating in the 1970s to 7.2 percent. It declined in the 1980s to 4.2 percent, and in the 1990s fell to 2.2 percent (World Bank 2015).

In analyzing the persistent growth slowdown that got under way in Kenya around the 1980s, a shortlist of plausible determinants includes the global recession, commodity price decline, delayed structural adjustment policies, political succession in the country, as well as other, slow moving candidates such as institutional quality and distributional politics (O'Connell 2008). The country also experienced several negative shocks that undermined growth and contributed to the weak performance. Measures to reduce Kenya's susceptibility to exogenous shocks, hence, are necessary for improved economic growth (World Bank 2013). However, the scope for untangling the contributions of a large number of potentially relevant determinants is limited in a country case study (O'Connell 2008). For this reason, we focus on a few factors that will help explain the current period.

Kenya's Economic Performance since 2000

In explaining Kenya's economic performance since 2000, we focus on three dimensions: first, the role of political economy; second, the macro-growth story that sheds light on how much of Kenya's experience is explicable in terms of growth regressions; and finally, the role of markets in explaining Kenya's growth process.

Since the early 2000s (figure 4-1), the economy has experienced some recovery consistent with the Africa Rising narrative of resurgent

FIGURE 4-1. *Economic Growth in Kenya since 1980*

Percent change

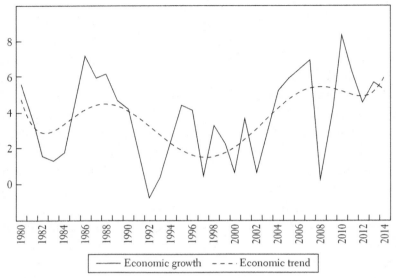

Source: Republic of Kenya, Economic Survey (various issues).

economic growth in the region. The rapid growth in Africa has been attributed to a whole range of factors (Robertson 2013): better government finances and fiscal policies reflected in reduced debt and general government expenditures ratios; booming commodity exports, especially to China, although the region runs a trade deficit with the country; increased FDI; new discoveries of oil and other minerals; the increased role of telecoms; ease of doing business reforms; increased investment in education; and democratization of the continent. Some of these factors have also applied to Kenya, especially the rapid expansion in telecommunication and financial services, although the country started from dismally low growth rates.

Political Economy of Kenya's Growth Process

In 2000, the economy recorded an all-time low growth rate of 0.6 percent, increasing to 3.8 percent in 2001 but declining to 0.5 percent in 2002. Following a peaceful change of government in December 2002 from the Kenya African National Union (KANU), which had ruled the country since independence, to the National Rainbow Coalition (NARC) under Mwai Kibaki, the growth rate accelerated. The economy expanded steadily from 2.9 percent in 2003 to 5.1 percent in 2004, 5.9 percent in 2005, and 6.3 percent in 2006, to reach a peak of 7.1 percent in 2007, the highest in over two decades and the only episode of five-year growth acceleration in Kenya's independence history (World Bank 2014). The good economic performance was bolstered by the implementation of bold economic and structural reforms under the Economic Recovery Strategy (ERS) and a favorable external environment. The ERS was a five-year blueprint prepared to address Kenya's macroeconomic vulnerabilities and structural weaknesses.

The Kibaki government put in place economic policy and governance reforms that enhanced economic performance. The average World Bank Country Policy and Institutional Assessment (CPIA), published since 2005, which rates twenty aspects of governance and policies, for example, generally improved over the study period. It improved in 2005–06 (from 3.52 to 3.58); declined in 2007–08 (to 3.55 and 3.52, respectively) as a result of the post-election violence, drought, and the global financial crisis; and improved in 2009–13 (from 3.67 to 3.80).[1] In the absence of poverty measurements, the World Bank (2014) estimates that poverty declined from 46 percent in 2006 to around 42 percent by 2013.

Despite the relatively good performance, the failure to develop an inclusive political agenda widened divisions in the country. The coalition of parties that formed NARC splintered after only three years, following disagreements over proposed constitutional reforms (Collier and others 2010). The subsequent 2007 elections were followed by a serious outbreak of ethnic violence, significantly disrupting the economy. About 1,300 people were killed and nearly 600,000 displaced. A group of eminent persons, led by former United Nations secretary-general, Kofi Annan, brokered a peaceful solution to the political stalemate, leading to a power-sharing agreement between Mwai Kibaki and Raila Odinga.

The events that followed the 2007 general election left a difficult legacy by exacerbating inter-ethnic mistrust and lack of confidence in the rule of law, which can be expected to have detrimental economic effects. Collier and others, therefore, recommend revamping efforts at building supervisory institutions, such as the electoral commission and judiciary, in which the country's citizens can have confidence. The efforts in strengthening the institutions in the country since the promulgation of the new constitution in 2010 led, in part, to a peaceful change of government in March 2013.

In 2008, the growth rate declined to 0.23 percent as a result of the post-election violence, drought in the country, and the global financial crisis, eroding the achievements of the previous half-decade. Following countercyclical demand management policies and favorable weather conditions that improved agricultural performance, growth subsequently picked up, to 3.31 percent in 2009 and to 8.41 percent in 2010. As a result of a surge in global food and oil prices and a drought in the country, growth declined to 6.12 percent in 2011, to 4.45 percent in 2012, to 5.74 percent in 2013, and 5.30 percent in 2014. With an average economic growth of only 4.37 percent over 2000–14, not very significantly above the population growth rate of 2.7 percent, the country continued to operate below its potential.[2] This growth was lower than the average for Sub-Saharan Africa (4.88 percent).

Macro-Growth Performance

The Kenya story is one of missed opportunities. Kenya, for example, did not exploit globalization to increase manufactured exports, given its coastal location, relatively cheap labor, and basically market-friendly orientation. The share of manufactured exports in manufacturing output has historically remained quite low (at less than 15 percent). While the economy was liberalized in the 1980s and 1990s, the trade liberalization policies were not credible and were subject to frequent reversals. Manufactured exports were also subject to serious supply constraints, such as unavailability and/or high cost of credit and foreign exchange, infrastructural deficiencies, and an adverse regulatory framework, increasing transaction costs and undermining the country's competitiveness. This makes it difficult to overcome the threshold of cost-competitiveness to sell in the global market arising from the Asian countries' agglomeration economies (Collier and O'Connell 2008). There is agreement that manufactured exports are mainly constrained by high transaction costs, not endowments, at least in the medium term. The poor performance has not been confined to manufactured exports only, but encompasses exports in general.

What differentiates Kenya from peer countries, in particular those outside the East Africa region, is the clogged "exports engine" (World Bank 2014). Exports of goods, as percent of GDP, have been declining since the mid-2000s, from 21.7 percent in 2006–10 to 18.9 percent in 2011–14, while imports of goods have been increasing. In contrast, services exports have been expanding, but not enough to offset the widening gap between exports and imports of goods. Kenya has, in the last decade, therefore, experienced a large increase in the current account deficit. The current account recorded an average deficit of 1.75 percent of GDP in 2006, generally widening in subsequent years. By 2012, the deficit had risen to an average of 10.6 percent of GDP, and by July 2015 to 10.8 percent of GDP, mainly due to increased imports in the context of a stagnant export sector. Imports of machinery and other equipment have, however, continued to account for a higher proportion (about one quarter) of the import bill. These are essential for enhancing future productive capacity of the economy.[3]

The high overall current account deficit is mainly financed by short-term net capital inflows. This is a major source of potential vulnerability for the economy and for financial stability. The easy reversibility of these inflows increases the risk of a "sudden stop" or a reversal as a shift in market sentiments creates a flight away from domestic assets (O'Connell and others 2010).

The growth literature, however, takes cognizance that economic growth is a multi-faceted process and that the rapid economic growth in East Asia from the 1960s to 1990s is attributable to a wide range of factors. Rapid economic growth requires the positive interaction of multiple factors, such as the "prevalence of primary education, agricultural development, macroeconomic stability, the role of public policies, the existence of regional dynamism, and so on" (Kurihara and Yamagata 2003, p. 6). Achieving rapid growth and shared prosperity requires continued action on multiple fronts. Improving on the key determinants to growth necessitates not only enactment of legislation, but also its

FIGURE 4-2. *GDP Growth Rate and Gross Capital Formation/GDP Ratio, 1964–2014*

Percent

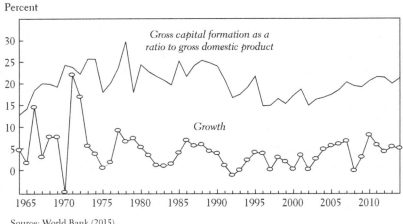

enforcement; more public investment and better execution of capital projects; greater political and economic stability; and improved governance (World Bank 2014).

The rate of investment is one of the most important influences on economic growth in Kenya. As seen in figure 4-2, there is close correlation between growth and the gross capital formation ratio (0.3), with causality running from the investment ratio to growth.[4] Since 2000, there was a general increase in the investment ratio, from 17.4 percent in 2000 to 21.3 percent in 2014. These are, however, relatively low investment rates, driven by low private and public saving rates, as well as low foreign direct investment. Savings, for example, did not keep up with investment. The gaps increased from near zero to a deficit equivalent to 8.9 percent of GDP in 2011 (World Bank 2013). An obvious policy implication is that macroeconomic policies should be geared toward stimulating more private and public investment rates (World Bank 2013). The Second Medium Term Plan of Vision 2030 sets ambitious targets for augmenting public and private investment. To this end, it envisages an increase in the investment rate to 31 percent of GDP by 2018, an ambitious 11 percent increase from the 2013 level. While foreign savings can finance some of the investment, the stated target cannot be achieved in a sustainable manner without higher national savings.

Role of Markets in the Growth Process

Markets are crucial for providing the incentive structure of the economy and shaping the direction of economic change toward growth, stagnation, or decline. Markets and their accessibility are important for inclusive growth. It is difficult to map out specific policies for each of the markets in Kenya, but the general trend was that major controls were introduced in the 1960s and 1970s and dismantled in the 1980s and 1990s. From being largely syndrome free in the 1960s, regulatory syndromes of soft (mild) controls were introduced in the 1970s, which persisted into the 1980s (Collier and O'Connell 2008).[5] These controls acted as an easier response in controlling balance of payments and inflationary pressures in the economy. However, the 1980s and 1990s are characterized by economic reforms to aid markets to work better: structural adjustment policies. There were also parastatal and civil service reforms. Whereas market reforms started in the 1980s with a slow pace and then accelerated in the 1990s, institutional reforms were a phenomena of the 1990s.

By the new millennium, therefore, most of the markets were fully liberalized, although, more recently, in December 2010, price controls were re-introduced in the oil industry. As well, legislation that allows the government to determine and gazette price controls on essential commodities like maize flour, kerosene, and cooking oil was passed by parliament. In other areas, liberalization has continued. Privatization of state corporations like the defunct Kenya Post and Telecommunications Company, for example, which resulted in East Africa's most profitable company (Safaricom), has led to their revival because of massive private investment. But removing controls does not guarantee rapid economic growth (Collier and O'Connell 2008). First, there are lags between reforms and private investment. Second, agglomeration economies by Asian countries make it difficult for African countries to break into international markets for manufactures and services. Third, success requires "big push" actions by the state, such as the provision of physical and social infrastructure.

To summarize, there are various lessons to be learned reviewing Kenya's growth experience over the past decade. While the economy has become fairly dynamic and innovative, the economic outcomes have not been transformative. Agriculture remains the mainstay of the economy and three quarters of the population continue to live in rural areas. Manufacturing has been disappointing, and service industries, such as finance or communications, account for only a marginal share of employment. Kenya's modest growth performance is not surprising when the country is benchmarked against the most important determinants of growth (World Bank 2014). Countries at similar levels of development typically have greater macro-stability, higher urbanization, are more open, invest more, spend more on health, have better governance, and have more developed higher education system than Kenya.

Kenya's challenges in enhancing its growth performance, as noted by Robertson (2013), include identifying competitive advantages; delivering the energy and transport infrastructure required to achieve the Vision 2030 development goals; enhancing investment in education to support rapid growth; and ensuring sustainable fiscal policy and a stable macroeconomic environment. Achieving the desired growth targets, therefore, entails improvements simultaneously on two fronts: increased physical and human capital, and faster productivity growth.

THE PROMISING FUTURE

The rapid population growth in Kenya is a phenomenon of the 1960s to the 1980s: its growth was on average above the real GDP per capita growth. But in the decades that followed, it is the age cohort analysis that has been amenable to interesting policy debate and presents an opportunity for a promising future. Four outcomes have been observed in the Kenyan analysis: first, Kenya has witnessed a youth bulge that has increased the labour force, we observe that 67.8 percent of the working age is comprised of youth. Second, urbanization in Kenya has increased over time, it stands at 25.2 percent and is projected to increase to over 32 percent by 2030. Third, the analysis does show that Kenya is reaping the demographic dividend. Finally, a combination of the above three factors strengthen the outcome of an emerging middle class in Kenya. This is a class of innovators and investors who have taken advantage of digital financial services to build savings and accumulate capital. It is a class that presents opportunities for social, economic transformation and growth in Kenya.

Kenya's Population Structure, Transition, and Demographic Dividend

Kenya has been disadvantaged by a more rapid population growth (Mwega and Ndung'u 2008). Up to the 1980s, Kenya had one of the most rapid population growth rates in the world. Population growth rate increased from 3 percent in the 1960s to 4 percent in the 1970s and 1980s, whereas that of Highly Performing East Asian Economies (HPAEs) declined from 3 percent in early 1960s to 2 percent thereafter. In the 1990s, the average population growth rate was 2.9 percent, declining to about 2.7 percent in the new millennium.

World Bank statistics show an increasing trend in population age ranges 0–14 years, 15–34 years, and 35–64 years since 1960, while the population age sixty-five years and above has stagnated. The population aged 0–14 years continues to remain higher than the other age groups, followed by the youth population (ages 15–34 years) and those age 35–64 years. This trend indicates that Kenya is likely to experience a youth bulge as more of those age 0–14 years move into the youth age group. In 2014, the population age 0–14 years stood at 19.1 million, while the 15–34 years group stood at about 16.1 million. The population group age 35–64 years stood at about 8.9 million. On the other hand, the population age sixty-five years and above has remained at below 3 percent of the total population since 1981, with the 2014 figure being 1.2 million.

Kenya has also experienced a steady rise in urbanization. In 1950, the share of urban (rural) population was 5.5 percent (94.41 percent). In 2014, urban population was estimated at 25.2 percent of the total population. So urbanization has steadily increased in Kenya. It is projected that by 2030 the urban population will be at 32.83 percent, while the rural population will have declined to 67.17 percent of the total population due to rural–urban migration resulting from the pull factors in urban areas (quality of life and economic opportunities in urban areas, among others). The trend reveals that while, indeed, urbanization will continue at a steady rate, rural areas will remain home to the vast majority of the population for the foreseeable future.

An important feature of the population structure that relates to labor markets outcomes is the relative size of the youth population to that of the total working-age population (ages 15–64). The United Nations defines youth as a person between the ages of 15 and 24 years, while in Kenya, youth is defined as a person between 15 and 35 years old, according to the Kenya National Youth Policy (Republic of Kenya 2006). The youth population has constituted more than half of the working-age population in Kenya since 1950; in 1950, the youth population comprised 57.5 percent of working-age population. The share of the youth population increased steadily over time, reaching a peak of 67.7 percent of the working-age population in 2002. Since 2006, the ratio of the youth population to the working-age population has been declining. In 2014, the share of the youth population to the working-age population stood at 64.2 percent and is projected to decline gradually to 59.0 percent in 2030. The youth population can be disaggregated into two cohorts; that is, those who are age 15–24 years (most of whom are still in school and are considered inactive in the labor market) and those age 25–34 years (most of whom have completed school and are employed or actively looking for jobs). Figure 4-3 presents the trend and projections for these cohorts of youth population in the country.

Figure 4-3 shows that the population of youth age 15–24 years has been higher than that of those age 25–34 years since 1950, and this is projected to continue toward 2050. In 2014, the share of the youth population age 15–24 years was 35.2 percent of the working-age population, while the share of the youth population age 25–34 years was 29.1 percent of the working-age population. The share of both cohorts of youth population in the working-age population has been declining since 2006 and is projected to decline further as we move to 2050. This decline is expected to reduce the youth dependency ratio as more of the working-age population will be composed of those aged between 35–64 years as we move to 2050. The fact that the working-age popula-

FIGURE 4-3. *Share of Youth Population*

Youth (millions)
Youth in working population (percent)

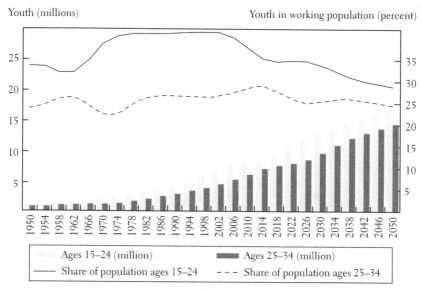

| Ages 15–24 (million) | Ages 25–34 (million) |
| Share of population ages 15–24 | Share of population ages 25–34 |

Source: United Nations (2013).

tion is not homogeneous is important to note in developing policies to ensure that most of them are actively involved in the labor market activities in one way or another.

The second feature of the population structure, related to the labor market, is the share of working-age population (ages 15–64) to the dependent population (ages 0–14 and above sixty-four). In 1950, the dependent population was 2.7 million. In 2014, the dependent population was estimated at 20.4 million (44.75 percent of the total population), while the working population was 25.2 million (55.25 percent of the total population). Figure 4-4 shows the trends in the working-age population and the dependent population in Kenya.

From 1960, the dependent population was slightly higher than the working-age population until 1994, when the working-age population overtook the dependent population. The figure indicates that, since 1994, the working-age population has been growing faster than the dependent population, and this trend is projected to continue into the next decades. As noted, the population age 0–14 years continues to

FIGURE 4-4. *Trends in Kenya's Working Age and Dependent Population*

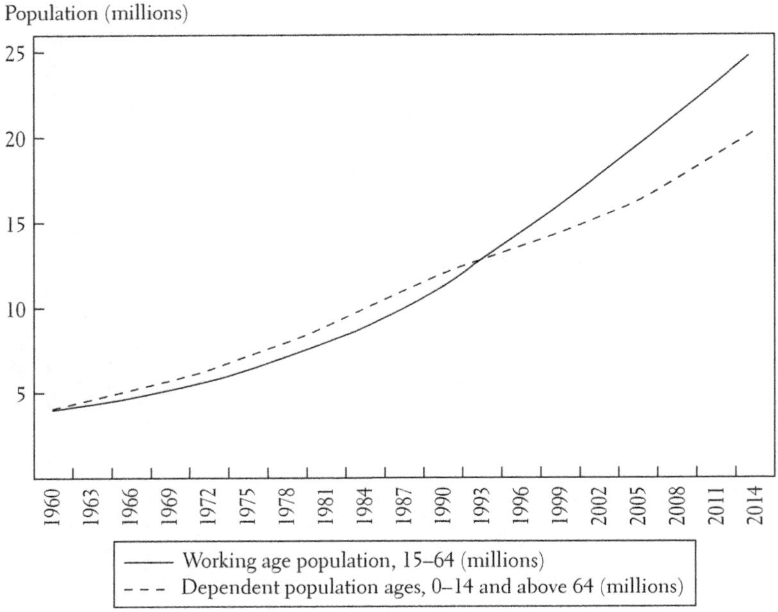

Population (millions)

Source: World Bank (2015).

remain higher than the other age groups, followed by the youth population (ages 15–34 years) and those age 35–64 years. As more of those
age 0–14 years move into the youth age group, the working-age population in the country is expected to continue expanding, leading to further
decline in dependent population and a larger working-age population
that would accumulate savings and increase investment in the economy.

It is also worth noting that Kenya has witnessed declining fertility
rates, from eight births per woman in the 1960s to seven births per
woman in the 1980s and, finally, to 4.4 births per woman in 2013. In
2014, Kenya had 46 percent contraceptive prevalence rate (all methods)
and a fertility rate of 4.6 children per woman (Republic of Kenya 2014).
The crude mortality rate has also declined from twenty per 1,000
people in 1960 to eight per 1,000 people in 2013. Consequently, the life
expectancy has improved from 46.4 years in 1960 to 61.7 years in 2013.
With the increase in the share of the working-age population, which

has accelerated since 1993 from 49.8 percent of the total population to 55.1 percent in 2013, these trends indicate that demographic transition has taken effect in Kenya. This sets the country on the path to realization of demographic dividend, if other contributing factors are adequately provided for. Bloom and Canning (2008) observe that, as the dependency ratio falls, opportunities for economic growth tend to rise, creating a demographic dividend.

A demographic dividend is a temporary opportunity for faster economic growth that begins when fertility rates decline, leading to a larger proportion of working-age population compared to young and retired dependent population (Republic of Kenya 2014). Bloom and others (2014) note that factors that can facilitate the reaping of demographic dividend for a country include integrated family planning, education, and economic development policies. From Bloom and others (2014), the emphasis is that, for a demographic dividend to be realized, there should be a decline in birth rates and mortality rates, followed by an increase in labor supply. This seems to describe what Kenya has gone through. The increase in labor supply must then find a macroeconomic setting that will absorb this labor force (Gribble and Bremner 2012). With a low share of dependent population, the larger working-age population would be able to save and invest more in the economy. At the same time, they are able to produce more per work, hence boosting the national income per capita.

Computation of the demographic dividend focuses on the relative changes of the dependent and working-age populations. Based on the data of the working-age and dependent populations, the support ratio is obtained by dividing the dependent population by the working-age population. The support ratio shows the average number of dependents per worker. Figure 4-5 presents the prospects of Kenya's earning demographic dividend, to which the change in support ratio is a key contributing factor.

Figure 4-5 shows that the change in support ratio has been positive but declining from 1960 to early 1980s, when it became negative. Since then, the change in support ratio has remained negative, with a negative change of about 0.6 percent in 2011, 0.3 percent in 2012, and 0.4 percent in 2013. The consistent negative change in support ratio implies that the dependence on the working population in the country is

FIGURE 4-5. *Prospects of Earning Demographic Dividend*

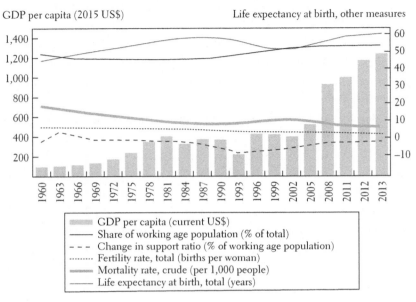

GDP per capita (2015 US$)   Life expectancy at birth, other measures

Source: World Bank (2015).

declining. With less dependence, the working-age population is able to save and invest more in the economy, hence creating opportunities for economic growth.

Lee and Mason (2006) and Bloom and others (2003; 2007) acknowledge the fact that demographic transitions do not in themselves guarantee a demographic dividend unless there is a quality institutional environment to enhance the productivity of the working-age population. Kenya has made positive steps in strengthening its institutions since the promulgation of the new constitution in 2010. Significant steps have been made in reforms in the public service, the police, the judiciary, the electoral system, and in devolving power. The CPIA public sector management and institutions cluster average (1 = low to 6 = high) for Kenya has averaged at 3.58 since 2005, improving to 3.80 in 2014.[6] Though more still has to be done, Kenya can be said to be on the right path in strengthening its institutional quality, a move that will enhance the chances of the country realizing the demographic dividend even before the year 2050.

The sustained increase in the GDP per capita since 2008, after the post-election violence shock, is an indication that the prospects of Kenya reaping demographic dividend by 2050 is real with improved political and economic framework. A demographic dividend model (DemDiv), developed by the USAID-funded Health Policy Project (HPP), predicts that Kenya will benefit from demographic dividend by 2050 if the institutional qualities are ensured. The DemDiv model integrates key elements needed for Kenya to achieve a demographic dividend that include family planning, education, and economic policies, especially on financial efficiency, ICT use, imports, labor flexibility, and public institutions. The DemDiv model presents a base scenario with no investment in family planning and a combined scenario of investments in family planning, education, and economic policies. In the base scenario, with no investments in family planning, the fertility rate would be the same in 2050 as it is today, more than four children per woman. Kenya's age structure would remain very young and be dominated by dependents. In contrast, the combined scenario, which includes increased use of family planning, produces a youth bulge, which moves into the working-age years in 2050. An increase in a healthy, educated, and productive working-age population will put Kenya on the path to realization of a demographic dividend (Republic of Kenya 2014).

Another notable feature of Kenya's working-age population that should be factored in the growth debate is the emerging middle class population and its role in driving economic growth in the country. According to the African Development Bank, the middle class are those who spend between US$2 (approximately 200 Kenyan shilling [Ksh]) and US$20 (approximately Ksh2,000) a day or earn an annual income exceeding US$3,900 (approximately Ksh390,000). In 2011, the middle class in East Africa was estimated to be about 29.3 million, representing an average of 22.6 percent of the population: 44.9 percent of Kenya's population, 18.7 percent in Uganda, 12.1 percent in Tanzania, 7.7 percent in Rwanda, and 5.3 percent in Burundi (AfDB 2011).

The emergence of the middle class presents an opportunity for social and economic growth in Kenya, since the middle class has been argued to play a key role as a conduit for advancing social progress, an agent of change for institutional reforms, a catalyst for the realization of inclusive growth, innovation, and entrepreneurial drive (Ncube and Shimeles 2012). The rise in the middle class population in Kenya has boosted the purchasing power in the country, leading to the thriving of the wholesale and retail sector (evidenced by the growing shopping mall culture) in the country. Additionally, the rise in the middle class population has led to an increase in demand for housing, giving rise to the boom in the housing market. It has also contributed to growth and innovation in the financial sector that finances the increased consumption by the middle class population. Moreover, the growing middle class is increasingly appealing to both domestic and foreign investors, thereby presenting Kenya with an opportunity for wealth creation and increased investment in the country.

The Labor Market, Employment, and Growth

In this section, we focus on some important aspects of the Kenyan labor market. We note that analysis of the Kenyan labor market is severely constrained by the paucity of data necessary to fully capture and analyze the dynamics of the labor market and, especially, the link between economic growth, employment, and poverty reduction. Nevertheless, the available data reveals some key features of the labor market and points to some specific policy proposals.

Labor Market Structure, Employment, and Wages

To provide a broad picture of Kenya's labor market, we start by looking at the trend of total employment and sectoral distribution of wage employment, as shown in table 4-1 and figure 4-6, respectively. The Kenyan work force is categorized into the modern (or formal) sector, the informal sector, and the small-scale agriculture and pastoralist sector. This section focuses mainly on the modern (formal) sector alongside the informal sector employment in view of the challenges of availability of data on small-scale agriculture and pastoralist sector. Table 4-1 shows that in 1985 total employment, excluding employment in small-scale agriculture and pastoralist activities, was estimated at 146,200 persons. Out of this, 80.33 percent were in wage employment. The self-employed and unpaid family workers were about 2.26 percent,

TABLE 4-1. *Shares of Kenya's Total Employment, 1985–2014*

Percent unless otherwise noted

		Modern sector		
Year	Wage employment	Self-employment and unpaid family workers	Estimated informal employment	Total employment (number)
1985	80.33	2.26	17.41	146,200
1988	77.47	2.54	20	173,140
1991	56.38	2.04	41.58	255,710
1994	44.86	1.74	53.41	335,620
1997	35.06	1.36	63.57	469,840
2000	28.68	1.1	70.22	591,160
2003	23.53	0.9	75.57	733,940
2006	20.66	0.75	78.6	899,340
2009	19.13	0.65	80.23	1,045,650
2012	16.87	0.6	82.53	1,278,110
2013	16.89	0.62	82.49	1,351,700
2014	16.56	0.72	82.73	1,431,670
For the period 1985–2014	169,582 (26.55%)	6,179 (0.97%)	463,036 (72.49%)	

Source: Republic of Kenya, Economic Survey (various issues).

while those in informal employment were estimated to be about 17.41 percent of the total employment.

Over the period under review, wage employment grew by an annual average of 2.5 percent, self-employment and unpaid family workers grew by an annual average of 3.7 percent, while informal employment grew by an annual average of 11.6 percent. Over the same period, the share of wage employment declined to 16.56 percent in 2014, and that of self-employment and unpaid family workers declined to 0.72 percent of the total employment in the same year. On the other hand, the share of estimated informal employment increased from 17.41 percent in 1985 to 82.73 percent in 2014. Informal employment increased from 1989 into the 1990s, surpassing the wage employment in 1994. Since then, the composition of employment in Kenya has progressively tilted toward informal employment. Generally, since 1985, the trend in informal employment has defined the overall trend in growth of total employment in the country. This increased rate of growth of informal employment can be attributed to a multi-dimensional matrix of reasons. These reasons include but are not limited to the government promotion of the informal sector and better informal sector data capture (Omolo 2010); limited capital, which hinders small entrepreneurs from venturing into large formal firms; the relatively high cost of doing business, which pushes employers to cut on labor costs (such as social contributions) through informal employment; and occasional freezes and/or rationalization of government employment, pushing labor to the informal sector.

The informal sector, commonly referred to as the *jua kali* sector, therefore, currently dominates and plays a critical role in the labor market in Kenya. Over the years, the sector has expanded into activities of manufacturing, transport and information, communication, and technology (Republic of Kenya 2003). However, there has been a lot of debate on the quality of employment in the informal sector. Additionally, Kenya's informal sector enterprises tend to remain small with limited labor absorption capacity. A look at the informal sector units in the period reviewed shows an increasing number of informal business units rather than expansion of existing units. This could be as a result of increased self-employment in the sector, an indication that the sector has not been dynamic enough to absorb the excess labor in the country. This suggests that focus should be on how to make the informal sector more dynamic while, at the same time, seeking to make it easier to do business in the formal sector. Bigsten and Wambugu (2010) argue that the formal sector employment expansion, on the other hand, has been constrained by the inability of the country to achieve rapid capital accumulation to improve on the capital–labor ratio and the labor market regulations that have tended to increase labor costs relative to productivity in the sector. They noted that the increase in informal sector firms leading to the employment expansion in the sector is mainly made possible by the limited capital requirements for new jobs in the sector.

In the modern sector employment, a notable feature has been the increasing number of casual workers as compared to regular employment workers. Casual workers are individuals whose terms of engagement provide for payment at the end of each day and who are not engaged for a period longer than twenty-four hours at a time (Republic of Kenya 2007). This category of workers enjoys the same rights as other employees to a large extent, but may be excluded from certain crucial benefits, such as leave entitlement, medical coverage, and pension contributions. Most employers in Kenya, including the public sector, have resorted to the increasing use of casual, temporary, part-time, contract, subcontracted, and outsourced workforces to reduce labor costs, achieve more flexibility in management, and exert greater levels of control over labor (Omolo 2010). According to a report by the International Labor Organization (ILO 2013), regular employment grew by only 7.0 percent between 2003 and 2011, while casual employment grew by 87 percent over the same period. Additionally, the proportion of casual formal jobs increased from 20 percent in 2003 to 30 percent in 2011 (Republic of Kenya 2014).

Until the end of 1980s, expansion of employment in the modern sector of the economy was largely attributed to the absorption of employees into the public sector. However, in 1994, there was a turnaround in this trend with employment in the private sector expanding faster than that in the public sector. The share of the private sector in wage employment has been on the rise since 1991, dominating wage labor progressively, to stand at 70.4 percent of wage employment in 2014. On the other hand, the share of the public sector in wage employment has declined from 49.6 percent in 1991 to 29.6 percent in 2014. A comparison of the wage earnings in the public and private sector is presented in table 4-2, which shows the real average annual earnings per employee in selected sectors in the Kenyan economy.

As is evident, there is a wide variation in earnings across sectors, with workers in financial and insurance activities earning the highest and those in agriculture, forestry, and fishing sectors earning the lowest. In essence, workers in agriculture, forestry, and fishing, mainly rural workers, have low earnings, hence dominate the bracket of the working poor. Furthermore, the gap between public and private sector earning varies widely within the sectors. Earnings in the public sector are relatively higher than in the private sector for most of the selected sectors, as evidenced by the percentage divergence in table 4-2. The sectors of specific concern are the wholesale and retail trade sector and the

TABLE 4-2. *Estimated Real Average Wage Earnings Per Employee, Kenya, 2014*

KSh per annum, unless otherwise noted

Sector	Private sector	Public sector	Divergence (%)
Agriculture, forestry, and fishing	153,904	217,789.60	70.7
Mining and quarrying	229,400	205,021.70	112
Manufacturing	233,304	472,230.60	49.4
Electricity, gas, steam, and air conditioning supply	831,991	747,447.10	111.3
Construction	366,160	365,919.60	100.1
Wholesale and retail trade	346,494	1,042,822.50	33.2
Transportation and storage	702,651	819,062.60	85.8
Financial and insurance activities	1,003,456	950,288.80	105.6
Education	553,722	270,131.30	205
Human health and social work activities	436,270	600,710.20	72.6
Arts, entertainment, and recreation	353,746	424,133.10	83.4
Information and communication	498,375	410,726.60	121.3

Source: Republic of Kenya, Economic Survey (various issues).

education sector. In the wholesale and retail sector, private sector employees' real average earning is approximately a third of their counterparts in the public sector. In the education sector, private sector employees' real average earning is slightly more than twice that of their public sector employees.

These wage inequalities explain the frequent agitation for wage adjustments by trade unions, such as Kenya National Union of Teachers (KNUT), which has seen the public wage bill spiral in the last two decades. The high wage bill in the public sector has turned out to be a constraint to economic growth, as it tends to crowd out resources available for development expenditure in the country. A study commissioned by the Salaries and Remuneration Commission (SRC) and carried out by the Kenya Institute for Public Policy Research and Analysis (KIPPRA) found that, generally, the public sector pays slightly higher than the private sector when comparing basic salary and allowances. However, the private sector pays a higher basic salary. The study also found

FIGURE 4-6. *Labor Productivity*

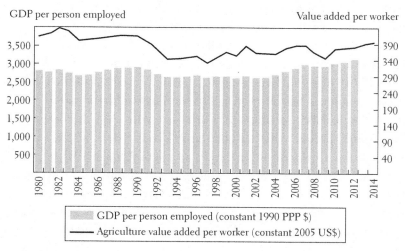

Source: World Bank (2015).

that there is a large vertical wage inequality in both the public and private sectors between the lowest and highest cadres (**KIPPRA** 2013). The wage differentials between the public and private sectors indicate that there are barriers to mobility of labor between the sectors and that the Kenyan labor market is not efficient in allocation of labor.

Labor Productivity and Human Capital Returns

In this section, we focus on labor productivity and human capital returns. Labor productivity measures the amount of real GDP produced by an hour of labor. In Kenya, labor is the abundant factor of production for the various economic activities. Labor productivity growth is important in measuring the efficiency of labor and in signaling an improvement in the standard of living in the country. Figure 4-6 shows productivity in terms of GDP per person employed (for the period 1980–2012) converted to 1990 constant international dollars using Purchasing Power Parity (PPP) rates and agriculture value added per worker in constant 2005 dollars (for the period 1980–2014). Agriculture value added per worker is a measure of agricultural productivity. In the analysis, agriculture is comprised of value added from forestry, cultivation of crops, hunting, fishing, and livestock production. Since agriculture is the dominant sector of the Kenyan economy, agricultural productivity provides a good estimate of the labor productivity in the country.

In the period under review, GDP per person employed has experienced a sluggish, inconsistent growth, dropping from 2,810 in 1980 to a low of 2,615 in 2000, then rising to 3,134 in 2012. Since 2008, GDP per person employed has been on a consistent upward trend, an indication of growth in labor productivity in the economy. On the other hand, agricultural productivity has been quite erratic over the period under review, dropping inconsistently from a high of 429.5 in 1983 to a low of 331 in 1997. Since 2009, agricultural productivity has consistently grown from 347.5 to 395.8 in 2014. The trends of GDP per person and agricultural productivity in recent years are an indication of growing labor productivity in the country. This is essential for enhancing economic growth of the country.

The growth in labor productivity in the country comes partly as a consequence of the improvement in education attainment since independence. Barro and Lee (2010) show that educational attainments (average years of schooling) in Kenya increased significantly, from 0.3 years in 1960 to about 4.4 years in 2000, then to 6.5 years in 2010. This was mainly driven by attainments in primary education (47.8 percent) when compared to secondary education (7.9 percent) and tertiary education (2.8 percent), due to the introduction of free primary education in 2003. Tertiary education has also expanded rapidly in the last two decades, mainly driven by demographic pressures as well as pressures from the high subsidization of primary and secondary education, the upgrading of colleges to universities, and the introduction of what is referred to as "parallel programs," where students pay tuition for part-time or distance learning programs (World Bank 2014). These trends suggest an improvement in the supply of quality labor that has positive effects on growth.

Information on the human capital returns is scarce. Kimenyi and others (2006) use data from the 1994 Welfare Monitoring Survey (WMS) to estimate human capital returns for workers with different levels of education using the Mincer (1974) earnings function. The sample used in the study includes only individuals in the working-age group 15–65

TABLE 4-3. *Human Capital Returns, Private Returns to Education, Kenya*

Percent of population

	Completed primary	Completed secondary	College	University
National	7.7	23.4	23.6	25.1
Urban	9.3	34.4	26.2	34.8
Rural	7.8	21	22.4	14.2
All Males	4.4	21.2	12.8	23.3
Urban	6.1	25.6	17.9	30.7
Rural	4.2	20.2	12.4	12.6
All Females	13.2	36.3	43.5	62.5
Urban	6.2	44.9	28	66
Rural	16	30.3	51.5	18.6

Source: Adapted from Kimenyi and others (2006).

years who are full-time employees. The sample size consisted of 6,140 observations covering individuals both in the rural (4,878) and urban (1,262) areas.

Table 4-3 shows private returns to education for different levels of education by region and gender categories determined by Kimenyi and others (2006). The results reveal large differences in returns between levels of education, with the largest difference in returns observed between primary and secondary education. The human capital return for those who have completed primary schooling was estimated at 7.7 percent, while the return for those with secondary schooling was estimated at 23.4 percent. The human capital returns for those with secondary education are about thrice the returns of those with primary schooling. This has influenced the education policies in the country, as evidenced by the increased allocation for development of secondary schools to improve on their enrollment rates and the current push to review the education system. The results also indicate that returns to education are greater for females than for males. For example, the return for females with primary education was 13.2 percent compared to 4.4 percent for males. Human capital returns to females with secondary education were estimated at 36.3 percent, while returns to males were

21.2 percent. This informs the increased focus on girl-child education as the government endeavors to provide an equal opportunity for all children to access basic education and to increase enrollment rates, especially for girls in secondary schools and institutions of higher learning. Additionally, the returns for urban workers were found to be higher, except for the case of females with primary education, where returns are higher for those in rural areas. The rising productivity since 2009 and the results for returns on human capital indicate an improvement in the efficiency of labor in the country. With the improvements in labor quality and efficiency, additional capital accumulation will propel the country to a rapid economic growth path.

Growth and Employment

We have outlined Kenya's growth profile and recent performance. One important question is whether growth has been effective in creating employment. In this section, we provide evidence on the relationship between growth and employment. As noted previously, this analysis is severely hampered by the lack of accurate and updated data; hence, we rely on available data and anecdotal evidence to draw some conclusions. Policies aimed at generating employment opportunities in Kenya have consistently promoted economic growth as the panacea to employment creation in the country. The relationship between economic growth and employment is estimated using a simple employment elasticity (which is a measure of the percentage change in employment associated with a one percent change in economic growth). The employment elasticity summarizes the ability of a country's economy to generate employment opportunities for its population as its economy grows, and can also provide an insight into trends in labor productivity in the country. According to ILO (2009), employment elasticity for Kenya has been generally higher than that for the world and also for Sub-Saharan Africa. Nevertheless, employment elasticity varies greatly over different periods, with the highest elasticity of 1.77 recorded for the period 1996–2000, when the growth rate was low (–1.6 percent). The lowest employment elasticity, 0.5, was recorded during the period 2004–08, when the economic growth rate was high at 5.3 percent. Thus, in the latter high-growth period, employment response was weak.

FIGURE 4-7. *Growth-Employment Elasticity*

Source: Republic of Kenya, Economic Survey (various issues).

This has been explained by the fact that growth in this period was driven by efficiency gains.

It is evident from figure 4-7 that employment elasticity for Kenya has been erratic, especially in the late 1980s and early 1990s, after which it stabilized between 1993 and 1998, before declining to a low of −4.7 in the year 2000. It then rose again to 5.4 in 2002. Since then, Kenya's employment elasticity has stagnated, ranging between 0.5 and 1.6. In 2014, the employment elasticity was at 0.56. This means that a 1 percent increase in the country's GDP would trigger a 0.56 percent increase in employment in the economy. The decline in employment elasticity since 2009 shows the declining responsiveness of Kenya's employment to growth in GDP as more labor is pushed into the informal sector. From the analysis earlier, the informal sector is a reservoir of self-employed, unemployed, and underemployed, and so may have a weak relationship to economic growth.

Figure 4-7 also shows that the growth in total employment in the country has closely tracked the economic growth in the country from 2004 to 2014. The GDP growth witnessed between the years 2003–2007

can be related to the strategies employed by the government as per
the Sessional Paper of 2003 on Economic Recovery for Employment
and Wealth Creation (Republic of Kenya 2003), but the growth experienced up to 2007 was related to the efficiency gains in the economy.
However, the unemployment rates still remain high in the country.
The employment and GDP growth dynamics indicate that the nexus
between economic growth and reduction of unemployment in the
country is weak. This can be explained by the fact that labor force
growth (mainly attributed to increase in working population and increased labor participation) in the country outpaces employment growth,
leading to an increase in unemployment despite the positive economic
growth witnessed in most of the years in the period under review (which
averaged 3.87 percent in the period 1986–2014 and 5.45 percent in the
period 2003–07, which had the highest growth episode). However,
economic growth seems to be a key factor in generating wage employment in the country. The growth in wage employment tracks GDP
growth closely. However, there is no clear pattern in the relationship
between GDP growth and growth in informal sector employment or
growth in self-employment and unpaid family workers.

EMERGING OPPORTUNITIES AND PITFALLS
TO ECONOMIC GROWTH AND EMPLOYMENT

As discussed, Kenya has recorded robust growth over the last decade
and is expected to sustain growth rates above 5 percent in the next
few years. However, the growth achieved so far is still below what is
necessary to achieve the targets set in the country's Vision 2030 to make
Kenya an upper-middle country by 2030. But there are many opportunities the country can exploit to maintain and raise its growth performance.
An important one is to take advantage of being a regional financial hub
and having a set of port and airport facilities and an efficient road and
railway networks that would serve the landlocked countries and generate economic rents and employment. As the largest economy in the
East Africa community, Kenya stands to gain from removal of barriers
to trade. Advancement with the trilateral agreement between Southern

Africa Development Community (SADC), East African Community (EAC), and Common Market for Eastern and Southern Africa (COMESA) is bound to boost opportunities for trade and enhance economic growth in the entire region, including Kenya. Kenya has also diversified her commercial relationships to a wide array of partners, especially in Asia and, increasingly, in the Middle East. These new relationships offer new opportunities to boost economic growth through expanded trade and investment and also other dimensions of development cooperation.

Kenya has embarked on the implementation of an ambitious new constitution, the Constitution of Kenya 2010. The key aspect of this constitution is devolution, which has resulted in the creation of forty-seven constituent county governments. The devolution process is a significant shift from the previous system, where power was concentrated with the central government. Devolution is particularly important because it provides for individual counties to deliver specific services and to design policies to promote growth. The counties have different resource endowments that can be used once devolved policies and resources are efficiently employed but, also, those disadvantaged by resource endowments have a compensatory mechanism in line with shared growth. If well implemented, devolution holds the potential to significantly support growth. Each county has different resource endowments, so policies and the provision of services closer to the populace will spur economic vibrancy at the periphery.

Kenya has also discovered new natural resources, with oil being the most important. The exploitation and possible exportation of oil by Kenya is expected to support the country's transformation process by reducing the cost of energy and stimulating manufacturing of petrochemicals, plastics, and related products. These are expected to drive economic growth and generate more employment opportunities in the country.

The large youthful population in the country presents the country with an opportunity to accelerate its growth. There is an increasing number of educated youth, and this group has been active in various mobile phone-based financial services innovations that have created job opportunities. With a supportive environment, Kenyan youth hold great potential for economic growth. Coupled with the growth in youth population, the emerging middle class in Kenya forms a large market, a group of innovators, investors, consumers, and early adapters. The middle class population prefers and preserves stable policy and political environment. They have everything to lose with violence and civil wars, hence are major contributors in creating a supportive environment and market that drive investment and employment creation in the country.

However, the country also faces serious pitfalls that present real risks to growth potential. A serious challenge to economic growth in the long run pertains to the limited transformation of the economy. Although there have been important shifts in terms of sectoral contribution from agriculture to services, the economy has undergone only limited transformation. In agriculture, which is the primary source of livelihood for the vast majority of the population, productivity remains low, and most subsectors are characterized by traditional production methods. Likewise, productivity in manufacturing is low, and the growth in this sector has been stunted. The share of manufacturing output to GDP has remained relatively flat. The expectation given the resource endowment pattern in Kenya was that agri-industries would transform agricultural production downstream and expand the manufacturing sector and product demand upstream. The failure to transform the economy is a major threat to economic growth and job creation.

The fragile democracy in Kenya is also a challenge to sustained economic growth in the country. The sporadic ethnic violence observed during elections has been a major concern, and private investors seem to have adopted a waiting option, driven by election cycles. This is the pattern that was observed in most ethnically heterogeneous constituencies in 1992, 1997, 2002, and even in 2007 general elections (see Kimenyi and Ndung'u 2005). This can only be resolved by strong institutions of governance and obedience to the rule of law. Other risk factors include the emerging terrorist attacks by the Al-Shaabab group based in Somalia, which has adversely impacted the country's economy and directly affected the tourist sector. The youth bulge could also easily turn out to be a curse instead of a blessing if not enough jobs are created for the increased youth population. Likewise, poverty and inequality and, more so, inequality at the regional levels remain high and pose threats not only to sustained growth but also to stability. Empirical evidence has shown that inequality can choke a growth momentum. In addition, internal institutional weaknesses and governance challenges threaten the gains of the new constitution. These and other risk factors are of concern to the country's ability to sustain growth and retain its position as a dominant economy.

CONCLUSIONS

The objective of this study was to analyze the recent drivers of economic growth in Kenya and to evaluate the impact of growth on labor market prospects, as well as population growth dynamics. This is in recognition that Kenya, as the ninth largest economy in Africa and the fourth largest in Sub-Sahara Africa, presents some lessons that can boost its capacity and take advantage of its location and policy environment to drive growth in the region. We advance from Mwega and Ndung'u (2008), but also review the challenges as well as the opportunities that are likely to influence the country's growth trajectory. We have provided a background to Kenya's economy and some important policy and political developments that have a bearing on economic performance. The discussion and analysis dwell on the macroeconomic performance and the role of political economy and markets in Kenya's growth process. The most important conclusion to be drawn here, to relate it to the micro-analysis, is one of institutional and policy failures. The study then focuses on the country's population growth, its structure and transition, and the prospects of reaping the demographic dividend. The interest here was primarily on those aspects of the population that have a bearing on economic performance and, specifically, on the labor markets. We focus on the working-age and youth populations, and the implication for population dividend, in addition to analyzing the trends in urbanization and the implication for economic growth.

The analyses of Kenya's population trends reveal a high rate of population growth, though the rate of population growth is expected to continue on a downward trend. Urbanization is expected to continue at a steady rate, even though the vast majority of the population will remain in rural areas. Increased urbanization and expanding cities has

been shown to increase economic growth if accompanied with enhanced infrastructural development and decongestion of the urban
areas. The demographic transitions experienced over the years in the
country put Kenya on the path to reaping demographic dividend. If
measures are put in place to enhance institutional quality and provide
productive employment opportunities to the large working population,
Kenya is likely to realize her demographic dividend even before 2050.
The emergence of the middle class in the country, which is driving
innovations in the country, is also increasingly appealing to investors,
hence presents an opportunity for economic and social–political growth
through advancement of social progress, realization of inclusive growth,
innovation, and entrepreneurial drive.

The Kenyan labor market is dominated by the informal sector employment, which has been rising since the early 1990s. On the other
hand, employment in the modern (or formal) sector has remained stagnant over the period. In view of the insufficient capital accumulation in
the country, labor tends to move into the informal and self-employment
sectors, which require limited capital as compared to the capital-intensive
modern sector and capital-intensive agricultural activities. To enhance
long-term growth prospects, the rapid growth in labor supply should
be accompanied with rapid growth in capital accumulation. Labor market growth and dominance of informal employment has reduced the capacity of the economy to deliver quality employment and output growth
via productivity. Over the years, there has been an increase in the number of informal units rather than expansion of the existing ones. The
private sector is best positioned to drive labor demand in the future, having increasingly dominated the provision of employment opportunities
over the public sector. Therefore, continued implementation of measures
to boost private sector investments should be highly encouraged.

Earnings across the various sectors of the economy and even within
the sectors (between public sector employees and private sector employees) were found to vary. This reflects barriers to mobility of labor
between the informal and formal labor market, resulting in labor with
similar skills being rewarded differently in the two markets. This is an
indication that the different segments of the labor market in Kenya are
not fully integrated and are less efficient, since labor mobility is impor-

tant in ensuring efficient allocation of the labor force in the market. The rising productivity since 2009 and the results related to returns on human capital indicate an improvement in the efficiency of labor in the country. With the improvement in labor efficiency, additional capital accumulation will propel the country to a rapid economic growth path.

Growth-employment elasticity has slightly declined in recent years. However, growth in wage employment and, by extension, growth in total employment has tracked GDP growth closely since 2004. On the other hand, there has been no clear pattern in the relationship between GDP growth and growth in informal sector employment or growth in self-employment and unpaid family workers. This affirms the fact that the key to growth in formal sector employment is capital deepening, which is fundamental for economic growth.

Finally, it is the middle class that seems to drive the economy. A developing country with a large middle class is likely to enjoy peace, stability, and increased private investments that will drive overall growth. That is where the Kenyan economy is at the moment.

NOTES

1. In 2014, Kenya had an average score of 3.76, above Africa's average of 3.20.

2. Recent growth rates have been revised as a result of the rebasing of the economy in September 2014. This involved revisions in sector classifications and the base year to 2009. Rebasing increased the GDP by 25 percent in 2013 so that indicators such as the Debt/GDP, current account balance/GDP, and fiscal deficit/GDP improved (Central Bank of Kenya, Monetary Policy Statement, October 2014).

3. According to a Central Bank of Kenya (CBK) estimate, excluding heavy machinery and industrial equipment would reduce the current account deficit to a sustainable 4.2 percent of GDP in the year to July 2014.

4. This is based on our own analysis. Only at six lags is there a two-way causality between growth and gross capital formation.

5. "Syndrome free" refers to a situation where a country avoids four broad anti-growth regimes: 1) severe controls or regulations that distort production activities and reward rent-seeking behavior; 2) ethno-regional redistribution that compromises efficiency in order to generate resource transfers to subnational political interests; 3) inter-temporal redistributions that aggressively

transfer resources from the future to the present, especially in resource-rich countries; and 4) state breakdown characterized by civil war or intense political instability during which the government fails to provide security or to project a coherent influence in a substantial portion of the country.

6. The public sector management and institutions cluster includes property rights and rule-based governance, quality of budgetary and financial management, efficiency of revenue mobilization, quality of public administration, and transparency, accountability, and corruption in the public sector.

REFERENCES

African Development Bank (AfDB). 2011. "The Middle of the Pyramid: Dynamics of the Middle Class in Africa." Market Brief (AfDB). 20 April. (www.afdb.org/fileadmin/uploads/afdb/Documents/Publications/The%20Middle%20of%20the%20Pyramid_The%20Middle%20of%20 the%20Pyramid.pdf).

Barro, R. J., and J. W. Lee. 2010. "A New Dataset of Educational Attainment in the World, 1950–2010." Working paper 15902 (Cambridge, MA: National Bureau of Economic Research).

Bigsten, A., and A. Wambugu. 2010. "Kenyan Labour Market Challenges," in *Kenya: Policies for Prosperity*, edited by C. S. Adam, P. Collier, and N. S. Ndung'u (Oxford University Press).

Bloom D. E., and D. Canning. 2008. "Global Demographic Change: Dimensions and Economic Significance." *Population and Development Review*, vol. 34.

Bloom, D. E., D. Canning, G. Fink, G., and J. Finlay. 2007. "Realizing the Demographic Dividend: Is Africa any Different?" Program on the Global Demography of Aging Working Paper 23 (Harvard University).

Bloom D. E., D. Canning, and J. Seville. 2003. "The Demographic Dividend: A New Perspective on the Economic Consequences of Population Change. Population Matters." Monograph MR-1274 (Santa Monica, Calif.: RAND).

Bloom D. E., S. Humair, L. Rosenberg, J. P. Sevilla, and J. Trussell. 2014. "Capturing the Demographic Dividend: Source, Magnitude and Realization," in *One Billion People One Billion Opportunities: Building Human Capital in Africa*, edited by A. Soucat and M. Ncube (Tunis: African Development Bank).

Central Bank of Kenya. 2014. "Monetary Policy Statement." (www.centralbank.go.ke/index.php/monetary-policy/monetary-policy-statements).

Collier, P., R. Gutierrez-Romaro, and S. M. Kimenyi. 2010. "Democracy and Prosperity," in *Kenya: Policies for Prosperity*, edited by C. S. Adam, P. Collier, and N. S. Ndung'u (Oxford University Press).

Collier, P., and Stephen A. O'Connell. 2008. "Opportunities and Choices," chapter 1 in *The Political Economy of Economic Growth in Africa, 1960– 2000, Volume 1,* edited by Benno J. Ndulu, Stephen A. O'Connell, Robert H. Bates, Paul Collier, and Chukwuma C. Soludo (Cambridge University Press).

Gribble, J. and J. Bremner. 2012. "Challenges of Attaining Demographic Dividend." Policy Brief (Washington, D.C.: Population Reference Bureau), September.

International Labour Organization (ILO). 2009. *Key Indicators of the Labour Market.* KILM 2009, 6th ed. (Geneva: ILO).

———. 2013. *Kenya: Making Quality Employment the Driver of Development* (Geneva: ILO).

Kenya Institute for Public Policy Research and Analysis (KIPPRA). 2013. "A Comparative Study on Public-Private Sector Wage Differentials in Kenya." Policy Paper 5 (Nairobi: KIPPRA).

Kimenyi, S. M., G. Mwabu, and D. K. Manda. 2006. "Human Capital Externalities and Private Returns to Education in Kenya." *Eastern Economic Journal,* 32(3), pp. 493–513.

Kimenyi, S. M. and N. S. Ndung'u. 2005. "Sporadic Ethnic Violence: Why Has Kenya not Experienced a Full-blown Civil War?" in *Understanding Civil War (Vol. 1: Africa),* edited by P. Collier and N. Sambanis (Washington, D.C.: World Bank).

Kurihara, M., and T. Yamagata. 2003. "Pro-Poor Growth in Asia and its Implications for Africa: Which Sector Increases the Employment of the Poor?" JBIC Institute and Institute of Developing Countries Research Paper (Tokyo: Japan Bank for International Cooperation).

Lee, R., and A. Mason. 2006. What is Demographic Dividend? *Finance and Development,* 43(3).

Mincer, Jacob A. 1974. "Schooling, Experience, and Earnings." NBER 74-1.

Mwega, F. M., and N. S. Ndung'u. 2008. "Explaining African Economic Growth Performance: The Case of Kenya," in *The Political Economy of Economic Growth in Africa, 1960–2000. Volume 2: Country Case Studies,* edited by B. J. Ndulu, S. A. O'Connell, J. P. Azam, R. H. Bates, A. K. Fosu, J. W. Gunning, and D. Njinkeu (Cambridge University Press).

National Council for Population and Development (NCPD). 2012. "Reaping Socio-Economic Benefits from Kenya's Population." Policy Brief 40 (Nairobi: NCPD).

Ncube, M., and A. Shimeles. 2012. "The Making of the Middle Class in Africa." Research Paper (Tunis: African Development Bank).

O'Connell, S. A. 2008. "Overview," in *The Political Economy of Economic Growth in Africa 1960–2000. Volume 2: Country Case Studies,* edited by

B. J. Ndulu, S. A. O'Connell, J. P. Azam, R. H. Bates, A. K. Fosu, J. W. Gunning, and D. Njinkeu (Cambridge University Press).

O'Connell, S. A., B. O. Maturu, F. M. Mwega, N. S. Ndung'u, and R. W. Ngugi. 2010. "Capital Mobility, Monetary Policy, and Exchange Rate Management in Kenya," in *Kenya: Policies for Prosperity*, edited by C. S. Adam, P. Collier, and N. S. Ndung'u (Oxford University Press).

Omolo, J. 2010. "The Dynamics and Trends of Employment in Kenya." Research Paper series 1/2010 (Nairobi: Institute of Economic Affairs).

Republic of Kenya. 2003. *Economic Recovery Strategy for Wealth and Employment Creation 2003–2007* (Nairobi: Government Printers).

———. 2006. Kenya National Youth Policy (Nairobi: Government Printers). (www.youthpolicy.org/national/Kenya_2006_National_Youth_Policy .pdf).

———. 2007. "Employment Act 2007, No. 11 of 2007." (Nairobi: Government Printers).

———. 2014. "Demographic Dividend Opportunities for Kenya: Results from the DemDiv Model." Policy Brief (Nairobi, Kenya: National Council for Population and Development, and Health Policy Project) (http:// www.healthpolicyproject.com/pubs/384_KenyaDemDivBrief.pdf).

———. Economic Survey, Various Issues. (Nairobi: Kenya National Bureau of Statistics.

Robertson, C. 2013. "Kenya: The Next Emerging Market." Paper Presented at High Level Conference on Kenya Successes, Prospects, and Challenges (Nairobi), September 17–18.

United Nations Development Program (UNDP). 2013. "Kenya's Youth Employment Challenge. UNDP, Bureau for Development Policy." Discussion Paper (New York: UNDP).

World Bank. 2013. *Achieving Shared Prosperity in Kenya*. (Washington, D.C.).

———. 2014. "Kenya: A Sleeping Lion or Speedy Lioness?" *Country Economic Memorandum* (Washington, D.C.: World Bank).

———. 2015. "World Development Indicators" (Washington, D.C.: World Bank). (http://data.worldbank.org).

FIVE

Mozambique

Growth Experience through an Employment Lens

Sam Jones and Finn Tarp

M ozambique's economy has experienced substantial change over the past twenty years. In the early 1990s, the country emerged from a devastating and prolonged conflict. Since then, aggregate economic growth has been sustained at high rates, making the country one of the top economic performers of the region. Other studies have noted that, while Mozambique's growth until the mid-2000s largely reflected a process of post-war recovery, sustained growth since then is a testament to solid macroeconomic management, pursuit of a wide range of economic governance reforms, and substantial inflows of foreign aid and political stability.[1] This is underscored by recent access to external commercial debt markets. In 2013, Mozambique made its debut $850 million U.S. dollar-denominated commercial bond issue with a coupon of 8.5 percent.[2]

Below the surface of strong aggregate economic performance lie a number of ongoing concerns. Principal among these is evidence suggesting that the pace of poverty reduction may have weakened. Data collected from household budget surveys suggest that, while poverty reduced significantly from 1996–2003, there is no clear evidence of significant reductions at a national level from 2003–09.[3] Although this partly reflects temporary shocks, it is the absence of a convincing process of structural transformation of the economy that is more worrisome from a longer-term development perspective. Indeed, the majority of Mozambique's (growing) workforce remains reliant on low-productivity agricultural activities, and the agricultural sector has shown few signs of transformation that might provide a basis for future growth and upgrading.

Positive or growth-enhancing structural transformation is characterized by a shift of workers out of lower productivity activities and into higher productivity and less vulnerable employment. Existing experience from a range of middle and high income countries indicate that such transformation often involves comparatively rapid growth of both employment *and* labor productivity in modern, industrial enterprises. In so doing, modern firms operate as an engine of growth for the entire economy. However, structural transformation of this sort is also typically accompanied by productivity growth in the agricultural sector; for example, as surplus or marginal labor is released. Concerns regarding the absence of structural transformation are not unique to Mozambique and this theme has been raised in many other countries in Sub-Sahara Africa (SSA).[4]

Existing labor market decomposition analyses for SSA nations are useful in describing general trends both at regional and country-levels.[5] However, in taking a cross-country perspective, they typically are unable to take advantage of the latest data and neglect important details in individual countries, such as divergent sectoral changes. As a result, careful analysis of developments *within* individual countries over time remains vital, and doing so with a focus on Mozambique constitutes the objective of the present study. Specifically, this chapter has three main aims. These are to: 1) provide an overview of recent economic developments in Mozambique at both the macroeconomic and microeconomic levels; 2) apply labor market decomposition tools to investigate the apparent disconnect between macroeconomic trends (GDP growth) and changes in household well-being (poverty reduction); and 3) consider relevant policy priorities to support a more pro-poor pattern of future growth.

The chapter contains three main sections. First, we elaborate on recent economic trends in Mozambique, provide a brief historical background, and compare trends across a range of macroeconomic and microeconomic indicators. As already hinted, such analysis raises concerns regarding the structure of growth and the extent to which growth is effectively promoting the well-being of the poorest. The second main section contains the analytical core of the chapter. It begins by describing the data and empirical methods used to decompose changes in Mozambique's labor market. Due to the limitations of regular official data on employment, aggregate GDP data must be combined with irregular information on employment patterns taken from household surveys. With respect to the latter, we take advantage of preliminary data from a recent household survey. Thus, the derived data encompasses the period 1996–2014, which provides an extensive view of recent labor market changes to the present.

The labor market decomposition is elaborated next, focusing on the distinction between within-sector productivity growth and productivity growth driven by structural change in the labor market. The results clearly show that labor reallocation effects have played a relatively small role in Mozambique's post-conflict productivity growth. Moreover, there is little evidence that sectors with relatively faster productivity growth are adding jobs at a faster rate than other sectors. In contrast, recent aggregate growth appears to have been driven by capital-intensive growth in the mining sector and by comparatively rapid growth of employment in services but, typically, in activities that are lower productivity than the sector average. Following this examination, the third main section looks ahead. We focus first on a set of inevitable demographic issues. These suggest that the supply of new entrants to the labor market is of a massive scale in the coming years, which underlines the need to boost the demand side of the labor market. We subsequently discuss the policy implications of the trends inherent in our labor market decomposition, taking into account, as well, our demographic projections. The final section provides our conclusions.

BACKGROUND

Mozambique lies in southeastern Africa, and borders South Africa in the south and Tanzania to the north. Similar to other countries in the region, Mozambique experienced a long period of colonial rule. Portuguese interests in the country began in the sixteenth century and were maintained over the course of the next two centuries through military posts, settlements, and trading companies. Expansion of Portuguese interests began in earnest in the nineteenth century, leading to the emergence of a settler economy based primarily on the production of cash crops (for example, cotton and tea). In addition, Mozambique's major ports became important hubs for trade into other southern African nations, especially South Africa and Zimbabwe. Following the Second World War, and as global demand increased, the Mozambican economy grew rapidly and became a destination for foreign direct investment and large inflows of Portuguese migrants.

The 1960s saw the emergence of Mozambique's national independence movement. Based in newly independent Tanzania, the Mozambique Liberation Front (Frente de Libertação de Moçambique, FRELIMO) began launching guerilla attacks into the north of Mozambique. With support from the local populace and facing a relatively weak Portuguese military presence, FRELIMO was able to gain effective control of substantial territory. Although FRELIMO had a relatively small number of active troops, their knowledge of the terrain and extensive use of land mines were effective in resisting significant Portuguese counter-insurgencies. According to one historian, white settlers in Mozambique began to feel "panic, demoralization, abandonment, and a sense of futility" as the conflict continued.[6] Facing costly and unsuccessful overseas conflicts, as well as increasing international isolation, the Portuguese government in Lisbon was overthrown in 1974. This quickly led to a retreat from its African colonies, and Mozambique achieved independence in 1975.

The new Mozambican government faced huge challenges in the early independence period. Perhaps most critically, mutual mistrust between the white settlers and the (elite) Mozambican population led to a huge exodus of those with Portuguese heritage (passports) and destruction of their business capital. As virtually all managerial and skilled positions throughout the economy had been dominated by these settlers, skills shortages were immediate and acute. Adding to this, the neighboring "white economies" of Rhodesia and South Africa viewed Mozambique's independence as an existential threat. Consequently, they sought to destabilize their neighbor by funding and training a resistance movement, RENAMO (Resistência Nacional Moçambicana). Global economic instability further undermined initial economic progress and, with economic support from the Soviet Union to FRELIMO, the conflict widened during the 1980s.

Without exaggeration, the 1980s were miserable for most Mozambicans. No less than one million people lost their lives, the economy shrank severely, many rural areas became highly insecure, and a large share of the population was internally displaced. Food shortages affected thousands such that, by the early 1990s, Mozambique had one of the lowest levels of per capita caloric availability in the world. Data from the FAO's food balance series shows a clear trend of decline in food availability per capita over the period 1975–92, even from an initially low base. A sharp upward break in the series from 1992 marked the end of hostilities, reflecting exhaustion on both sides and the end of significant external support to RENAMO, which coincided with the move to democracy in South Africa.[7] The transition to peace was quick and largely successful. Supported by a large UN presence, active troops were demilitarized and some integrated into a single national army.

Macroeconomic Trends

The first multi-party elections were held in 1994, giving victory to Frelimo, which has retained a parliamentary majority in all subsequent general elections, the most recent one held in 2014.[8] Postwar economic restructuring and rebuilding began under the auspices of significant international donor support, including extensive World Bank and IMF programs, initiated in the 1980s.[9] Figure 5-1 provides an indication of Mozambique's economic turn-around over the past two decades. As previously described, ongoing conflict had wrecked the economy and Mozambique was among the poorest countries in the world as it

FIGURE 5-1. *Trends in Real GDP per Capita*

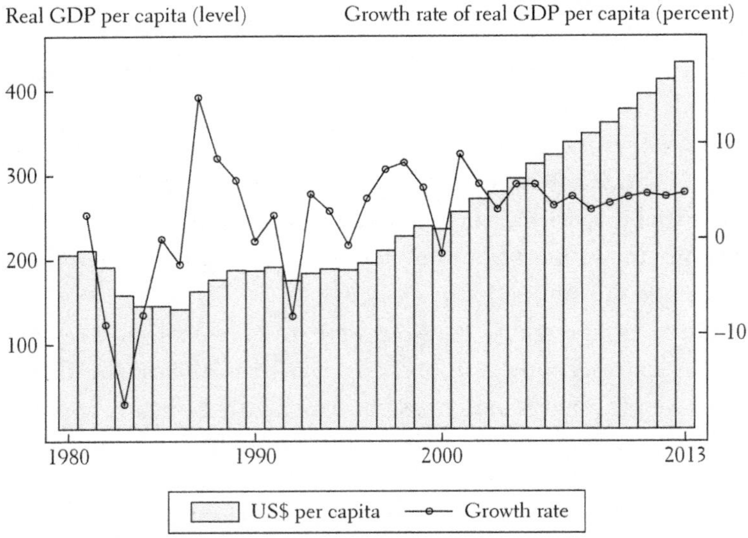

Real GDP per capita (level)   Growth rate of real GDP per capita (percent)

Source: Authors' calculations using World Bank, WDI series.

embarked on the task of reconstruction. Using the World Bank's World Development Indicators, figure 5-1 reports real GDP per capita (in 2005 U.S. dollars) and associated per capita growth rates from 1980 (the earliest observation) to 2013. This shows that average mean incomes doubled over the period, driven by sustained and stable real rates of growth equal to about 4.5 percent per person per year for 1993–2013 (or over 7 percent on aggregate).

Mozambique's impressive rate of economic growth is substantiated by a range of other aggregate indicators.[10] Robust positive trends are found with respect to control of inflation, reducing the current account deficit, and expanding government spending. These are not small achievements and compare highly favorably with trends in the rest of Sub-Saharan Africa. Indeed, most commentators agree that Mozambique's macroeconomic management was competent and provided a critical foundation to growth performance until recently.[11] Additionally, while foreign aid flows have been and continue to be significant, at more than 10 percent of GDP, Mozambique's aid dependence has fallen significantly over recent years. This is due to a combination of the mechanical impact of sustained GDP growth (rising more quickly than the value of aid), domestic revenue growth, and inflows of alternative sources of external finance, such as foreign direct investment and international capital investment. As noted in the introduction, Mozambique's debut international bond launch in 2013 marked its place as a frontier investment destination.

The post-conflict period can be roughly divided into two main phases. The first, lasting from 1992 until the mid-2000s, was characterized by a focus on stabilization, reconstruction, and consolidation of a market-oriented economy. Government intervention in the economy was scaled-back through privatization of state enterprises and removal of price controls and other explicit distortions, in essence completing the work started in the 1980s. As early as 1997, the World Bank triumphantly noted that the proportion of GDP subject to price controls had been reduced from over 70 percent in 1986 to around 10 percent.[12] Mozambique's privatization program was extensive and rapid, prompting a chorus of criticism and concerns regarding political interference.[13] Nonetheless, and despite the emergence of winners and losers from this process, robust rates of aggregate economic growth were sustained.

This period of consolidation was largely complete within about a decade. Echoing trends across the region, by the mid-2000s the natural resources sector had become an explicit focus of development. In the absence of sufficient domestic capital or expertise, the focus has been on attracting foreign investment to the sector. An early project of this sort was exploration of an inshore natural gas field. This was developed by the South African company SASOL, which also financed an 865-kilometer-long pipeline (completed in 2004) to take the gas for processing to South Africa. Large deposits of thermal and coking coal, abandoned after independence, became the next priority and prompted large investments by Vale (Brazil) and Riversdale (Australia), among others. More broadly, given attractive global commodity prices and political and economic stability in the country, Mozambique witnessed an explosion of interest in its minerals sector. Foreign Direct Investment (FDI) increased from a moderate level in the 1990s and early 2000s, growing to over 30 percent of GDP in the most recent period,

FIGURE 5-2. *Trends in Sectoral Shares of Real GDP, 1996–2014*

Percent of real GDP

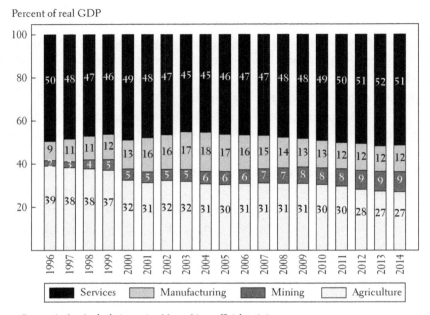

Source: Authors' calculations using Mozambican official statistics.

far outstripping aid inflows. This reflects investments in the coal sector, as well as exploration of offshore gas deposits.

It is worth noting that, since most resource projects remain in a start-up or preliminary phase, inflows of FDI have substantially supported acquisition of offices and equipment and on-site construction. As a result, the share of recent growth attributable to this resource boom is difficult to estimate and is likely to be reflected in other sectors, such as services and construction. According to official figures, depicted in figure 5-2, the relative contribution of aggregate economic sectors to GDP has remained broadly stable during the post-conflict period. While mining has increased in relative terms over the past few years, this is from a very low base. Today, as in 1996, the economy remains dominated by agriculture (27 percent) and private and public services (51 percent). The growth in manufacturing seen from 1998–2004 is largely explained by the establishment of the Mozal aluminum smelter (phases one and two), operated by BHP Billiton under highly favorable tax arrangements.

Over the period 2005–14, manufacturing grew more slowly than other sectors and, thus, declined as a share of GDP from its high of 18 percent in 2004.

Microeconomic Questions

Mozambique's aggregate economic track record since the early 1990s has been widely applauded. An outstanding question, however, is how and to what extent these trends have been reflected in improvements in well-being across the population. Here, something of a puzzle emerges. On the one hand, since the mid-1990s, there is good evidence of steady progress on a range of social indicators. Data from Demographic and Health Surveys (DHS) support this view and are summarized in table 5-1, panel (a). They show significant reductions in infant/child mortality, as well as clear gains in access to education, particularly among women and girls. Moreover, the table suggests that the pace of improvement appears to have quickened; that is, annual proportional changes are larger over the period 2003–11 than for 1997–2003. This is likely to reflect a number of factors, including continued improvements in service delivery (and access), as well as the cumulative effect of ongoing investments and spillovers through achievement of greater scale.

Positive trends in social indicators are also found in other survey data, as well as in administrative statistics on coverage of basic services.[14] The same data sources also show broad increases in asset ownership and access to transport.[15] From this perspective, there appears no immediate disconnect between the macro and micro trends. Deeper questions emerge, though, when we review the evidence on poverty reduction. This is summarized in table 5-1 panel (b), using household budget survey data. The first row reports the official poverty estimates, which is the share of population considered poor according to their estimated level of consumption, calculated following a cost of basic needs approach. This shows a sharp reduction in poverty from 1997–2003, consistent with the narrative of post-war recovery, but no clear progress from 2003–09.

Admittedly, consumption poverty estimates are subject to both sample and non-sample measurement error; therefore, they cannot be taken as exact. Multidimensional poverty metrics, which are based on

TABLE 5-1. *Trends in Selected Microeconomic Indicators, Mozambique*

Percent

(a) DHS surveys	Group	1997	2003	2011	Annual change 1997–03	2003–11
No education	Male	26.2	25.4	19.3	−0.1	−0.8
	Female	47.4	44.4	32.8	−0.5	−1.5
Infant mortality	Boys	153	127	75	−4.3	−6.5
	Girls	142	120	67	−3.7	−6.6
Under 5 mortality	Boys	225	181	113	−7.3	−8.5
	Girls	213	176	103	−6.2	−9.1
Total fertility rate	Adults	5.2	5.5	5.9	0.1	0.1

(b) Budget surveys	1996–97	2002–03	2008–09	Annual change 1997–03	2003–09
Consumption poor	69.4	54.1	54.7	−2.6	0.1
Asset poor	73.8	73.6	66.7	0.0	−1.2
Asset and consumption poor	54.0	42.6	40.1	−1.9	−0.4
Non-poor	11.8	14.8	19.0	0.5	0.7

Source: Authors' calculations using DHS and household budget surveys.

Notes: "No education" and budget survey (poverty) figures all refer to population shares; mortality figures are per 1,000 children; fertility rate is expected number of births per adult woman. Changes are calculated on a mean annual basis.

more directly observable factors such as asset ownership and housing quality, provide complementary insights.[16] These indicate that the share of households deprived in multiple dimensions has followed a slightly different pattern—slow progress in the immediate post-war period and more rapid reductions since then. Combining these insights, two main points emerge. First, the share of the population that is in some way deprived or poor remains large. According to the metrics in table 5-1, in 2008–09, less than 20 percent of the population in 2008 was found to be above both asset and consumption poverty thresholds. This underlines the need to keep in mind the severity of conditions Mozambique found itself in by the beginning of the 1990s. That is, what might appear to be a disconnect between welfare outcomes and aggregate growth is, in part, a reflection of the low base from which

Mozambique has grown and the fact that processes of accumulation are necessarily cumulative and take time.

Even so, and second, whatever metric we use, the elasticity of improvements in welfare to aggregate economic growth appears relatively low. In the second period (2003–09), the share of households not in so-called asset poverty fell by around 1.2 percent per annum in absolute terms, or 9 percent over the period. This compares to average real GDP growth per capita of over 4 percent per year, or a cumulative gain of 30 percent over the six years. The implication is that the pattern of growth has not so far favored the poorest segments of society. Moreover, in-depth analysis of the household surveys suggests this concern applies particularly to rural areas that are more distant from the capital city, Maputo, which is located in the far south.

These points raise concerns regarding the structure or nature of growth in Mozambique, especially over recent years. To what extent are these concerns justified? On the one hand, the existing set of three budget surveys, which are now dated, represents a limited basis to make such claims. Thus, it would clearly overstep the evidence base to claim that Mozambique has taken a fundamentally wrong turn in its development path. The need for caution gains force from the argument that the weak consumption poverty performance in the period 2003–09 was significantly driven by a combination of climatic and external price (terms of trade) shocks in 2007–08.[17] Since consumption is a relatively short-term concept and safety nets, including savings, are limited among the poor and vulnerable, it is not surprising that the scope for consumption smoothing is limited. Thus, we observe sharp (regional) variations in consumption over time. At the same time, these shocks have not persisted. So, in light of continued aggregate growth, it is reasonable to expect that new household survey data (in the field 2014–15) will reveal gains in poverty reduction since 2009.

Despite these reservations, complacency regarding the extent to which aggregate growth is mapping into welfare gains for Mozambique's poorest is not warranted. An insight into recent developments comes from the Afrobarometer surveys of adults, conducted in Mozambique in 2002, 2008, and 2012.[18] These surveys have collected information (among other things) on subjective perceptions of well-being, the

TABLE 5-2. *Insights from Afrobarometer Surveys, by Region, Mozambique*

Percent

	Urban			Rural		
	2002	2008	2012	2002	2008	2012
(a) Fairly or very good living conditions now						
South	23.2	27.2	18.8	26.8	28.4	26.2
Center	40.1	18.8	24.7	45.4	24.5	25.8
North	35.1	23.2	29.9	51.7	35.3	24.7
All	31.6	23.6	23.7	44.3	28.9	25.5
(b) Better or much better living conditions now versus 12 months ago						
South	32.3	40.1	47.0	15.3	43.2	36.7
Center	38.3	39.9	28.8	47.0	42.3	30.9
North	34.4	47.8	46.0	48.2	41.8	31.8
All	34.8	42.1	41.4	42.0	42.3	32.2
(c) Often or always without a cash income						
South	25.5	28.0	33.3	66.7	53.0	55.4
Center	23.6	27.4	36.8	53.4	35.7	48.7
North	46.7	32.9	36.9	37.2	50.1	60.4
All	30.3	29.1	35.4	49.5	43.5	54.1
(d) Has a job that pays a cash income						
South	57.1	43.1	53.0	42.4	26.2	36.3
Center	51.8	36.7	51.0	35.1	42.1	38.7
North	30.1	21.9	39.2	28.5	18.7	26.7
All	48.9	34.8	48.2	34.2	31.3	33.8

Source: Authors' calculations using Afrobarometer surveys, Mozambique.

types of deprivations experienced by households, and access to employment. Summary statistics from these surveys are reported in table 5-2. These report the share of households, split by region and location, responding in specific ways to selected questions. Panels (a) and (b) refer to perceptions of own living conditions; panels (c) and (d) refer to access to some form of cash income. While the patterns are somewhat complex, there is no clear evidence of rapid or distinct improvements in either perceived living conditions or access to cash incomes over time. In rural areas, perceived conditions appear systematically lower in 2012 versus earlier periods. Also, the share of the adult population with access to employment that provides a cash income has displayed no major changes over time (2002–12) in either rural or urban areas on aggregate. Perhaps the only systematic tendency is greater convergence between regions in both perceptions and experiences. Nonetheless, it is notable that considerably less than half of the adult population has access to a cash income; and many households regularly struggle to find any cash.

The Afrobarometer findings rely on subjective perceptions and are based on relatively small samples; for example, the proportions in table 5-2 are based on between 104 and 760 observations. Nonetheless, they point to substantial stability in the broad structure of economic activities pursued by households across the economy. Despite changes at the intensive margin, there is little to suggest there have been significant transformations in how workers make a living; for example, the same series of household budget surveys, as well as a one-off labor force survey, show minimal changes to the aggregate structure of employment over the period 1997–2009 in Mozambique.[19] In particular, the vast majority of workers do not earn a stable wage income, even in urban areas. There are also large and persistent differences in well-being between households whose income derives from different aggregate economic sectors, with the largest gap being between formal sector urban wage earners, who are predominantly found in service industries, and the large share of households who are uniquely reliant on smallholder agriculture. This is indicative of large productivity differentials between sectors. Additionally, contrary to what one would expect if a dynamic process of structural transformation were under way, there is no sign of inter-sectoral productivity convergence.[20] In line with the recent Afrobarometer data, these concerns motivate a deeper investigation of recent labor market trends. This issue is taken up below.

LABOR MARKET ANALYSIS

The aim of this section is to analyze labor market trends in Mozambique over the post-conflict period. Before doing so, a remark on data sources is necessary. As in other low-income countries, the majority of work effort occurs in the informal sector in both rural and urban areas. This sector is not monitored on a regular basis, meaning that official labor force statistics derived from administrative data, such as business or taxation records, do not provide a complete picture of trends in the labor market. Rather, irregular micro-data surveys must be used for this purpose. As alluded already, three household budget surveys have been completed in Mozambique to date. These are the "Inquéritos aos Agregados Familiares" (IAFs) of 1996–97 and 2002–03; and the "Inquérito ao Orçamento Familiar" (IOF) undertaken in 2008–09. These surveys provide relatively detailed information about the labor market activities of each adult member of the household (for example, employment status, sector of activity, type of work performed). More recently, a new IOF went to the field and basic, preliminary data is available from this for the first quarter.[21]

Given the value of undertaking an up-to-date analysis of labor market trends, we combine available employment data from the series of four household surveys and match it to the official aggregate sectoral GDP data, which is also available through 2014. This is the first attempt to use this latest data source in this way. Due to the preliminary nature of the 2014 IOF data, however, it is only possible to classify individual workers into one of four aggregate sectors.[22] These are: 1) agriculture, which includes forestry and fisheries; 2) extractive industries (*indústria de extração mineira*), which also includes construction and utilities; 3) manufacturing (*indústria transformadora*); and 4) services, combining public administration, education, health, and a range of private commercial and financial activities. The rationale for combining utilities and construction with the extractive industries segment is that, in general, all these activities are intensive in capital. Moreover, and as discussed above, many of the new resource extraction projects are currently in a construction phase.

Matching the macro- and micro-data sources by aggregate sector provides a sector-specific time series on employment and output (value added). While the employment data is not observed annually, we make a simple linear interpolation between the survey years to fill the series. To deepen the analysis, it would have been useful to split the aggregate sectors into contributions from formal and informal activities.

However, this is problematic from the output side since the survey data only captures consumption at the household level, not income. Aside from a bespoke survey of the informal sector in 2005, as well as a survey of informal manufacturing firms in 2011, very little detail is available on informal sector enterprises in Mozambique (urban or rural).[23] This reflects a more general problem of weak enterprise data, which suggests that the sectoral classification of GDP is likely to be rather crude. In turn, this justifies retaining a focus on very aggregate sectors.

Methods

To analyze the employment and output series, we start by describing general trends. Here the focus is on average labor productivity, given simply by the ratio of output to employment:

$$P_{it} = Y_{it}/L_{it}$$

where i indexes sectors; t is time; Y is value added at constant prices; and L is the number of individuals identifying i as their primary sector of economic activity. Absolute values of P are not of particular interest. Rather, we report changes over time and compare labor productivity in each sector to the economy-wide average, denoted 0_t. This provides an initial view into the structure of recent growth, and is given by the ratio of output to employment shares:

$$\frac{P_{it}}{P_t} = \frac{(Y_{it}/L_{it})}{(\bar{Y}_t/\bar{L}_t)} = \frac{(Y_{it}/\bar{Y}_t)}{(L_{it}/\bar{L}_t)}$$

Other descriptive statistics, such as a comparison of changes in labor shares to the level of labor productivity, have been used elsewhere and provide complementary insights.[24] To go further, however, a more formal decomposition is warranted. This aims to identify the principal drivers of changes in aggregate labor productivity over time. These changes arise from different sources: differential trends in employment growth (within and between sectors), as well as output gains occurring through acquisition of capital (technology). Put differently, it is instructive to learn whether sectors with rapid productivity growth are also sectors that are significantly attracting new workers. Identifying the

drivers of changes in aggregate labor productivity indicates the extent
to which aggregate GDP growth is associated with transformation in the
underlying structure of the economy.

Following other studies, changes in aggregate labor productivity can
be decomposed into three main components: within-sector productivity
changes (the intra-effect); the contribution due to the reallocation of
labor across sectors, holding productivity fixed (the Denison effect);
and a dynamic structural reallocation effect given by the interaction between productivity growth and relative labor growth (the Baumol effect).[25]
The second effect is positive when workers are moving from lower to
higher productivity sectors, yielding a static gain. The third term is positive when those sectors experiencing employment growth are also experiencing positive productivity gains. Not only is the overall magnitude of
these three effects of interest, we are also concerned to understand how
different sectors contribute to each component. Thus, with four sectors
and three effects (per period), there are twelve quantities of interest.

The three components can be calculated relatively easily from the
output and employment time series. To do so, note that aggregate labor
productivity is a weighted sum of sector-specific labor productivities:[26]

$$\bar{P}_t = \sum_{i \in I} Y_{it} \Big/ L_t = \sum_{i \in I} \frac{P_{it} L_{it}}{L_t} = \sum_{i \in I} P_{it} \omega_{it}^L$$

Thus, the change in aggregate labor productivity between two periods (t and $t-1$) can be separated into the contributions from pure
changes in productivity in each sector and changes in labor shares.
That is, denoting the absolute productivity change in a given sector as:
$P_{it} - P_{it-1} = \Delta P_{it}$, we have:

$$\Delta \bar{P}_t = \sum_{i \in I} \left(P_{it} \omega_{it}^L - P_{it-1} \omega_{it-1}^L \right)$$
$$= \sum_{i \in I} \left(\Delta P_{it} \omega_{it-1}^L + P_{it} \Delta \omega_{it}^L \right)$$

The above expression for the absolute change in labour productivity
is reminiscent of the Oaxaca–Blinder decomposition technique. The
first term on the RHS captures changes in labor productivity holding
labor shares constant, which is the intra-effect. The second term captures changes in employment shares holding labor productivity fixed,
which refers to labor reallocation effects.

This decomposition can be re-expressed as relative contributions to productivity growth. Dividing the previous expression by aggregate productivity at time $t-1$ gives:

$$\bar{g}_t^p = \frac{\Delta \bar{P}_t}{\bar{P}_{t-1}} = \sum_{i \in I} (\Delta P_{it} \omega_{it-1}^L + P_{it} \Delta \omega_{it}^L) / \bar{P}_{t-1}$$

$$= \sum_{i \in I} \left(\frac{\Delta P_{it}}{P_{it-1}} \frac{P_{it-1}}{\bar{P}_{t-1}} \omega_{it-1}^L + \frac{P_{it}}{P_{it-1}} \frac{P_{it-1}}{\bar{P}_{t-1}} \Delta \omega_{it}^L \right)$$

$$= \sum_{i \in I} (g_{it}^P \omega_{it-1}^P \omega_{it-1}^L + \Delta \omega_{it}^L [1 + g_{it}^P] \omega_{it-1}^P)$$

$$= \sum_{i \in I} \omega_{it-1}^P (g_{it}^P \omega_{it-1}^L + \Delta \omega_{it}^L [1 + g_{it}^P])$$

$$= \sum_{i \in I} (g_{it}^P \omega_{it-1}^Y + \Delta \omega_{it}^L \omega_{it-1}^P + \Delta \omega_{it}^L g_{it}^P \omega_{it-1}^P)$$

As required, the three terms on the RHS of the above productivity growth decomposition respectively denote the relative contributions to aggregate productivity growth of: within-sector productivity growth, static labor reallocation, and dynamic labor reallocation.

Results

Previously, we outlined a range of analytical tools that can be used to investigate how the structure of output and employment have coevolved over time. Applying these to the Mozambican series, figure 5-3 illustrates trends in sectoral employment shares. Combining these with sectoral shares of real output (figure 5-2), figure 5-4 indicates trends in the relative productivity of each sector versus economy-wide labor productivity (ω_{it}^P). Stated in log terms, bars less than zero indicate sectors with below-average productivity. Also, a unit change on the y-axis is consistent with an approximate doubling of labor productivity relative to the mean.

The figures are informative. Consistent with earlier data, we find that the majority of Mozambicans continue to be employed in (smallholder) agriculture. As shown in figure 5-3, this sector accounts for more than two in every three workers. Nonetheless, the agricultural labor share appears to have fallen rapidly between the two most recent surveys, from 79 percent of workers in 2009 to 72 percent in 2014. While part of this difference may simply reflect the preliminary nature

FIGURE 5-3. *Trends in Sectoral Shares of Employment, 1996–2014*

Percent of employment

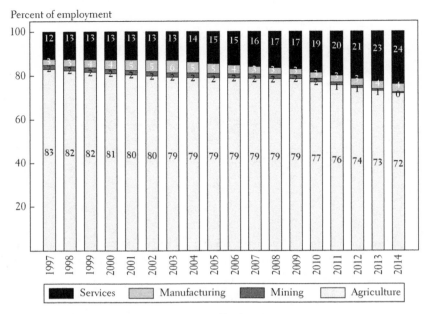

Source: Authors' calculations using Mozambican official statistics.

FIGURE 5-4. *Sector-Specific and Aggregate Labor Productivity*

Productivity ratio (log)

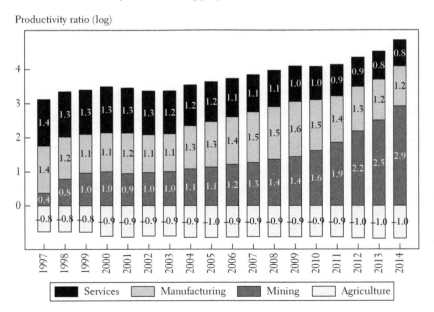

Source: Authors' calculations using Mozambican official statistics.

of the 2014 data, it is consistent with indications from agricultural survey data of a trend shift out of agriculture in certain areas, especially the south. This decline has been offset by a corresponding increase in the labor share of the services sector. The other aggregate sectors, mining and manufacturing, account for less than one in every twenty workers and show no material changes in their overall shares of employment.

Figure 5-2 indicates that, aside from a small increase in the output share accounted for by the mining sector and a small decline in the contribution from manufacturing over the most recent period, output shares have remained broadly constant over time. In turn, figure 5-4 indicates that productivity differences *between* sectors have diverged, particularly in the latest period (2009–14). This has been driven by two trends: a significant increase in labor productivity in the mining sector and a relative decline in labor productivity in both services and manufacturing. At the same time, agricultural labor productivity has remained low and stable (in relative terms) at around half of the economy-wide level of productivity. This does not mean that labor productivity in agriculture has been stagnant. Rather, it has roughly tracked aggregate productivity growth. Specifically, between 2009 and 2014, the latter grew by around 25 percent, or an average of around 4 percent per annum. For the same period, we estimate agricultural productivity grew by around 3.5 percent per annum. However, labor productivity in mining grew by an average of over 35 percent per annum during this period, increasing about fivefold.

Figure 5-5 plots the relative level of labor productivity against changes in labor shares for the four sectors for two periods: 1997–2005 and 2006–14. Of particular interest are sectors located in the positive quadrant, those that show relatively high labor productivity and increases in their share of employment. In transition and developing economies we typically see large differences in labor productivity between sectors.[27] However, for those economies undergoing positive and dynamic structural transformation, we often see that it is higher productivity sectors that are able to attract more labor. The Mozambican data suggests the economy is in transition. Labor productivity in agriculture is lower than productivity in any other sector by a factor of at least two. Consequently, movement of workers out of agriculture and into other

FIGURE 5-5. *Relative Labor Productivity vs. Changes in Labor Shares, by Sector, 1997–2005 and 2006–14*

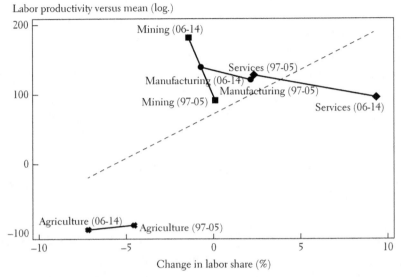

Source: Authors' calculations using Mozambican official statistics.
Note: Labor productivity (y-axis) is given by the period mean of: $[100 \times \ln(\omega)_{it}^p]$.

sectors (or relatively faster employment growth in the latter) is consistent with a trend increase in economy-wide labor productivity. Even so, the figure gives rise to concerns. First, the only sector in the positive quadrant is the services sector. Moreover, labor productivity is falling in this sector, which suggests that new workers in this sector tend to operate on an informal basis and undertake more precarious activities relative to existing workers. Additionally, sectors experiencing the highest labor productivity growth, namely mining, are not creating new employment posts in line with the pace of new entrants to the economy. Not only is this a small sector in employment terms; it is getting smaller as the working population expands.

The previous discussion hints at results from the decomposition analysis. This is summarized in table 5-3, which reports mean absolute and relative contributions to average annual aggregate productivity growth by component (intra-sector productivity effects [intra], static

TABLE 5-3. *Decomposition of Contributions to Aggregate Productivity Growth, by Period, Mozambique*

Percent

		Absolute				Relative			
		Intra[a]	*SRE*	*DRE*	*Total*	*Intra*	*SRE*	*DRE*	*Total*
1997–2002	Agriculture	1.40	-0.29	-0.01	1.10	22.2	-4.5	-0.2	17.5
	Manufacturing	0.06	1.94	-0.01	2.00	1.0	30.8	-0.2	31.6
	Mining	0.67	0.06	0.01	0.73	10.5	0.9	0.2	11.6
	Services	2.15	0.32	0.01	2.48	34.0	5.1	0.2	39.3
	Total	4.28	2.04	0.00	6.32	67.7	32.2	0.0	100.0
2003–08	Agriculture	1.15	-0.08	0.00	1.06	27.6	-2.0	-0.1	25.5
	Manufacturing	2.04	-1.44	-0.21	0.39	48.9	-34.5	-5.0	9.5
	Mining	0.66	-0.07	-0.01	0.58	15.8	-1.7	-0.2	13.8
	Services	0.19	1.94	0.00	2.13	4.5	46.6	0.1	51.2
	Total	4.04	0.35	-0.22	4.17	96.8	8.4	-5.2	100.0
2009–14	Agriculture	1.02	-0.44	-0.02	0.56	24.2	-10.5	-0.4	13.3
	Manufacturing	-0.20	0.49	-0.08	0.20	-4.8	11.6	-1.9	4.8
	Mining	2.97	-1.57	-0.69	0.71	70.5	-37.3	-16.4	16.8
	Services	-0.39	3.16	-0.03	2.74	-9.2	75.0	-0.7	65.1
	Total	3.40	1.64	-0.82	4.21	80.6	38.9	-19.5	100.0

Source: Authors' calculations.

a. Intra = within-sector productivity effect; SRE and DRE are static and dynamic reallocation effects, respectively.

reallocation effects [SRE], and dynamic reallocation effects [DRE]), by sector and by period (1997–2002, 2003–08, 2009–14). For the absolute estimates, in each period the sum of the component-sector cells gives that period's total aggregate productivity growth, or 100 percent in the case of the relative contributions. For instance, in the latest period aggregate productivity growth averaged 4.2 percent per year, composed primarily of the intra effect (81 percent). Labor reallocation (structural change) effects in the same period, given by the sum of SRE and DRE, contributed less than 20 percent of overall productivity growth.

Four key findings emerge. First, as already indicated, labor reallocation effects have played a relatively small role in Mozambique's postconflict productivity growth. Compared to later periods, reallocation made the largest relative contribution in the immediate reconstruction period (1997–2002), at around 32 percent. This underlines the thesis that the underlying drivers of Mozambique's growth have shifted over time. Second, the same point is supported by evidence that the composition of these labor reallocation effects have altered. In particular, the dynamic component has turned negative, which reflects the finding that sectors with the fastest rates of growth in employment are also sectors with falling relative productivity, while those with the slowest rates of employment growth show increasing relative productivity. In the most recent period, this negative dynamic effect reduced the contribution of structural change to aggregate productivity growth by around 20 percent. It is important to keep in mind, however, that the static reallocation effect in the latest period (absent the negative dynamic effect) was reasonably large and positive. This means that sectors are adding jobs at quite different paces (either through new entrants or through job changes) relative to 2003–08; even so, the marginal worker added in the services sector is not as productive as existing workers.

Third, a related issue is that while the intra effect remains the predominant overall contributor to aggregate productivity growth compared to structural change, within-sector productivity growth—which also captures workers moving within the same sector from lower to higher productivity activities (for example, from smallholder to commercial farming)—is highly uneven. Of most concern is that in all sectors excluding mining, the sector-specific intra effects are smaller in magnitude in the latest period versus the two earlier periods. Put differently, absent the mining sector, inherent within-sector productivity growth appears to be weakening. Indeed, this growth has turned negative in services and manufacturing, meaning that workers are less productive in these sectors, on average, than before. This raises profound questions regarding the sustainability of Mozambique's current rapid rates of aggregate economic growth, particularly given current slack in global commodity prices. Additionally, such trends corroborate earlier disquiet regarding the extent to which growth is translating into widespread improvements in well-being.

Fourth, the analysis suggests that aggregate productivity growth has become increasingly dependent on dynamics in the services sector. This is indicated by the "total" columns of table 5-3. These report the sum of the component effects for each sector and show that services accounted for two thirds of aggregate productivity growth in 2003–08, compared to 51 and 39 percent in the earlier two periods. The corollary of this insight is that the contribution of other sectors, including both agriculture and manufacturing, have declined over time. Indeed, the strong contribution of manufacturing witnessed in the first period was almost entirely dependent on the establishment of a single large firm (Mozal), attracted by a highly preferential taxation structure. Also, despite providing the majority of the population with a livelihood, agriculture contributed just 25 percent to aggregate productivity growth in 2003–08. Again, this endorses concerns regarding the extent to which growth in Mozambique is pro-poor.

LOOKING AHEAD

We have just analyzed past developments in the labor market to shed light on Mozambique's recent growth experience. The results highlighted important changes in the structure of growth and raised concerns regarding both the sustainability and the poverty-reducing capacity of the current growth mode. The latter appears to be dominated by two main currents: first, rapid productivity growth in the mining sector, intensive in capital and contributing relatively few new jobs; and second, expansion of the services sector, largely in lower productivity activities. Given that the vast majority of the workforce is engaged in low-productivity informal activities (for example, smallholder agriculture), a guiding assumption of this section is that the qualitative nature of growth will need to change to achieve rapid improvements in well-being across the population. Moreover, such changes are likely to be necessary to sustain high rates of growth *per se*.

Challenges

Future challenges need to be considered in light of demographic trends. Fertility rates remain high in Mozambique. This means it is inevitable that the working-age population will expand rapidly over the next generation. The UN's baseline projections for the working-age population (ages 15–64), for the period 2010–50, predict that the total number of potential workers will rise from around 15 million in 2015 to 36 million in 2050. This represents a growth rate of about 3.6 percent per annum, meaning that, by 2025, more than 500,000 new workers will enter the labor market each year. Given the present structure of growth, this represents a significant challenge and raises the specter of conflicts over productive resources (for example, land) and even social unrest if levels of well-being do not improve.

At the same time, there is a potential demographic dividend. This comes from a relative reduction in the share of dependents (nonworkers) in the population. The current dependency ratio is over 45 percent, meaning there is approximately one dependent for every *potential* worker. According to the projections, this ratio is expected to decline to around 35 percent by 2050, thereby reducing the effective burden on workers and raising possibilities for greater productive investments in the economy. Furthermore, the quality of the working population is set to change as access to schooling continues to increase. To model this shift, we use secondary data that estimates the average years of schooling of fifteen- to nineteen-year-olds in multiple countries since the 1950s at five-year intervals.[28] Using this data, we estimate the expected rate of growth in years of schooling conditional on its current level. This is necessary since years of schooling is bounded, meaning that as one approaches a theoretical maximum of (around) fifteen years, growth rates must decline. We undertake these estimates at the 25th, 50th, and 75th percentiles of the distribution of cross-country human capital growth rates.[29] These imply different paths for how the mean years of schooling of any given country will evolve, conditional on the starting level. The path at the 75th percentile would be consistent with the top 25 percent of all historically observed conditional growth rates (regardless of country or period).

We apply these estimates to the demographic projections for Mozambique. Specifically, we allow the mean years of schooling of the 15–19 age cohort, which are taken as (potential) new labor market entrants, to evolve according to either the 25th, 50th, or 75th percentile estimated growth paths. The latter is taken as a reasonable upper bound on what Mozambique might achieve, and the first a lower bound.[30] We additionally assume that years of schooling remains fixed after the age of twenty. As a consequence, growth in the overall mean years of schooling, encompassing all members of the working-age population, is uniquely generated by new labor market entrants. Thus, the overall mean years of schooling will change only gradually over time. Starting values for 2010 are taken directly from observed mean years of schooling for each age group of five years (as per the projections) from the 2008–09 survey.

Table 5-4 reports aggregate results of our projections using the median (50th percentile) growth path. Figures 5-6 and 5-7 plot the same estimates, including the confidence interval (that is, 25th lower and 75th upper bounds), plus a disaggregation by gender. A first point to note is that years of schooling are presently low; only around one in four workers has completed primary education (seven or more years of schooling). This reflects the predominantly rural nature of the work force and historical legacies. At the median of the observed historical conditional cross-country human capital growth rate distribution, average years of schooling should double to 6.6 years by 2050. In turn, this implies that over 40 percent of the working-age population should have attained a basic level; under the upper bound scenario this share reaches around 50 percent by 2050. Assuming increased literacy and numeracy implies a greater capacity to adopt (and effectively use) modern technologies, this raises hope for greater innovations and transformations across sectors.

TABLE 5-4. *Decomposition of Contributions to Aggregate Productivity Growth, by Period, Mozambique*

| Year | | Working-age population (in millions) | | | Median forecast | |
		Total	Completed primary	Not completed primary	Years of schooling	% completed primary
2010	Male	6.0	1.8	4.2	4.9	29.8
	Female	6.6	1.2	5.5	2.9	17.5
2030[a]	Male	11.2	4.1	7.1	6.1	36.5
	Female	11.7	3.3	8.4	4.7	28.5
2050[a]	Male	17.7	7.6	10.1	7.1	42.9
	Female	18.1	6.8	11.3	6.2	37.5
2010	All	12.6	3.0	9.7	3.9	23.4
2030[a]	All	22.9	7.4	15.4	5.4	32.4
2050[a]	All	35.8	14.4	21.4	6.6	40.1

Source: Authors' calculations using UN baseline demographic projections and human capital growth estimates based on data from Barro and Lee (2013).

a. Projected numbers. Human capital forecasts are projections at the median growth path.

FIGURE 5-6. *Trends in Working Population and Labor Force Quality*

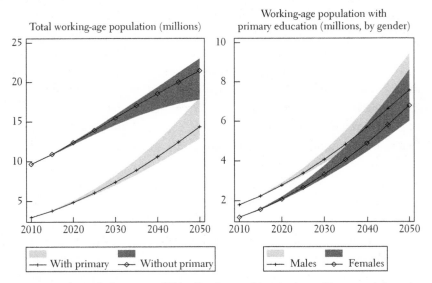

Source: Authors' calculations using UN baseline demographic projections and human capital growth estimates based on data from Barro and Lee (2013).

Note: Shaded regions represent confidence intervals defined as the 25th and 75th percentile conditional growth paths; solid lines are the projections at the median growth path (see text); all population figures are in millions.

FIGURE 5-7. *Trends in Mean Years of Schooling of Working-Age Population*

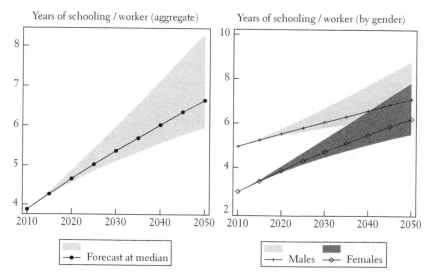

Years of schooling / worker (aggregate)   Years of schooling / worker (by gender)

— ● — Forecast at median   —+— Males —◇— Females

Source: Authors' calculations using UN baseline demographic projections and human capital growth estimates based on data from Barro and Lee (2013).
Note: Shaded regions represent confidence intervals defined as the 25th and 75th percentile conditional growth paths; solid lines are the projections at the median growth path (see text).

Moreover, these developments portend the likely emergence of thicker and more qualified markets for labor (in both rural and urban areas), which may stimulate larger-scale investments. Even so, the flipside is that many workers will remain poorly educated. Transformation in the quality of the labor force will be slow and possibly uneven.

Policy Priorities

Looking forward, a key question is what kinds of government policies are most likely to alter the shape or pattern of growth toward a configuration that is more pro-poor. Here an important distinction is between macro-structural policies and microeconomic sectoral policies. The former can be best described as policies that affect economic incentives and behavior across large swathes of the population (people, firms, and sectors), without necessarily targeting specific markets or subgroups.[31] Examples include public investments in infrastructure, general legal or tax reforms, as well as monetary and exchange rate policies. Micro-economic sectoral policies refer to more specific, targeted interventions that often seek to address market failures or efficiency losses in specific sectors. Examples include active labor market policies, such as employment subsidies, or investments in labor market information systems.

Without ruling out the role of microeconomic policies, there are good reasons to suggest that efforts should focus on deploying macro-structural policies to enhance the quality of growth. A main reason is simply the massive scale of the jobs challenge. The demographic projections already noted mean that Mozambique needs to run just to keep up. The number of projected new labor market entrants per year is larger than the absolute number of workers currently found in the formal sector (that is, who receive a regular wage). Consequently, it is difficult to see how targeted microeconomic policies, which naturally tend to be directed toward legally incorporated entities and/or the visible (formal) sector, can have an adequate footprint even if undertaken on a large-scale.

A second reason to focus on macro-structural policies is that state capacity is weak. Not only are there few examples of unambiguously effective microeconomic development interventions in present-day Mozambique; the government also plays a minimal role in most sectors, except as a major purchaser of goods and services. Thus, in the short- to medium-term, any kind of step change in the role and effectiveness of sector-specific microeconomic interventions is not realistic.

What can be done to raise the quality of growth? In keeping with previous studies, we recommend that very considerably increased priority must be given to raising productivity in the agricultural sector.[32] Since the majority of households are reliant on agriculture and this sector shows significantly lower levels of labor productivity relative to other sectors, progress must be made in transforming agriculture to achieve significant poverty reduction. In this view, any broad-based interventions in agriculture are macro-structural in nature since they cut across the rural sector and feed into urban dynamics, for example, through living costs. Also, raising rural incomes will be important to moderate migration out of agriculture into urban informal activities.

We believe two main rural policy initiatives merit attention. The first is to draw in private sector expertise and creativity to raise rural incomes. Presently, modern private sector entities face few incentives to engage directly with rural producers. Among other things, this reflects poorly coordinated and integrated value chains, high transaction costs, and low market predictability (for example, due to climatic and other factors). Lessons can be learned from various Asian countries regarding how structural interventions in staple food markets played a crucial role in their development successes. This does not necessarily require large-scale public interventions in food markets. Rather, the creation of a clear and stable set of incentives for private buyers is needed, which in turn supports domestic price stability.[33] Existing pockets of agricultural success in Mozambique point in this direction. For instance, contract farming schemes in tobacco, cotton, and cassava (used to produce beer) have been shown to boost incomes. There also has been success in establishing a more integrated value chain running from production of chicken feed (soya) by emergent commercial farmers to domestic chicken production.[34]

A second and related macro-structural intervention is to focus a larger share of public investments on rural areas, with a key aim of fostering market linkages. A recent infrastructure diagnosis notes that: "Mozambique's connectivity among urban and economic clusters is quite limited, lacking linkages that connect parallel corridors to each other. . . . Additionally, rural population accessibility to domestic markets . . . is an enormous challenge, and lags behind what is observed in the region."[35] Supporting this view, research shows that, relative to other countries, such as Vietnam, poor rural infrastructure in Mozambique contributes to much lower agricultural income multipliers.[36] Ensuring a network of high-quality all-weather roads to connect all major towns in Mozambique, as well as an expansion of rural feeder roads, requires sustained political commitment over the long-term.

A third issue is policy distortions that limit demand for domestic labor. A first example of this is the real exchange rate. A recent analysis associated with the IMF suggests that the Metical was overvalued by between 26 and 41 percent in real effective terms, and this preceded a phase of significant devaluation of the South Africa Rand relative to the Metical.[37] While a strong Metical may be "good" for urban consumers in the south, who rely largely on food imports from South Africa, there are potentially damaging longer-term consequences for the rural sector and job creation in labor-intensive exports. Research into price competitiveness suggest that certain cash crops, cotton and soya, could be seriously affected by any further sustained appreciation of the currency.[38] The point is that maintenance of a reasonable and stable level of external price competitiveness provides a broad-based incentive to exporting activities and use of domestic factors of production. Determined pursuit of such competitiveness is necessary given Mozambique's current resource boom and high levels of external financial inflows.

Another distortion is minimum wage policies. National minimum wages are set for individual occupational sectors in Mozambique each year. Not only do these minimum wages differ by a large factor between sectors, it is clear they have increased much more rapidly than labor productivity growth. Stated in constant 2009 prices, average minimum wages have increased by a factor of nearly four since 1996; that is, from 28 to 138 U.S. dollars; and over the period 2009–14, they increased at an annual rate of over 10 percent. This compares to average aggregate labor productivity growth of below 5 percent.

These trends are problematic for a number of reasons. First, high minimum wages constitute a bias toward certain types of labor; namely, skilled urban workers. This bias also appears to be material since labor productivity in the majority of Mozambican manufacturing firms is well below that implied by the minimum wage.[39] Second, as a national price, these minimum wages ignore the large regional differences in prices (as well as urban–rural differences). Significant spatial price disparities are found in Mozambique due to high transport costs, reflecting long distances between centers of production and consumption, and weakly competitive intermediaries.[40] The extent to which minimum wage policies directly affect job creation (for example, in manufacturing) is hard to assess and merits additional research. Nonetheless, it is representative of a more general policy stance that tends to promote a structure of growth that has weak capacity to reduce absolute poverty. We recommend careful consideration of this and other policies and subsequent action in practice.

CONCLUSION

This chapter has reviewed recent macroeconomic and microeconomics development trends in Mozambique. The overall aim was to make sense of the apparent disconnect between rapid aggregate growth and weaker trends in poverty reduction. While part of this disconnect reflects temporary factors, such as a conjunction of price shocks and climate events in 2008–09, more worrisome is a lack of growth-enhancing structural change in the economy. This motivated a detailed decomposition of trends in labor productivity for the period 1996–2014. This represented the primary analytical contribution of the chapter and was able to take advantage of recent household data from 2014.

Four main findings emerged from the labor productivity decomposition. First, labor reallocation effects have made a relatively small contribution to productivity growth over this period. Moreover, when the full post-war period is split into phases of around six years, labor reallocation was found to have made the largest relative contribution, at around 32 percent, in the immediate reconstruction period (1997–2002). Second, the composition of labor reallocation effects has altered over time. More recently, dynamic structural reallocation effects have become negative, reflecting the point that sectors with the fastest rates of growth in employment (primarily, services) show falling levels of relative productivity. Third, within-sector productivity growth remains a predominant overall contributor to productivity growth, yet is highly uneven across sectors. We also found that, with the exception of mining, sector-specific intra productivity growth has been falling over time and even is negative in services and manufacturing. This implies that each worker is becoming less productive in these sectors than before, raising concerns regarding the sustainability of Mozambique's current growth path. Fourth, aggregate productivity growth appears to be increasingly dependent on the services sector. Despite large investments in mining and related industries, and associated within-sector productivity growth, this has not translated into large aggregate labor productivity benefits due to the weak contribution (negative) of these new activities to employment.

The final section of the chapter reflected on what these findings mean for policy. We highlighted unavoidable demographic trends that suggest both forthcoming opportunities and also challenges, particularly concerning the sheer number of new workers that will enter the labor market and that average worker quality (years of schooling) will only evolve slowly. We suggested that macro-structural policies should be a primary though not exclusive focus of initiatives compared to sector- or firm-specific interventions. This reflects both the scale of the jobs challenge and weak state capacity to intervene at the microeconomic level. Three specific macro-structural interventions were recommended. The first is efforts to raise agricultural productivity, particularly by establishing larger and more stable incentives for the private sector to engage directly with rural smallholders. Second, investments in rural infrastructure and rural–urban connections will be critically important to exploit gains from trade and specialization. Third, we recommend efforts to minimize distortions that act against export-oriented and labor-intensive activities. Distortions that merit specific attention are external price competitiveness (via the exchange rate) and minimum wage policies.

We have argued that Mozambique's economic development challenges remain significant. However, it is important to emphasize that substantial and laudable progress has been made in sustaining two decades of rapid growth and establishing a stable macroeconomic and political environment. Moreover, the challenges Mozambique faces reflect, in part, the cumulative impact of historical experiences, as well as global interest in SSA commodities. Nevertheless, Mozambique must push back against trends that favor a capital-intensive path of development. Instead, we believe greater priority must be given to finding a more labor-intensive, and thus pro-poor, growth path in which rural producers play a prominent role.

NOTES

1. See Jones (2006); Arndt and others (2007); Nucifora and da Silva (2011).
2. This chapter was written in 2015, before the emergence of information regarding a number of large, commercial government guaranteed external loans that had not been declared to the IMF. Together with falling commod-

ity prices, these events have cast doubt on the sustainability of Mozambique's recent growth path and have led to significant economic and political turmoil, including substantial exchange rate depreciation since October 2015.

3. Arndt and others (2012a).

4. McMillan and Rodrik (2012) use decomposition methods to argue that growth-enhancing structural transformation was largely absent in Africa over the period 1990–2005; de Vries and others (2013) extend the analysis to 2010.

5. For example, see African Development Bank (2013).

6. Quoted from Henriksen (1983, p. 44).

7. For further details, consult Jones and Tarp (2012, 2015).

8. In line with local practice in Mozambique, "Frelimo" is now written in lower case to mark the distinction between the independence movement and the post-independence political party.

9. For additional details see Pitcher (2002); Arndt and others (2007).

10. See also Jones and Tarp (2015).

11. Jones (2008); Nucifora and da Silva (2011).

12. World Bank (1997).

13. Cramer (2001); Pitcher (2002).

14. Republic of Mozambique (2010).

15. For a review of this evidence see Arndt and others (2015).

16. For elaboration, see Jones and Tarp (2012, 2013).

17. Set out in Arndt and others (2012a, 2015).

18. A further round was undertaken in 2005; however, the rural/urban structure of this survey was distinct and appears less comparable.

19. Jones and Tarp (2012, 2013).

20. Gemmell and others (2000).

21. Instituto Nacional de Éstatistica (2015).

22. In part, this reflects changes in the occupational categories and codes used in the questionnaires. As a result, further work will be needed to make the 2014 data consistent with previous rounds when a final dataset is released.

23. Rand and Tarp (2013).

24. For example, see African Development Bank (2013).

25. See Dumagan (2013); de Vries and others (2013).

26. Superscripts on the share terms denote the variables from which they are derived; that is, $\omega_{it}^{L} = L_{it}/\bar{L}_t$, $\omega_{it}^{P} = P_{it}/\bar{P}_t$, etc.

27. For a similar exercise, see African Development Bank (2013).

28. This data is taken from Barro and Lee (2013).

29. These estimates are based on quantile regressions where the dependent variable is the observed (annualized) growth rate in the mean years of schooling over a five-year period, and the explanatory variables are the initial level of schooling and population size. Coefficient estimates from these regressions are used to construct our growth paths.

　　　　　　　　　　　　　Jones and Tarp

30. The notion here is that Mozambique must sustain rates of growth in mean years of schooling according to these paths over a period of forty years. Since the growth paths are estimated from the full distribution of schooling year growth rates, the upper (lower) part of this distribution is populated by country-period observations that are often not sustained over long periods. Thus, our focus on the 25th–75th band is reasonable.

31. Macro-structural policies include certain elements of industrial policy, including infrastructure investments and exchange rate management, since these affect multiple sectors at once.

32. For an early view of this thesis, see Tarp and others (2002); also Jones and Tarp (2012, 2013).

33. See Timmer and Dawe (2007).

34. Hanlon and Smart (2014).

35. Dominguez-Torres and Briceño-Garmendia (2011, p. 8).

36. Arndt and others (2012b).

37. See Vitek (2009). Note that in 2015, Mozambique has experienced significant devaluation pressure.

38. Salinger and Ennis (2014).

39. Rand and Tarp (2013).

40. Arndt and others (2015).

REFERENCES

African Development Bank. 2013. *African Economic Outlook 2013, Special Thematic Edition: Structural Transformation and Natural Resources* (African Development Bank, Organisation for Economic Co-operation and Development, United Nations Development Programme, Economic Commission for Africa).

Arndt, C., A. Garcia, F. Tarp, and J. Thurlow. 2012a. "Poverty Reduction and Economic Structure: Comparative Path Analysis for Mozambique and Vietnam." *Review of Income and Wealth*, 58(4), pp. 742–63.

Arndt, C., M. A. Hussain, E. S. Jones, V. Nhate, F. Tarp, and J. Thurlow. 2012b. "Explaining the Evolution of Poverty: The Case of Mozambique." *American Journal of Agricultural Economics*, 94(4), pp. 854–72.

Arndt, C., S. Jones, and F. Tarp. 2007. "Aid and Development: The Mozambican Case," in *Theory and Practice of Foreign Aid*, Vol. 1, edited by S. Lahiri (Amsterdam: Elsevier B.V.), pp. 235–88.

———. 2015. "Mozambique: Off-Track or Temporarily Side-Lined?" Working Paper 2015/044 (UNU-WIDER: Helsinki).

Barro, R. J., and J. W. and Lee. 2013. A New Data Set of Educational Attainment in the World, 1950–2010." *Journal of Development Economics*, 104(2013), pp. 184–98.

Cramer, C. 2001. "Privatisation and Adjustment in Mozambique: A 'Hospital Pass'?" *Journal of Southern African Studies*, 27(1), pp. 79–103.

Cunguara, B., G. Fagilde, J. Garrett, R. Uaiene, and D. Heady. 2011. Growth Without Change: The Elusiveness of Agricultural and Economic Transformation in Mozambique." Paper presented at Dialogue on Promoting Agricultural Growth in Mozambique, 21 July (Maputo).

de Vries, G. J., M. P. Timmer, and K. De Vries. 2013. "Structural Transformation in Africa: Static Gains, Dynamic Losses." Research Memorandum 136 (University of Groningen, Groningen Growth and Development Centre).

Dominguez-Torres, C., and C. Briceño-Garmendia. 2011. "Mozambique's Infrastructure: A Continental Perspective." Technical Report, Africa Infrastructure Country Diagnostic (AICD) (Washington D.C.: World Bank).

Dumagan, J. C. 2013. "A Generalized Exactly Additive Decomposition of Aggregate Labor Productivity Growth." *Review of Income and Wealth*, 59(1), pp. 157–68.

Gemmell, N., T. A. Lloyd, and M. Mathew. 2000. "Agricultural Growth and Inter-Sectoral Linkages in a Developing Economy." *Journal of Agricultural Economics*, 51(3), pp. 353–70.

Hanlon, J., and T. Smart. 2014. *Chickens and Beer: A recipe for Agricultural Growth in Mozambique* (Maputo: Kapicua).

Henriksen, Thomas. 1983. *Revolution and Counterrevolution* (London: Greenwood Press).

Instituto Nacional de Éstatistica (INE). 2015. Household budget survey, 1st Trimester, August to October. Technical Report (Maputo: INE).

Jones, S. 2006. "Growth Accounting for Mozambique (1980–2004)." Discussion Paper 22E (National Directorate of Studies and Policy Analysis, Ministry of Planning and Development, Republic of Mozambique).

———. 2008. "Sustaining Growth in the Long Term," chapter 3 in *Post-Stabilization Economics in Sub-Saharan Africa: Lessons from Mozambique*, edited by J. Clément and S. J. Peiris (International Monetary Fund).

Jones, S., and Finn Tarp. 2012. "Jobs and Welfare in Mozambique." Background study for the 2013 World Development Report (Helsinki: UNU-WIDER).

———. 2013. "Jobs and Welfare in Mozambique." Working Paper 2013/045 (Helsinki: UNU-WIDER).

———. 2015. "Understanding Mozambique's Growth Experience through an Employment Lens." Working Paper 2015/109 (Helsinki: UNU-WIDER).

McMillan, M. S., and D. Rodrik. 2012. "Globalization, Structural Change, and Productivity Growth." Discussion Paper 01160 (International Food

Policy Research Institute [IFPRI]). (www.ifpri.org/sites/default/files/publications/ifpridp01160.pdf).

Nucifora, A. M., and L. A. P. da Silva. 2011. "Rapid Growth and Economic Transformation in Mozambique 1993–2009," chapter 3 in *Yes, Africa Can: Success Stories from a Dynamic Continent*, edited by Punam Chuhan-Pole and Manka Angwafo (Washington, D.C.: World Bank), pp. 65–80.

Pitcher, M. A. 2002. *Transforming Mozambique: The Politics of Privatization, 1975–2000* (Cambridge University Press).

Rand, J., and F. Tarp. 2013. "Inquérito às Indústrias Manufactureiras (IIM 2012): Relatório Descritivo." Technical Report (Maputo: Ministry of Planning and Development).

Republic of Mozambique. 2010. "Poverty and Well-Being in Mozambique: The Third National Assessment." Discussion Paper 2010/3 (Maputo: Ministry of Planning and Development).

Salinger, L., and C. Ennis. 2014. "Manufacturing Competitiveness and the Resource Boom." Report 017 (SPEED: DAI and Nathan Associates).

Tarp, F., C. Arndt, H. T. Jensen, S. Robinson, and R. Heltberg. 2002. Facing the Development Challenge in Mozambique: An Economy-Wide Perspective. Research Report 126 (International Food Policy Research Institute [IFPRI]).

Timmer, C. P., and D. Dawe. 2007. "Managing Food Price Instability in Asia: A Macro Food Security Perspective." *Asian Economic Journal*, 21(1), pp. 1–18.

Vitek, F. 2009. "An Assessment of External Price Competitiveness for Mozambique." Working Paper 2009/165 (International Monetary Fund).

World Bank. 1997. "Memorandum of the President of the International Development Association to the Executive Directors on a country assistance strategy of the World Bank Group for the Republic of Mozambique." World Bank Report No. 17180 MOZ (International Development Association). (http://documents.worldbank.org/curated/en/1997/11/727079/mozambique-country-assistance-strategy).

SIX

Nigeria

The Relationship between Growth and Employment

**Olu Ajakaiye, Afeikhena Jerome, David Nabena,
and Olufunke Alaba**

Nigeria has maintained remarkable growth over the last decade, recording an average growth rate of 6.8 percent from a large economic base, and the potential for further growth is reasonably high. Real gross domestic product (GDP) growth was estimated at 6.23 percent in 2014, compared to 5.49 percent in 2013. The rebasing of its GDP in April 2014 by the National Bureau of Statistics, to better reflect the size and structure of the economy, saw it surge past South Africa to become Africa's largest economy, with a rebased GDP estimate of US$454 billion in 2012 and US$510 billion in 2013. The rebased GDP, using updated prices and improved methodology, also reveals a more diversified economy than previously thought, with rising contributions of previously undocumented services (including the entertainment industry) to GDP. In addition, as a result of banking sector reforms, especially the bank consolidation exercise of 2004, an increasing number of private Nigerian banks are present in many African countries.

However, given the country's high population, per capita GDP was only US$2,688 in 2013, ranking 121st compared to South Africa, which, at 69th, had a per capita GDP of US$7,507. The rebasing also indicated that the Nigerian economy is transforming from an agrarian economy to a tertiary service economy, without going through the intermediate stage of industrialization. This atypical transition, the so-called tertiarization that has so far failed to deliver quality jobs, poses challenges for the sustainability and inclusiveness of economic growth in Nigeria.

Recent growth has also not translated into significant social and human development, contrary to the postulates in the development literature that associate faster economic growth with poverty reduction. The 2010 Nigeria Poverty Profile Report by the Nigeria National Bureau of Statistics (NBS 2010a) estimated the poverty incidence at 69 percent in 2010, up from 54.4 percent in 2004, using the Harmonized National Living Standard Survey (HNLSS) of 2009–10. The country's performance is at odds with the general international trend of poverty reduction, in particular in other countries experiencing rapid economic growth (Ajakaiye and others 2014).

Nigeria's socioeconomic indicators are also poor. The level of unemployment increased from 23.9 percent in 2011 to 25 percent in 2014, while the country's human development index (HDI) value increased by only 8.1 percent in the last decade, from 0.466 in 2005 to 0.504 in 2013, positioning the country at 152 out of 187 countries. Albeit marginal, Nigeria has made some progress in other development indicators. According to the United Nations Development Programme (UNDP) (2014) HDI, which takes into account life expectancy and literacy as well as per capita GDP, life expectancy at birth increased by 6.9 years between 1980 and 2013, mean years of schooling increased by 0.2 years, and expected years of schooling increased by 2.3 years. Gross National Income (GNI) per capita also increased by about 25.7 percent between 1980 and 2013.

The country remains highly dependent on the oil sector, which accounts for about 70 percent of government revenues and 85 percent of exports. While oil revenues have helped support the country during times of boom, the oil sector also presents a major challenge during bust periods.

For example, crude oil prices lost over 50 percent in the last quarter of 2014 and traded close to US$50 dollar per barrel at the end of the year.

This has had a devastating effect on Nigeria, with major fiscal contractions among the three tiers of government, and a slowdown in overall economic growth. The economy has been particularly hard hit by some major external shocks, including the rebalancing of the Chinese economy, which brought with it lower commodity prices; the slow global economic recovery; and other global financial developments. They have impacted the Nigerian economy through trade, exchange rates, asset markets (including commodity prices), and capital flows, further aggravating the country's longstanding vulnerabilities, including inadequate infrastructure, high unemployment, and high poverty rate.

In a bid to shore up the Naira value and preserve the external reserves, the Central Bank of Nigeria (CBN) devalued the Naira in November 2014 by 8.4 percent. However, with sustained pressure on the foreign exchange, the CBN shut down the official window in February 2015, implying another tactical devaluation of the Naira. This move led to relative stability in the currency market as the CBN intervened to meet excess demand through special interventions. Given continued efforts of the CBN to support the Naira in the face of declining oil prices, Nigeria's external reserves plummeted to US$30.3 billion as of March 17, 2015—barely enough to cover six months of imports—a threshold that posed a major threat to Nigeria's balance of payments transactions.

Perceived neglect and economic marginalization have also fueled resentment in the predominantly Muslim North. The militant Islamist group, Boko Haram, has grown increasingly active and deadly in its attacks against state and civilian targets, including the April 2014 abduction of 276 schoolgirls from Chibok, which attracted extensive international attention.

Meanwhile, Nigeria's democratic process was further consolidated with the relatively peaceful outcome of the general elections held in May 2015, which ushered in a new regime. For the first time in the country's history, power was successfully transferred from a ruling government to the opposition. Elected officials both at the federal and state level are already confronted with a perfect storm in the area of the economy as a result of dwindling revenues. The challenges that the Buhari administration has been trying to confront include the diversification of the economy, fighting corruption through blockage of fiscal leakages, prioritization of government expenditures to boost investment in critical infrastructure, and job creation. While intuition suggests that employment growth and poverty reduction are closely linked, there has been little research in this area in Nigeria apart from Treichel (2010) and World Bank (2016). This paper, therefore, tries to fill this gap by studying the experience of Nigeria, where average annual economic growth has reached 6.8 percent in the last decade but unemployment has been rising persistently. In line with the orientation of the project, the Nigerian case study intends to deepen our understanding of the character of Nigeria's non-inclusive growth experience and identify the potential limits and constraints to inclusive growth experience and the likely domestic and external economic growth opportunities available for Nigeria in the medium- to long-term, and explore how these can be exploited.

STYLIZED FACTS OF LABOR MARKETS, EDUCATION, AND GROWTH IN NIGERIA

Nigeria has continued to witness significant growth above the continental average in the last fifteen years. Table 6-1 shows that Nigeria's Gross Domestic Product (GDP) grew from 3.1 percent in the 1990s to an average of more than 5 percent beginning in 2000, largely driven by the value addition from the service sector.

Table 6-2 presents the sectoral composition of Nigeria's GDP. While the economy has traditionally been dominated by crude oil production, the sector accounted for only about 10 percent of the GDP in 2014.

Nigeria is still predominantly agrarian. Approximately 50 percent of the population engages in agricultural production at a subsistence level despite its steady decline and benign neglect as a result of the oil boom that the country experienced in the early 1970s. Agriculture as a percentage of GDP has stabilized at about 20 percent in 2014 (table 6-2), compared to about 40 percent in the mid-1980s. Agricultural holdings are typically small with low yields and low productivity.

TABLE 6-1. *Growth and Share of Sectors in Nigerian GDP Growth, Five-Year Averages, 1990–2014*

Percent of GDP

	1990–94	1995–99	2000–04	2005–09	2010–14
Agriculture value added	25.4	27.5	29.2	25.1	21.9
Industry value added	24.8	22.4	22.3	21.2	25.5
Services value added	49.8	50.1	48.4	53.7	52.6
Growth in GDP (%)	3.1	2.1	6.5	6.3	5.7

Source: Authors' computation from underlying data obtained from World Development Indicators 2015 (World Bank 2015a).

The industrial sector's contribution to the GDP declined from 27.7 percent to 24.2 percent in 2014. Of note is the manufacturing sector, which has been in a deplorable situation. Its contribution to GDP has been declining since the structural adjustment era, and currently hovers around 10 percent, as shown in table 6-2.

The decline in industrial capacity, especially in heavy industry, has had serious impact on Nigeria's long-term economic growth and poverty reduction. Nigeria's steel sector, especially the Ajaokuta Steel Company, no doubt represents a perfect illustration of why Nigeria's industrialization drive remains stunted. Despite having the second largest iron ore deposit in Africa, Nigeria has, curiously, failed to breathe life into the moribund Ajaokuta Steel Company in Kogi State, which was conceived as far back as September 1979 with the vision of generating important upstream and downstream industrial and economic activities critical to the diversification of the economy into an industrial one. While the project would directly employ about 10,000 workers at the first phase of commissioning, upstream and downstream industries are expected to engage over 500,000 employees.

Unfortunately, none of the benefits has accrued to Nigeria, even as the country continues to spend about $3.3 billion annually on steel importation, which is set to rise to at least $15 billion in the next ten years to meet its high infrastructure needs. The steel complex has become a subject of intense controversy and politicking by various interests, culminating in the termination of the concession agreement between

TABLE 6-2. *Sector Composition of Nigeria's Gross Domestic Product*

Percent of GDP

Sector	2011	2012	2013	2014	Q1 2015	Q2 2015
Agriculture	22.3	22.1	21.0	20.2	17.8	17.9
Industry	27.8	26.8	25.4	24.2	21.1	21.2
Oil and gas	17.5	15.8	12.9	10.8	6.6	7.6
Solid minerals	0.1	0.1	0.1	0.1	0.1	0.1
Manufacturing	7.2	7.8	9.0	9.8	10.2	9.3
Construction	3.0	3.1	3.3	3.6	4.2	4.2
Services	49.9	51.1	53.7	55.6	61.1	60.9
Information and communication	10.1	10.1	10.4	10.8	11.9	13.9
Finance and insurance	2.4	2.8	3.0	3.1	4.0	3.7
Real estate	7.3	7.7	8.3	8.4	7.8	8.7
Accommodation and food	0.4	0.5	0.8	0.9	1.3	0.7
Services, arts, entertainment, and recreation	0.1	0.2	0.2	0.2	0.3	0.2
Trade, wholesale and retail	16.4	16.5	17.1	17.6	20.1	18.9
Other services	13.2	13.3	13.8	14.5	15.8	14.8

Source: World Bank (2015b).

the federal government and Global Infrastructure Nigeria Ltd (GINL), an Indian firm, in 2008. Although the federal government had accused the Indian firm of breaching the provisions of the concession agreement and asset stripping, the company had gone to the International Court of Arbitration in London, challenging the revocation of the agreement. While the legal hurdles slowing down the project have been removed, the project has been a subject of legislative scrutiny following revelations that the country was paying huge sums of money to the company's idle staff.

As shown in table 6-2, tertiary activities have gradually been on the increase, rising from 50 percent in 2011 to almost 61 percent of Nigeria's GDP in the first half of 2015. The major service subsectors include retail and wholesale, real estate, and information and communication

(African Economic Outlook 2015). Trade, information and communications technology, and real estate together comprise almost 70 percent of the services sector output. The service sector trade, especially, is still dominated by informal sector activities operating at low margins and low levels of productivity.

Trade was the single largest sectoral component of GDP in the first quarter of 2015, at 20 percent, followed by agriculture (17.8 percent), information and communications technology (11.9 percent), manufacturing (10.2 percent), real estate (7.8 percent), with oil and gas contributing only 6.6 percent of the country's final output.

In sum, despite the high economic growth witnessed in the last decade and a half, the country has not yet been able to transform into an innovation-based, high-skilled, "knowledge" economy; hence, its trade composition and pattern has remained predominantly on primary production, with minimal participation in the global value chain.

The evidence in tables 6-1 and 6-2 suggests that the process of structural transformation, though in its formative stage, has commenced in Nigeria. The country is making the atypical transformation from agriculture to services, and this is not unique to Nigeria. Several developing countries in Sub-Saharan Africa and Latin America are witnessing what Rodrik (2015) described as premature de-industrialization, as the bulk of labor are absorbed in nontradable services operating at very low levels of productivity, in activities such as retail trade and housework. Industry, especially manufacturing, has transformed in several ways, especially with the dominance of global supply chains. As Rodrik (2014) established, manufacturing has become much more capital- and skills-intensive, with diminished potential to absorb large amounts of labor released from low-productivity agriculture This has sparked the debate on whether a services-led model can deliver rapid growth and good jobs in Africa in the way that manufacturing once did. Ghani and O'Connell (2014), using historical data, established that services can, indeed, be a growth escalator, while skeptics like Rodrik (2014) and Kormawa and Jerome (2015) posit that services can hardly deliver rapid growth and good jobs, especially in developing countries where most operate at low margins and low levels of productivity.

The result is slightly at odds with Adeyinka and others (2013). Based on an analysis of Nigeria's General Household Survey (GHS) from 2006 to 2009, they indicated that Nigeria has exhibited what one might consider the standard pattern of structural change, with labor leaving the agricultural and wholesale and retail trade sectors to join sectors such as manufacturing, communications and transportation, and services. Specifically, aggregate labor productivity grew by approximately 17 percent from 1996 to 2009 due to the movement of labor to higher productivity sectors. While positive, this is smaller than the growth in labor productivity arising from within-sector improvements, which resulted in aggregate labor productivity growth of approximately 62 percent.

The results are consistent for a resource-abundant country that has different relative price structures that impact on their structural transformation, especially through the so-called "Dutch disease," which makes nonnatural resource sectors unprofitable.

While aggregate labor productivity growth is positive, structural change has not proceeded at a pace consistent with the large gaps in labor productivity across sectors. The country's policy environment hampers structural transformation through restriction of agricultural productivity, and poor infrastructure has constrained the business environment and slowed down the expansion of manufacturing and business services.

Structure of Nigeria's Employment

In Nigeria, the total labor force is made up of persons age 15–64 years, excluding students, home-keepers, retired persons, stay-at-home parents, and persons unable to work or not interested in work (Kale and Doguwa 2015), while the unemployment rate is the proportion of the labor force who were available for work but did not work in the week preceding the survey period for at least thirty-nine hours. The labor market and employment situation as presented in figure 6-1 reveals that there was an average increase of 2.8 percent in the population growth between 2010 and 2014. Nigeria's population rose from 138.6 million in 2005 to 159.7 million in 2010, and to 178.5 million in 2014. In the same vein, the labor force, made up of the total number of employed and unemployed persons, increased by 2.9 percent on average, from 65.2

FIGURE 6-1. *Trend in Population and Labor Market Situation, 2005–14*

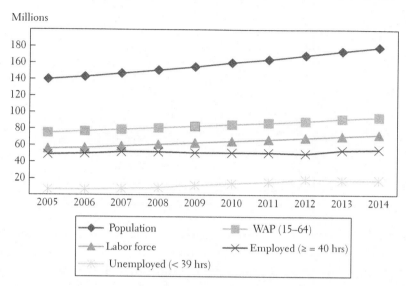

Source: Authors' computations based on underlying data from United Nations Department of Economic Social Affairs (2015) and NBS (2014 and 2015b).
WAP = working age population.

million in 2010 to 72.9 million in 2014. However, the total labor force in full remunerative employment increased at an average of 2 percent over the period, compared to 6.1 percent and 16.48 percent for the underemployed and unemployed population, respectively.

Figure 6-2 presents the data on employed persons in Nigeria by sectors from 1970 to 2014. Agriculture has continued to provide the most jobs for the country's labor force, although this is declining. In 2014, it accounted for 45 percent of all jobs, down from 51 percent in 2000. The services sector is the second largest job-providing sector, rising from 24 percent in 2000 to 44 percent in 2014, while the share of the manufacturing sector fell from 11 percent in 2000 to 6 percent in 2014. While the service sector is the fastest growing sector, the fall in employment in manufacturing industries explicates significant levels of de-industrialization. Its composition fell from 12.3 percent in 1970 to 9.3 percent in 2005 and 6 percent in 2014.

While information on the employment situation in Nigeria is still confined largely to the formal sector, with scant information on the

FIGURE 6-2. *Employment Trend by Sectors (Shares), 1970–2014*

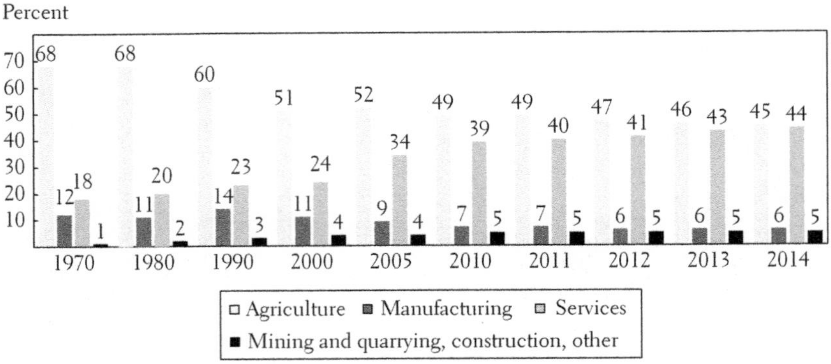

Percent

Source: Authors' computation from underlying data obtained from NISER (2015).

informal sector, it is generally acknowledged that the ascribed informal workforce has grown tremendously, both in real terms and in activity diversification since the Structural Adjustment Program (SAP) of 1986. Estimates suggest that the informal sector accounts for between 45 percent and 60 percent of the urban labor force, up from about 25 percent in the mid-1960s and the percentage is more in rural areas (Abumere and others 1995). A national survey carried out in the year 2000 puts the number of informal sector enterprises in the country at 8,604,048, employing 12,407,348 persons (Central Bank of Nigeria 2001). By 2010, the total number of people employed in the informal sector grew to 48,602,017 people, according to Nigeria's National Bureau of Statistics, as shown in table 6-3.

A cursory examination of table 6-3 indicates that employment in Nigeria's informal sector generally follows the same pattern as the formal sector. It is dominated by agriculture, wholesale and retail trade, and manufacturing. The three sectors contributed a whopping 66.4 percent of total employment.

While definitions and descriptions of the informal economy vary considerably, three successive national surveys recognize some noteworthy attributes of this sector, including its broad activity spectrum that spans the entire segment of the economy, its relatively low productivity, the dominance of youth in the age cohort, with the 20–40 years group accounting for over 50 percent of the workforce, ownership structure

TABLE 6-3. *Informal Sector Employment, 2010, Nigeria*

Sector	Number employed	Percent
Agriculture, forestry, and farming	14,837,693	30.5
Wholesale and retail trade, motor vehicle/motorcycle repair	12,097,189	24.9
Manufacturing	5,337,000	11.0
Other service activities	3,471,702	7.1
Accommodation and food services activities	2,730,308	5.6
Transportation and storage	2,009,183	4.1
Education	1,557,665	3.2
Construction	1,142,569	2.4
Administrative and support service activities	986,480	2.0
Public administration and defense, compulsory social security	800,333	1.6
Professional, scientific, and technical activities	779,209	1.6
Human, health, and social work	739,936	1.5
Activities of household as employers, undifferentiated goods	551,353	1.1
Information and communication	469,513	1.0
Arts, entertainment, and recreation	390,275	0.8
Financial and insurance activities	171,403	0.4
Electricity, gas steam, and air conditioning supply	152,610	0.3
Mining and quarrying	146,488	0.3
Water supply, sewage, waste management, and remediation activities	86,778	0.2
Activities of extraterritorial organizations and bodies	75,633	0.2
Real estate activities	68,697	0.1
Total	48,602,017	100.0

Source: National Bureau of Statistics, 2010c.

that is mostly sole proprietorship, and spatial location with a majority of informal enterprises neighborhood-based (Abumere and others 1995; Central Bank of Nigeria 2001; Oduh and others 2008).

Profile of Unemployment in Nigeria

The unemployment rate across Nigeria has been very high since the beginning of this century. The indicator that measures the proportion of active population that is without but is actively seeking work increased

FIGURE 6-3. *Unemployment Rate, Nigeria, 1967–2014*

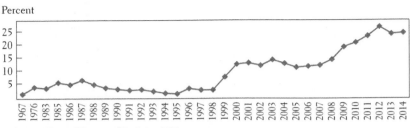

Source: National Bureau of Statistics, 2014.

to 25.1 percent in 2014 from 24.7 percent in 2013, as shown in figure 6-3. Since 2000, the rate of unemployment has grown at a compound annual average of 4.8 percent, even as it has continued to fluctuate and intensify.

Rising rural unemployment is also evolving sectorally, as opportunities are shifting away from agriculture despite the high prevalence of subsistence farming. Stagnating production and low productivity in the sector, where more than half of the rural population works, and the high growth witnessed in the services sector, are key reasons for the large variations across urban and rural labor groups. The unemployment rate is much higher in the northern part of the country, where two-thirds of the population engage in subsistence agriculture, and relatively lower in the southern part where more than half of the population is engaged in self-employed wage work (World Bank 2016).

Data from the National Bureau of Statistics (NBS) also shows that there is a higher incidence of unemployment for women than men; and in recent times, their access to quality job opportunities declined even further. While the number of unemployed males has hovered around seven to eight million in the past five years, the unemployed female population increased from 6.7 million in 2010 to over 10 million in 2014 (National Bureau of Statistics 2015b).

Youth unemployment, on the other hand, is intensifying. Large concentrations of youth, both trained and untrained, educated and uneducated, are idle and without any hope of securing a decent job. Youth unemployment was recorded as 45.8 percent in 2014. As can be seen from figure 6-4, unemployment is generally high regardless of level of education. For example, in 2014, unemployment rates among persons

FIGURE 6-4. *Unemployment Rate, by Educational Group, 2010–14*

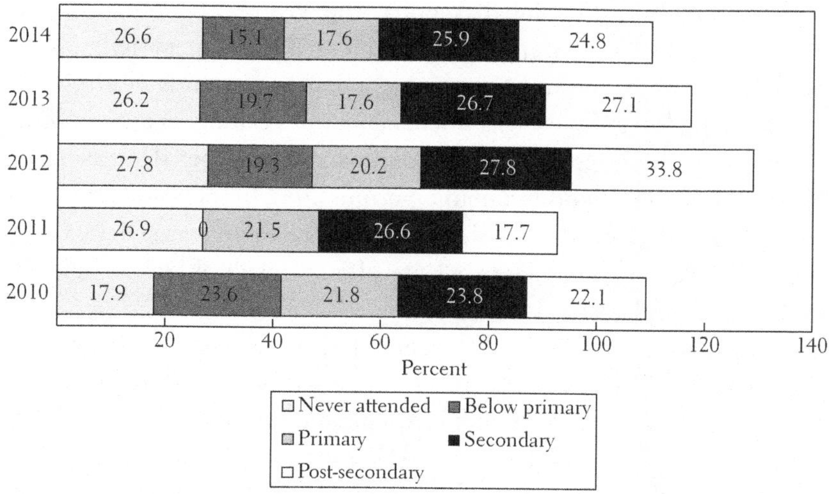

Source: Authors' computations based on data from NBS (2015b).

who never attended school and those with secondary and post-secondary education hover around 25 percent, while the unemployment rate among persons with primary education or below is somewhat lower, at 17.6 percent and 15.1 percent, respectively. Among those who have secondary and post-secondary education, skills gaps and job search barriers are major barriers to gainful employment.

BRIEF REVIEW OF THE LITERATURE

The current phenomenon of "jobless growth" witnessed across several developing economies, some in Africa, poses far-reaching challenges on the age-old economic assumption of growth in GDP directly resulting in an increase in employment. Okun's (1962) pioneering and seminal contribution provided some evidence in this regard. In his study of the statistical relationship between a country's unemployment rate and economic growth rate, he demonstrated that there is a positive relationship between output and employment, given the logical conclusion that output depends on the amount of labor used in the production process. However, economic realities have since evolved.

Today, jobless growth has emerged as a global phenomenon. In its outlook on the 2015 Global Agenda, the World Economic Forum (WEF) reports that deepening income inequality and persistent jobless growth are two of the most pressing challenges currently confronting mankind. Jobless growth exists where economies exiting recessions demonstrate economic growth while employment is either decreasing or barely stabilizing (World Economic Forum 2014). In such situations, unemployment remains stubbornly high despite economic growth. According to WEF, these characteristics are often a result of technologically derived job displacements.

Some papers have focused on sectoral patterns of economic growth. For instance, Hull (2009), in her investigation of the relationship between economic growth, employment, and poverty reduction, identifies sectors as "more productive" and "less productive," such that growth in a sector will not directly lead to general benefits to all sectors of the economy. This highlights the relevance of the productivity intensity of sectors as a tool for profiling growth. Using a sample of 106 growth periods covering thirty-nine countries, Gutierrez and others (2007) concluded that the sectoral growth pattern and employment/productivity profile vary significantly among countries. According to their study, the sectoral pattern of employment generation and productivity growth are key determinant factors of the rate of unemployment. Loayza and Raddatz (2010) also support this argument that growth in unskilled-intensive sectors contributes more to poverty reduction by providing better jobs.

The World Bank (2005), in its study of fourteen countries, noted that three countries that experienced pro-poor growth witnessed more labor-intensive growth. In another country-specific panel data analysis for the manufacturing industry carried out on eight Central and Eastern European countries, employment was completely de-linked from output, mostly in medium and low skilled sectors (Onaran 2008). This result was particularly apparent in the Czech Republic, Bulgaria, and Romania, not only in the first period of transition recession, but also in the post-recession period. Boeri and Garibaldi (2006) had also provided evidence that in the aftermath of 1996, the period of economic downturn in the CEE-10 led to significant job destruction, and growth in GDP did not result in statistically significant job creation. This study was also consistent with Lehmann (1995), who argued that capital and managerial shortages could lead to weak labor demand.

Based on recent studies on Africa, it has been observed that the continent's rapid growth over the last decade has so far not been able to create significant employment opportunities. Ancharaz (2010) alludes to the hypothesis that such growth has been driven largely by commodity exports. Export-led growth does not necessarily translate into higher employment levels, considering that extractive industries are generally capital-intensive and may not create many jobs, especially for women, as they expand. Resource-driven countries in the continent are further faced with lack of export diversification and equally concentrated markets. Ancharaz (2010) confirmed that export growth was strongly correlated with real GDP growth, particularly in Angola, Gabon, and Nigeria.

Olotu and others (2015) view the phenomenon as a result of an inability to fully utilize available factors of production. The study on Nigeria argues that jobless growth is increasing as a result of the very high number of graduates produced every year and the country's incapacity to absorb them. The country's growth and business environment, which has not been able to significantly expand the formal sector, has left the economy largely trapped in its pre-2001 trajectory, when it started to witness a sustained expansion in its non-oil economy.

On the empirical front, the World Bank has in recent years developed the Job Generation and Growth (JoGGs) decomposition tool to link "changes in employment, output per worker and population structure at the aggregate and sectoral level" (World Bank 2010). Using Shapley decompositions, the methodology decomposes growth in GDP per capita in two consecutive periods, in its employment, productivity, and demographic components to disentangle the sources of output-per-worker growth. The JoGGs decomposition tool has been adopted to analyze the incidence of jobless growth in Uganda (Bbaale 2013) and Rwanda (Malunda 2013). In Uganda, Bbaale proved that the industrial and services sectors have higher prospects for alleviating poverty through productivity and employment generation. On the other hand, Malunda's research on employment intensity in Rwanda showed that the country's manufacturing sector lagged behind other sectors in terms of output and productivity growth. His results also showed that growth in the East African country's dependency ratio impacted nega-tively on its per capita GDP growth.

Using the JoGGs decomposition tool, particularly in the context of economic structural transformation, Byiers and others (2015) recently studied employment means in a group of *Development Progress* coun-tries from Latin America, Africa, and Asia.[1] The paper showed that inter-sectoral shifts contributed more to growth than rising productivity within them. These labor movements were also toward the services sec-tor, including precarious, low-productivity jobs, rather than manufac-turing. Byiers and others additionally raised a rather crucial aspect of employment dynamics, underscoring the importance of politics as a key determinant of employment progress. New assessments of African government policies and institutions have emphasized governance as a crucial factor responsible for the uneven growth performance in most of Africa (African Development Bank 2013).

GROWTH AND LABOR MARKET ANALYSIS

This section provides a brief overview of the data and methodology adopted for the study.

The Data

To profile Nigeria's growth in terms of the employment and productiv-ity of sectors, we make use of aggregate data: total GDP, population, and employment from 2005–14, at five-year intervals of (2005–09) and (2010–14) as presented in table 6-4. Monetary data are sourced from the National Bureau of Statistics (2015a) and World Bank World Devel-opment Indicators (2015a). Population and labor statistics are sourced from the United Nations Department of Economic and Social Affairs (2015), the National Bureau of Statistics (2015b), and Nigerian Institute for Social and Economic Research (NISER) (2015).[2] The sectoral dis-aggregation of the economy into agriculture, mining, quarrying and construction, manufacturing, and services is due to data limitation. Re-sults are presented in the stepwise approach using the Job Generation and Growth (JoGGs) decomposition tool from the World Bank. The unit for all monetary values is 1 unless otherwise stated.

Methodology

We adopted the methodology of Gutierrez and others (2007)[3] and the World Bank stepwise decomposition approach using the Shapley decomposition method (World Bank 2010) to untangle the roles of output per worker, employment, and population structure in growth changes at the aggregate and sectoral levels. The Shapley decomposition method, presented in a stepwise manner, is used to decompose per capita GDP growth into output per worker, employment, and capital. Following this method of decomposition, GDP per capita, $Y/N = y$ can be written as:

$$\frac{Y}{N} = \frac{Y}{E}\frac{E}{A}\frac{A}{N}$$

Equation (1)

or

$$y = \omega^* e^* a$$

where Y is total value added, E is employment, A is the population of working-age, and N is the total population.

The ratio $\omega = Y/E$ is output per worker (labor productivity), $e = E/A$ is the ratio of people employed to the total working-age population (that is, employment rate),[4] and $a = A/N$ is the ratio of working-age population to total population (that is, dependency ratio).

Applying the Shapley decomposition approach to equation (1), the changes in per capita value added can be decomposed into changes in labor productivity, changes in employment rates, and changes in the dependency ratio. The approach is based on the marginal effect of eliminating the change in each of the contributory components in a sequence on the value of a variable and for each component, by considering all possible alternatives, thus eliminating residuals using weighted average. Each component, thus, has the interpretation of a counterfactual. For instance, from equation (1), the amount of growth that can be attributed to changes in output per worker (*w*) is obtained by calculating the resulting growth in per capita value added under the hypothetical scenario in which employment rate (*e*) and the share of the working-age population in total population (*a*) had "remained constant,"[5] but output per worker had changed as observed. The result between the hypothetical growth and the observed growth is defined as the contribution of changes in output per worker to per capita value added growth. The same interpretation applies to other components.

Shapley decomposition has the advantage of being additive. Therefore, if the marginal contribution of each component to the observed change in per capita value added, obtained through Shapley decomposition is $\bar{\omega}, \bar{e},$ and $\bar{a}$, then:

$$\frac{\Delta y}{y} = \bar{\omega} + \bar{e} + \bar{a}$$

Equation (2)

While $\bar{e}$ refers to changes in employment as a fraction of the working-age population (employment rate), the term $\bar{\omega}$ captures changes in output per worker, and $\bar{a}$ reflects changes in the demographic structure of the population, that is, changes in the dependency ratio. Observed increase in employment rates ($\bar{e}$) will reflect increases in participation and movements of people out of unemployment and into employment.

Although the term $\bar{\omega}$ captures changes in output per worker, the interpretation is not completely direct due to influence from: 1) increases in the capital/labor ratio; and 2) relocation of jobs from bad jobs sectors (low productivity) to good jobs sectors (high productivity). Under the constant returns to scale assumption, we can explain the first two influences: if $Y_t = \Phi_t f(E_t, K_t)$, where K_t is the capital stock at time *t*, Φ_t is a technological parameter, then we can imply that output per worker Y_t/E_t is equal to $\Phi_t f(1, K_t/E_t)$. Change in the parameter Φ_t will capture all other sources of growth not due to changes in capital/labor ratio (this is the Solow residual). It will, therefore, mainly capture changes in technology and relocation of production between sectors with different productivity levels (inter-sectoral shifts). However, we should note that it may also capture cyclical behavior of outputs; given that firms operating in economic downturns may have underutilized capital; when the demand rises again, this will be reflected as a rise in output per worker. The third influence is from workers moving to a high-productivity sector from a low-productivity sector, so that at the aggregate level, average output per worker increases.[6]

The last component in equation (2) reflects changes in the demographic structure of the population. For instance, due to growing dependency ratio, an increase in labor productivity and employment may affect per capita income negatively if the employment and productivity growth is not sufficient to counter the rapid growing young or ageing population.

A further analysis is to understand sectoral employment and productivity intensity in relation to aggregate intensity, and we can, therefore, rewrite equation (2) as follows:.

$$\frac{\Delta y}{y} = \sum_s \overline{\omega}_s + \sum_s \overline{e}_s + \overline{a}$$

Equation (3)

Here, $\overline{\omega}_s$ denotes the amount of growth in output per capita that can be linked to productivity changes in sector s while $\overline{e}_s$ is the amount of growth in output per capita that can be linked to changes in the share of employment of sector s. The productivity term captures growth, changes in the capital/labor ratio, and employment shifts within the sector. Most papers that analyze the sectoral growth pattern profiles aggregate growth in terms of sectoral growth with respect to productivity and employment. We can, therefore, say that Shapley decomposition simply sums growth in each sector multiplied by the average share of the sector in total value added. And this is equal to aggregate growth.

RESULTS

Following the Shapley procedure, Nigeria's growth episode is profiled by: 1) growth according to aggregate productivity, employment, and demographic change; 2) growth according to changes in sectoral productivity, employment shares, and aggregate demographic; and 3) growth profile according to its sectoral pattern.

TABLE 6-4. *Changes in Main Variables (Population, Employment, Output, and Productivity) in Nigeria, 2005–09 and 2010–14*

	2005	2009	% change 2005–09	2010	2014	% change 2010–14
GDP (value added) (million Naira)	37,789,508	50,058,959	32.50	54,612,264	67,152,785	23.0
Total population (million)	140	155	11.3	160	179	11.80
Total working-age population (million)	75	83	10.5	85	94	11.0
Total number employed (million)	50	51	2.30	51	53	4.4
GDP (value added) per capita	270,726	322,169	19.00	341,951	376,170	10.01
Output per worker (Naira)	762,612	987,175	29.45	1,066,144	1,255,779	17.79
Employment rate	66.1	61.23	-7.37	60.23	56.66	-5.93
Share of working-age population in total population	53.71	53.3	-0.41	53.25	52.87	-0.38

Source: Authors' calculations based on JoGGs decomposition tool.

Main Variables

Nigeria recorded a growth rate of 19 percent in per capita value added, for the 2005–09 period. However, there was a significant decrease between 2010 and 2014, to 10.01 percent. The growth in period one (2005–09) and two (2010–14) was accompanied by a 7.37 percent and 5.93 percent reduction in employment, and an increase in labor productivity by 29.5 percent and 17.8 percent in the two periods, respectively. The result indicates the phenomenon of jobless growth in Nigeria. In both cases, there was a reduction in the share of the employed in the total population of working-age, although now decreasing at a decreasing rate.

Decomposition of Growth Per Capita

The decomposition of aggregate per capita GDP growth into its main components using the Shapley decomposition for the two periods is presented in table 6-5. The table includes contribution in Naira value of 2010 to absolute observed growth in per capita GDP as well as the percentage contribution.

TABLE 6-5. *Decomposition of Growth in per Capita Value Added in Nigeria, 2005–09 and 2010–14*

	2005–09		2010–14	
	2010 Naira	*% total change in per capita value added growth*	*2010 Naira*	*% total change in per capita value added growth*
Total change in per capita GDP (value added)	51,443.48	100.00	34,219.55	100.00
Change linked to output per worker	76,495.76	148.70	58,809.93	171.86
Change linked to employment rate	−22,798.11	−44.32	−22,005.09	−64.31
Change linked to ratio of working-age population in total population	−2,254.17	−4.38	−2,585.29	−7.56

Source: Authors' calculations based on JoGGs decomposition tool.

According to table 6-5 and figures 6-A1 and 6-A2 in the appendix, while productivity was a dominant contributor, accounting for 148.7 percent and 171.9 percent of observed growth in the two periods, respectively, growth changes linked to employment were negative. The negative contribution of employment implies that 44.3 percent and 64.3 percent of the change in per capita value added can be linked to a decrease in the employment rate in Nigeria over the 2005–09 and 2010–14 periods, respectively. Thus, growth in Nigeria since 2005 was a jobless growth, a growth not followed by satisfactory job creation. Interestingly, changes in the structure of the population also contributed negatively to observed growth in both periods. It was –7.6 percent between 2010 and 2014 and –4.4 percent between 2005 and 2009. In other words, there were more dependents (minor and elderly) depending on each working-age adult. Given the negative effect on observed growth of high dependency ratio, there may be a need to investigate the increasing population growth in Nigeria. It is, however, important to note that the negative contributions of the employment rate and population structure to the growth in per capita value added were swamped by that of growth in labor productivity over the years.

Employment Generation and Productivity
by Economic Activity

Tables 6-6a and 6-6b present the data on employment by sector for 2005–09 and 2010–14. Total employment in Nigeria grew by 4.4 percent between 2010 and 2014, compared to 2.3 percent between 2005 and 2009. Although mining and services sectors registered absolute growths in the number of employed at both periods, only the service sector gained in the share of total employment in 2005–09 and 2010–14, increasing by 3.4 percent and 6 percent, respectively. An increasing marginal shift from the agricultural sector, which usually employs more than 50 percent of the population in both absolute figures and proportion of people working in the sector, can be observed. Agriculture, which is the leading employer in Nigeria, saw its output per worker increase only marginally (figures 6-A3 and 6-A4 in the appendix). This increase can, however, be attributed to the movement of persons to better paying jobs.

TABLE 6-6A. *Employment by Sectors of Economic Activity in Nigeria (Total Employment), 2005–09 and 2010–14*

				Total employment			
	2005	2009	% change	2010	2014	% change
Agriculture	25,938,722	25,241,535	−2.69	25,142,003	23,872,140	−5.05
Manufacturing	4,607,000	3,548,572	−22.97	3,469,912	3,197,316	−7.86
Mining and quarrying, construction, other	2,048,000	2,539,065	23.98	2,610,456	2,878,999	10.29
Services	16,959,000	19,380,145	14.28	20,001,744	23,526,545	17.62
Total	49,552,722	50,709,317	2.33	51,224,115	53,475,000	4.39

Source: Authors' calculations based on JoGGs decomposition tool.

TABLE 6-6B. *Employment by Sectors of Economic Activity in Nigeria (Employment/Working-Age Population), 2005–09 and 2010–14*

	2005	2009	Percent change	2010	2014	Percent change
Agriculture	34.6	30.48	−11.92	29.56	25.29	−14.44
Manufacturing	6.15	4.28	−30.28	4.08	3.39	−16.97
Mining and quarrying, construction, other	2.73	3.07	12.22	3.07	3.05	−0.62
Services	22.62	23.4	3.44	23.52	24.93	5.99
Total	66.1	61.23	−7.37	60.23	56.66	−5.93

Source: Authors' calculations based on JoGGs decomposition tool.

This phenomenon of inter-sectoral mobility, which has seen people leave the agricultural sector, explains a significant level of prolonged low productivity and underemployment in the sector, which, as the highest employing sector, affects the majority of the country's labor force. The widespread trend suggests that a greater problem lies in the quality of jobs created, where a huge percentage of people who cannot afford not to work engage in low productivity and low paying jobs.

Table 6-7 and figures 6-A5 and 6-A6 in the appendix are the result of the decomposition from equation (3). Table 6-7 shows how growth in employment (−4.5 percent) and (−3.6 percent) in 2005–09 and 2010–14, respectively, are distributed among economic sectors. Over the two periods to 2014, overall employment in the agricultural and manufacturing sectors fell significantly. However, while the number of people employed in the agricultural sector fell even faster over time, the fall in manufacturing employment slowed relatively from −22.97 percent between 2005 and 2009 to −7.86 percent between 2010 and 2014. Agriculture consistently had the largest negative contribution of 4.12 percent and 4.27 percent to the change in the employment rate in Nigeria over the 2008–09 and 2010–14 periods, respectively. The global financial crises of 2007–08 had varying impacts on Nigeria's employment distribution, while employment in electricity, gas and water, and mining and quarrying declined steadily, building and con-

TABLE 6-7. *Contribution of Employment Changes to Overall Change in Employment Rate in Nigeria, 2005–09 and 2010–14*

	2005–09		2010–14	
	Contribution to change in total employment rate (percent points)	Percent contribution of the sector to total employment rate growth	Contribution to change in total employment rate (percent points)	Percent contribution of the sector to total employment rate growth
Agriculture	−4.12	84.6	−4.27	119.5
Manufacturing	−1.86	38.2	−0.69	19.4
Mining and quarrying, construction, other	0.33	−6.9	−0.02	0.5
Services	0.78	−16	1.41	−39.4
Total employment rate	−4.87	100	−3.57	100

Source: Authors' Computation based on JoGGs decomposition tool.

struction expanded, as employment of persons in the subsector increased from just 1.3 percent of the total labor force in 2005 to 3.3 percent by 2014.

Sectoral Employment Changes to Growth in Total Per Capita Output

This section investigates each sector's contribution to observed growth and employment performance. Table 6-8 and figures 6-A7 and 6-A8 in the appendix present the contributions of employment from various sectors to growth in total per capita output. In the 2005–09 and 2010–14 periods, employment contribution shrank in all sectors except in the services sector, which more than doubled its contribution from 3,642.8 Naira in 2005–09 to 8,675.1 Naira in 2010–14. Of note is the fact that the contraction of employment in the agriculture sector led to a 76.9 percent reduction in its contribution to total change in per capita output.

TABLE 6-8. *Sectoral Employment Contribution to per Capita GDP (Value Added), Nigeria, 2005–09 and 2010–14*

	2005–09		2010–14	
	Contribution to change in per capita GDP (Naira)	*% of total change in per capita GDP*	*Contribution to change in per capita GDP (Naira)*	*% of total change in per capita GDP*
Agriculture	−19,295.1	−37.5	−26,298.0	−76.9
Manufacturing	−8,708.6	−16.9	−4,264.7	−12.5
Mining and quarrying, construction, other	1,562.7	3.0	−117.5	−0.3
Services	3,642.8	7.1	8,675.1	25.4
Total contribution	−22,798.1	−44.3	−22,005.1	−64.3

Source: Authors' calculations based on JoGGs decomposition tool.
Note: Monetary values are 2010 naira.

Understanding the Role of Inter-Sectoral Shifts

Structural shifts or changes are the movements of labor from low productivity sectors to high productivity sectors, and they have an important role in explaining the country's growth pattern. While an increase in the share of employment in sectors with above average productivity is expected to increase overall productivity and contribute positively to the inter-sectoral shift effect, the opposite effect occurs with labor movement out of above-average productivity sectors.

In other words, if sector i experiences productivity below the average productivity level (that is, a low productivity sector), and employment shares s_i decrease, it is expected that the sector's contribution will be positive, implying that the outflow from this low productivity sector has contributed to the increase in output per worker. However, if the same sector experiences an increase in s_i, then the inflow into this low productivity sector will decrease output per worker and, thus, have a negative effect on the inter-sectoral shift term.

Table 6-9 presents the inter-sectoral shift effect. The inter-sectoral shift captures the movement of labor between sectors, implying that, on average, labor moved from lower productivity sectors to higher pro-

TABLE 6-9. *Decomposition of Output Per Worker within Sector Changes in Output per Worker and Inter-Sectoral Shifts in Nigeria, 2005–09 and 2010–14*

	2005–09		2010–14	
	Contribution to change in total output per worker (Naira)	*Contribution to change in total output per worker (%)*	*Contribution to change in total output per worker (Naira)*	*Contribution to change in total output per worker (%)*
Agriculture	62,049.3	27.6	58,706.1	31.0
Manufacturing	34,588.8	15.4	67,542.6	35.6
Mining and quarrying, construction, other	−64,726.9	−28.8	−22,642.9	−11.9
Services	137,366.1	61.2	42,451.9	22.4
Inter-sectoral shift	55,285.4	24.6	43,577.9	23.0
Total change in output per worker	224,562.6	100.0	189,635.4	100.0

Source: Authors' calculations based on JoGGs decomposition tool.
Note: Monetary values are 2010 naira.

ductivity sectors. The inter-sectoral shift effect on output per worker was 55,285.4 Naira in the 2005–09 period. However, the effect reduced marginally within the 2010–14 period, to 43,577.9 Naira.

Tables 6-10a and 6-10b and figure 6-5 present a summary of the growth decomposition profile of Nigeria in percentage contribution and in Naira 2010, respectively. The demographic component accounted for a 4.4 percent negative contribution in the 2005–09 period, and a 7.6 percent negative contribution between 2010 and 2014. Also, the total value added per capita decreased from 51,443.48 Naira in 2005–09 to 34,219.55 Naira in 2010–14 (tables 6-10a and 6-10b). The table reveals that the services sector played the biggest role from 2005–09 to within-sector changes in output per worker and also highest contribution to employment changes (figure 6-5). Nigeria's growth is, thus, mostly explained by inter-sectoral shifts.

In summary, Nigeria's real GDP growth of 7 percent in the last decade was largely driven by the services sector, which experienced a

TABLE 6-10A. *Growth Decomposition: Contribution to Total Growth in GDP (Value Added) per Capita in Nigeria, 2005–09*

	2005–09			
Sectoral contributions	Within sector changes in output per worker**	Changes in employment	Inter-sectoral shifts	Total
Agriculture	21,136.66	−19,295.08	3,912.63	5,754.21
Manufacturing	11,782.43	−8,708.56	1,172.02	4,245.89
Mining and quarrying, construction, other	−22,048.78	1,562.70	10,906.87	−9,579.22
Services	46,792.85	3,642.83	2,841.08	53,276.76
Subtotals	57,663.17	−22,798.11	18,832.59	53,697.64
Demographic component	. . .	. . .	. . .	−2,254.17
Total change in value added per capita	. . .	. . .	. . .	51,443.48

Source: Authors' calculations based on JoGGs decomposition tool.
** Monetary values are 2010 Naira.
. . . = not applicable.

TABLE 6-10B. *Growth Decomposition: Contribution to Total Growth in GDP (Value Added) per Capita in Nigeria, 2010–14*

	2010–14			
Sectoral contributions	Within sector changes in output per worker**	Changes in employment	Inter-sectoral shifts	Total
Agriculture	18,205.98	−26,298.02	7,978.04	−14.00
Manufacturing	20,946.37	−4,264.71	−986.04	15,695.62
Mining and quarrying, construction, other	−7,022.05	−117.46	2,273.76	−4,865.75
Services	13,165.22	8,675.09	4,248.65	26,088.96
Subtotals	45,295.52	−22,005.09	13,514.41	36,804.84
Demographic component	. . .	. . .	. . .	−2,585.29
Total change in value added per capita	. . .	. . .	. . .	34,219.55

Source: Authors' calculations based on JoGGs decomposition tool.
** Monetary values are 2010 Naira.
. . . = not applicable.

FIGURE 6-5. *Growth Decomposition: Contributions Made to per Capita Income, by Sector, 2005–09 and 2010–14*

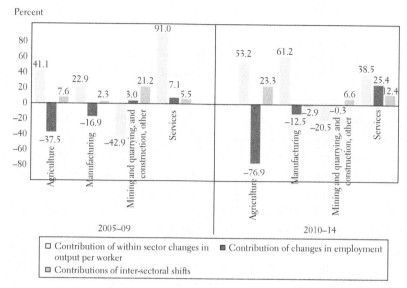

Source: Authors' computations based on JoGGs Decomposition tool (World Bank 2010).

significant increase in the total number of workers employed in the sector from 34 percent in 2000 to 44 percent in 2014 (an additional 9 million workers).

While 6.6 million workers moved into tertiary activities between 2005 and 2010, over 2 million workers left farming activities and around 1.4 million workers were disengaged from the manufacturing sector. Although the growth in services-led jobs cushioned the prevailing high labor redundancy, it was unable to offset the unemployment trend, which fell only marginally from 7.37 percent during the 2005–09 period to 5.93 percent between 2010 and 2014. Ironically, labor productivity also declined, from 7.37 percent to 5.93 percent over the two periods.

Growth in the country's working-age population from 75 million in 2005 to about 95 million in 2014, nearly half of its total population, contributed negatively to employment and slowed labor mobility. At the micro-level, this contributed to underemployment as additional workers became less able to find better paying jobs and improve their living situations. At the aggregate level, the phenomenon limited the

country's capacity to quickly adapt to technological changes and exploit
its competitive advantage for industries to develop.

EMPLOYMENT ELASTICITY OF GROWTH
IN NIGERIA, 1981–2014

A widely used indicator for analyzing the relationship between growth
and employment is the employment elasticity of growth, which gained
popularity following the seminal work of Okun (1962). Despite the
widespread use of this concept, especially in tracking sectoral potential
for generating employment, it has some notable shortcomings (see Hull
2009). First, it is incapable of stating the actual extent of job creation. For
instance, a country that grew by 1 percent and enjoyed a 1 percent increase in employment would have the same employment elasticity rate as
a country that had a 5 percent growth rate accompanied by a 5 percent
increase in employment. Second, the measure does not take demographic changes into account. Third, and most obvious, the employment
elasticity of growth is incapable of indicating the quality of new jobs created. In spite of these criticisms, employment elasticity of growth is a
convenient tool for summarizing the employment intensity of growth or
sensitivity of employment to output growth (Islam and Nazara 2000).

Two major approaches have been used in the literature to estimate
employment elasticity of output. The first is the simple arithmetic method
of computing the arc elasticity by dividing the proportionate change in
employment by the proportionate change in output during a given period, usually a year. While this methodology is computationally easy,
Islam and Nazara (2000) demonstrated that it tends to exhibit a great
deal of instability and may, therefore, be inappropriate for comparative
purposes. The base year or the terminal year may, for example, be ab-
normal, so that the elasticity obtained may not reflect the "normal"
technological relationship between labor and output for a given sector
(Ajilore and Yinusa 2011).

The second method involves applying the econometric method of
regression analysis, and there are different variants of this. This is the
approach adopted in this study. We compute a log linear regression
equation between employment and GDP to generate both aggregate as

TABLE 6-11. *Employment Elasticities of Growth in Nigeria*

Sector	Estimated elasticity
Overall	0.115240***
Agriculture	0.4810***
Manufacturing	0.3030
Services	0.8531***

Source: Authors' computation.
*** represents the significance at 1 percent.

well as sector-specific employment elasticities for Nigeria using annual data between 1981 and 2014. The results, presented in table 6-11, indicate that the elasticity of employment with respect to economic growth has been generally low except for services. The aggregate employment elasticity estimates for Nigeria is estimated at 0.11, which implies that with every 1 percent growth in GDP, employment increases by just eleven basis points. The implication is that the relative high growth has not led to an appreciable increase in employment.

The results from the sectoral analysis indicate that agriculture has elasticity of 0.48, while the services sector has generally been employment-intensive at 0.85. Manufacturing employment elasticity is 0.30 and insignificant. This is the sector that should constitute a repository of more productive, remunerative, and, hence, decent jobs. Consistent with the earlier results, the findings confirmed the low labor absorptive capacity of the Nigerian economy at the aggregate and at sectoral levels, especially manufacturing, supporting the notion that growth performance in Nigeria is, after all, a "jobless" one.

UNLEASHING ITS POTENTIAL

Although a number of factors have also naturally positioned Nigeria to be among the topmost economies, half a century following independence, however, Nigeria's economic growth has not only been disappointing until recently, but highly cyclical, sporadic, and non-inclusive (Ajakaiye and others 2014). From the aforementioned analysis, we can observe the influence of changes in the structure of the population on growth and the labor market as well as the movement to the low-productivity service sector. However, with the high level of human and natural resource endowments, Nigeria is yet to unleash its potential. Nigeria is Africa's most populous country, with about 170 million people in 2013, and the sixth most populous nation in the world. The current demographic structure of the country exhibits a growing youthful population with an estimated median age of 17.9 years (17.3 for males and 18.4 for females), as well as the fact that 42 percent of the population are younger than fourteen years, 29 percent are age 15–19 years, and 24 percent are in the age range of 30–59 years (National Population Commission (NPC) [Nigeria] and ICF International 2014).

Demographic Dividend

The observed demographic structure implies that Nigeria is on the verge of a major demographic transition in which the ratio of youth to other age groups is increasing (Bloom and others 2010). Total fertility, which is estimated to have fallen to 5.73 in 2015, is projected to slide further, to 5.10, by 2030. Hence, the working-age population, which is estimated at 52.9 percent in 2015, is expected to expand further, to 55.1 percent, by 2030, as the under-fifteen population contracts. This growth would mean that the working-age population (WAP) will grow from 97 million in 2015 to 151 million in 2030, representing almost 16 percent of Africa's labor force. This youth bulge is expected to stimulate growth and development, otherwise known as demographic dividend. Recent developments among the East Asian Tiger economies, such as Hong Kong, South Korea, and Singapore, suggest that a demographic dividend is possible for Nigeria (WEF 2014). The expansion in the number of people in the workforce relative to the number of dependents should provide a significant boost in economic productivity, not only in the production of manufactured goods, services, or agricultural produce, but also in the wake of an increasing purchasing power that fuels economic growth and development.

An empirical study carried out by Bloom and others (2010) estimated that not only will Nigeria's economy be three times larger than today in 2030, with GDP per capita increasing by more than 29 percent, but the country also has the capacity to lift about 31.8 million people out of poverty if it can overcome its challenges to collect its demographic dividend. In other words, if productively employed, the extra adults create a window of opportunity for significant inclusive economic growth in Nigeria. However, these dividends are not automatic (Olaniyan and others 2012). To reap this demographic dividend, the country needs concrete policy actions targeted toward the creation of productive jobs for youths. Increased investment in education is necessary given that the country's adult literacy rate is only 56.9 percent with huge variations between sex (male 65.1 percent and female 48.6 percent), regions, and states (NBS 2010b). Furthermore, there is a need for increased health investment in gender equality to improve women's opportunities and choices and achieve inclusive and sustained economic prosperity for all.

Apart from the population, Nigeria is endowed with highly educated individuals who mostly are in the diaspora, even though the country is increasingly experiencing a shortage of professionals due to human capital flight. In 2007, the emigration rate of Nigerians with tertiary education was estimated to be 36 percent, while, for physicians and nurses, the rates were about 13.6 percent and 11.7 percent, respectively (Ratha and others 2007). Long-term economic growth cannot be achieved in the absence of people with professional technical expertise and investment in the real sectors (agriculture and industry) (Mba and Ekeopara 2012). If the external human capital is harnessed alongside the internal capital, the growth trajectory is not only likely to be high but also inclusive.

CHALLENGES OF JOBLESS GROWTH IN NIGERIA

Our results show that the Nigerian economy is characterized by positive GDP growth, but it is a jobless one and this is due to a number of challenges.[7]

Challenge of Low Industrial Base

Industry is crucial to sustaining Nigeria's economic growth. This is why economic development policies (with each having a bearing on the industrial sector) were adopted ranging from the Import Substitution Strategy (ISS) through indigenization to the Structural Adjustment

Program (SAP). The country's recent growth rate is masking serious underlying deficiencies that must be addressed if there is to be any meaningful long-term transformation, a structural deficit that illustrates a reliance on primary production due to the absence of industrial capacity. Bringing this problem to an end would partly require focusing on efforts that will transform the largely agricultural economy into value added activities (Arrey 2013). Nigeria also cannot continue to depend on oil as the major source of its foreign exchange and revenue earnings. The recent crash in the price of oil and its effect on the economy further lends credence to this necessity.

Challenge of Infrastructural Deficits

Infrastructural services such as transport, water and sanitation, power, telecommunications, and irrigation have been critical in the structural transformation of advanced economies. They represent a large portfolio of expenditure in these economies, ranging from one-third to one-half of public investments. Besides proving that infrastructure capital has a significant positive effect on economic output and growth (Kessides 1993), studies have shown that where infrastructure appears to lead economic growth, the impact becomes relatively long-term. These structural impacts are further explicated through the effect on the quality of life of citizens, as well as the influence on the marginal productivity of labor and capital for both public and private investments. The current level of infrastructure deficit in Nigeria has been identified by Sanusi (2012) as the major setback to Nigeria's Vision 20:2020 of becoming one of the twenty largest economies in 2020. The absence of infrastructural services has hindered urbanization and the demographic dividends of the country's working population boom.

Challenge of Poor Governance and Weak Institutions

Governance is one of the key factors that explain the divergence in performance across developing countries (Khan 2007). This especially defines the level of inclusiveness that policies bring, as they are formulated and implemented by institutions. The role of the government does not depend solely on its involvement in the economic transformation process but, more important, on how it is able to govern development with a decisive ideological orientation and effective institutions and policies underpinned by adequate bureaucratic and organizational capacity and political will (Nkurayija 2011). Good governance, therefore, promotes democracy, human capital formation, and efficiency in the economy. Besides the weakness in the poor intermediation of production factors is the issue of the high cost of governance and administrative structures associated with the running of government. According to Warimeh (2007), the misuse of public funds is another cause of the increasing high cost of governance in Nigeria. This political economy eventually creates room for corruption and passiveness, thereby weakening government plans and policies for economic growth. For instance, Nigeria's rank in government effectiveness fell from its highest level in 2000 of 30.29 to 27.49 in 2013.

Challenge of Insecurity

Nigeria, in recent times, has witnessed an unprecedented level of insecurity. The phenomenon has found greater expression following the emergence of Boko Haram since 2011, which led to humanitarian crises particularly in the northeastern parts of the country (Jerome 2015). According to Nigeria's National Emergency Management Agency (NEMA), at least 470,500 people were displaced in 2013 alone by such violence, and there is very little information about their protection and assistance needs. The country ranked 151 out of 162 in the 2014 Global Peace Index for major factors such as society and security, as well as domestic and international conflict, with a national cost of violence estimated at US$28.5 billion.[8] There are also the associated effects of insecurity, including fear, coercion, loss of relatives, properties, and livelihoods, displacement, breakdown of production channels, and deprivation of basic needs, which worsen the already high level of poverty. Violence and insecurity have a global impact as they erode a country's human and social capital, reduce life expectancy at birth, destroy its productive and financial capital, and can threaten macroeconomic stability (Soares 2006; Geneva Declaration 2008). Security expenditures have the effect of eroding savings and investments in the broader economy, as well as labor productivity at the individual level. The World Development Report 2011 found that "a country that experienced major violence over the period from 1981 to 2005 had a poverty rate 21 percentage points higher than a country that saw no violence" and for every three years a country is affected by major violence, poverty reduction lags behind by 2.7 percent (World Bank 2011).

CONCLUSIONS AND PROPOSED REMEDIAL ACTIONS

Over the last decade, Nigeria has experienced a steady and unprecedented wave of growth, which came with unique structural changes in sectoral employment. Characteristics of this growth process in the light of findings of this study hold an important development policy interpretation, with the need for the reallocation of people to better-quality jobs to address unemployment, underemployment, and poverty. Nigeria will need to galvanize its policy space not only to stimulate job creation and productivity within sectors, but also to ensure sector growths that encourage labor shifts from low- to high-productivity sectors. Findings show that Nigeria's highest productivity sector is the manufacturing sector, which has lagged behind in terms of contributions to output and employment elasticity of output.

Although several factors have contributed to growth in Nigeria, foremost, growth has been driven by sectoral variations in terms of employment, sectoral development, and value added, but there is no significant structural change on the employment front. Even though the share of agriculture in total GDP has reduced, it is still the sector that employs the highest number of people, despite its low productivity and subsistence features.

Proposed Remedial Actions

Our results show that Nigeria has been experiencing jobless growth over the past decade and a half. The observed structural changes do not seem to be growth enhancing and seem to lack an employment generation capability. Thus, this type of growth is not inclusive.

Given the need for people to move out of less rewarding sectors (especially agriculture and rudimentary, informal services sectors) and the ongoing high rate of urbanization, underemployment has become entrenched rather than just a passing phenomenon. In the circumstances, unemployment has continued to increase, while underemployment has resurfaced as a bedeviling challenge facing the country's large youthful labor force.

To remedy the situation, Nigeria first needs to create more decent jobs. The World Bank has estimated that the Nigerian economy needs to create between 40 and 50 million jobs between 2010 and 2030 as a result of the continued high fertility rate, which is set to rapidly increase the working-age population by some 66 million people between 2010 and 2030, compared to an increase of 35 million people between 1990 and 2030 (World Bank 2016). These numbers roughly translate into over 2 million additional jobs per year, which will be mostly taken up by new entrants to the labor market. Emphasis should be on productive jobs that work well for development, as encapsulated in the World Development Report on Jobs (World Bank 2012). This could be sourced by: 1) promoting higher agricultural productivity, especially in smallholder farming; 2) spatially balanced investments that provide opportunities in the currently disadvantaged northern regions; and 3) bringing more girls into education and productive employment, which would contribute to higher family earnings, enhance family planning, and improve nutrition for children. For the foreseeable future, agriculture and small nonfarm household enterprises will continue to account for the bulk of new jobs. Nigeria must consider how to increase productivity in agriculture and non-farm enterprises and devise avenues of attracting youths into the sector. There should also be resolute commitment to raising productivity in the agricultural sector through sustained massive support for agricultural research and extension (as has been done in Brazil, China, India, and Malaysia), mechanization, commercialization of technologies, and enhanced value addition through effective support for agro-processors and agri-businesses.

Nigeria needs to invest more in building a skilled workforce through diverse measures, such as improving the quality of basic education; the removal of barriers to good-quality education; making education more

relevant to the labor market through better links between schooling
and job needs as well as strengthening the employability of graduate;
and emphasis on vocational education. These investments would help
increase the productivity of Nigeria's workforce. While Nigeria is already the sixth largest receiver of remittances in the world, with a tan-
gible $20.8 billion recorded in 2015 according to the World Bank
Group (2016) Migration and Remittances Factbook 2016, the diaspora
could participate more in Nigeria's development by bringing much
needed skills. The Nigeria Investment Promotion Commission estimated that each year, some 2,000 Nigerians who have been trained
outside the country return home to seek employment or business opportunities. Such "diaspora-tapping" also provides the rationale for the
TOKTEN (Transfer of Knowledge through Expatriate Networks) program of the United Nations Development Programme. These programs
need to be either formalized or scaled up.

Special attention should be paid to the development and technological upgrade of the manufacturing sector in general and
labor-intensive components in particular. In addition, effective programs for the modernization of the service sector, especially the
distributive trade subsector characterized by informality and low productivity, should be articulated, effectively implemented, regularly
monitored, and their impacts carefully evaluated to provide a basis for
evidence-based pragmatic and proactive modifications as may be
necessary. For Nigeria to benefit from its demographic dividend, developing the entrepreneurial potential of its youth population is an
important opportunity for growth. Specific labor-market interventions,
including federal and state-level youth skill-building institutions—for example, post-secondary trade schools, post-tertiary education skill building institutions (as in Canada), and innovative public works programs—
should be targeted toward the high number of poor and vulnerable
people.

Finally, an enabling business environment needs to be created by
tackling the obstacles to doing business, such as electricity, poor infrastructure, and corruption. Federal, state, and local governments should
focus on improving regulatory environments, infrastructure, and developing human capital as essentials for inclusive growth.

APPENDIX

FIGURE 6-A1. *Aggregate Employment, Productivity, and Demographic Profile of Growth in Nigeria, 2005–09*

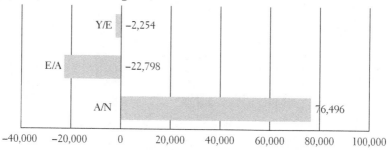

■ Contribution to growth in value added per capita (2010 Naira)

Source: Authors' computations based on JoGGs Decomposition Tool (World Bank 2010).
Note: Y/E = Output per worker; E/A = Employment rate and A/N = Demographic change.

FIGURE 6-A2. *Aggregate Employment, Productivity, and Demographic Profile of Growth in Nigeria, 2010–14*

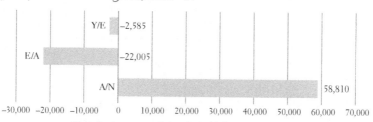

■ Contribution to growth in value added per capita (2010 Naira)

Source: Authors' computations based on JoGGs Decomposition Tool (World Bank 2010).
Note: Y/E = Output per worker; E/A = Employment rate and A/N = Demographic change.

FIGURE 6-A3. *Output per Worker by Sectors, 2005–09*

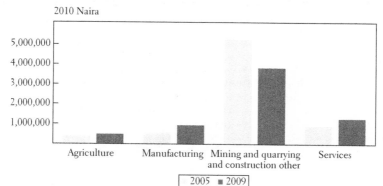

Source: Authors' computations based on JoGGs Decomposition Tool (World Bank 2010).

FIGURE 6-A4. *Output per Worker by Sectors, 2010–14*

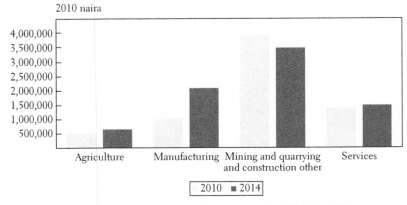

2010 naira

Source: Authors' computations based on JoGGs Decomposition Tool (World Bank 2010).

FIGURE 6-A5. *Contribution of Each Sector to Change in Employment-to-Population Ratio, 2005–09*

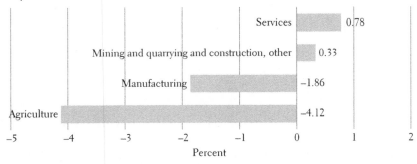

Source: Authors' computations based on JoGGs Decomposition Tool (World Bank 2010).

FIGURE 6-A6. *Contribution of Each Sector to Change in Employment-to-Population Ratio, 2010–14*

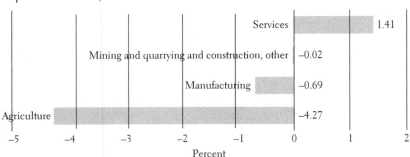

Source: Authors' computations based on JoGGs Decomposition Tool (World Bank 2010).

FIGURE 6-A7. *Contribution of Change in Employment-to-Population Ratio to Change in GDP (Value Added) per Capita, by Sector, Nigeria, 2005–09*

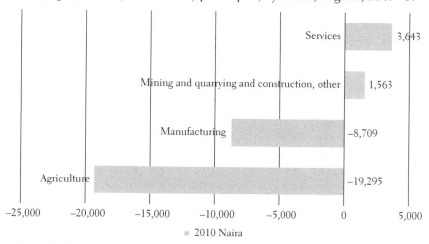

Source: Authors' computations based on JoGGs Decomposition Tool (World Bank 2010).

FIGURE 6-A8. *Contribution of Change in Employment-to-Population Ratio to Change in GDP (Value Added) per Capita, by Sector, Nigeria, 2010–14*

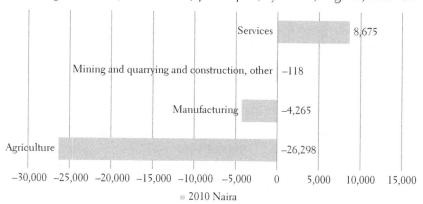

Source: Authors' computations based on JoGGs Decomposition Tool (World Bank 2010).

NOTES

1. Development Progress is a four-year research project embarked upon by the European Centre for Development Policy (ECDPM) to better understand and measure in concrete terms what has worked in development and why. The countries covered include Brazil, Cambodia, Chile, Ethiopia, India, Indonesia, Mauritius, Mongolia, South Africa, Sri Lanka, Thailand, Uganda, and Vietnam.

2. Employment and unemployment data are compiled by NISER from the erstwhile National Development Plan, 1980–84, the National Rolling Plans (1990–2003), NBS Statistical Fact Sheets, the database of the National Manpower Board, 1970–2005, and other publications.

3. The methodology followed the World Bank job generation and growth decomposition tool process. Detailed methodology is available in the tool's appendix.

4. Employment rate is defined by ILO measure as the population that "participates" in the labor market, and participation is defined as all those looking for jobs or already employed. But in developing countries, the definition of participation is very blurry because employment may be low due to agents that are seasonally unemployed. We, therefore, believe that, in the case of developing countries, a better measure of the labor force is the working-age population rather than those actively participating in the labor market.

5. Components can remain constant by treating them in various ways: by leaving them in the level observed in the initial year, or the start at the final year, or one of them can stay in the level observed in the initial year and the other start at the level observed in the final year. Choice of treatment depends on decomposition approaches but, as mentioned, the Shapley decomposition approach uses a weighted average of each possible alternative and, therefore, eliminates residuals.

6. Output per worker in this paper may be referred to as productivity under the assumption that it encompasses all three influences.

7. It should be noted that the challenges are inexhaustible and only a few selected ones are discussed in this study.

8. See www.visionofhumanity.org/#page/indexes/global-peace-index/2014 /NGA/OVER.

REFERENCES

Abumere, S. I., B. C. Arimah, and T. A Jerome. 1995. "The Informal Sector in Nigeria's Development Process: Lessons from the Literature." Vol. 95. Development Policy Centre.

Adeyinka, A., S. Salau, and D. Vollrath. 2013. "Structural Change and the Possibilities for Future Growth in Nigeria," Working Paper 24, July (International Food Research Policy).

African Development Bank (AfDB). 2013. "Africa Competitiveness Report 2013." (www.afdb.org/en/knowledge/publications/africa-competitiveness -report/africa-competitiveness-report-2013).

African Economic Outlook. 2015. "Nigeria Economic Outlook." (www.african economicoutlook.org/en/country-notes/west-africa/nigeria).

Ajakaiye, O., A. Jerome, O. Olaniyan, K. Mahrt, and O. Alaba. 2014. "Multi-dimensional Poverty in Nigeria: First Order Dominance Approach." Working Paper WP2014/143 (Helsinki: UNU-WIDER).

Ajilore, T., and O. Yinusa. 2011. "An Analysis of Employment Intensity of Sectoral Output Growth in Botswana." *Southern African Business Review*, 15(2), pp. 26–42.

Ancharaz, V. 2010. "Trade, Jobs, and Growth in Africa: An Empirical Investigation of the Export-Led Jobless Growth Hypothesis." (www.oecd.org/site /tadicite/48735521.pdf).

Arrey, O. B. 2013. "Industrialization and Economic Advancement in Nigeria: A Study of the Role of the Iron and Steel Sector." *GJMBR-A: Administration and Management*, 13(9).

Bbaale, E. 2013. "Is Uganda's Growth Profile Jobless?" *International Journal of Economics and Finance*, 5(11), p. 105.

Bloom, D., J. Finlay, S. Humair, A. Mason, O. Olaniyan, and A. Soyibo. 2010. "Prospects for Economic Growth in Nigeria: A Demographic Perspective." Paper presented at the IUSSP Seminar on Demographics and Macroeconomic Performance, 4–5 June (www.ntaccounts.org/doc /repository/BFHMOS2010.pdf).

Boeri, T., and P. Garibaldi. 2006. "Are Labour Markets in the New Member States Sufficiently Flexible for EMU?" *Journal of Banking and Finance*, 30(5), pp. 1393–1407.

Byiers, B., T. Berliner, F. Guadagno, and L.R. Takeuchi. 2015. "Working for Economic Transformation." Dimension Paper 03 (London: Overseas Development Institute).

Central Bank of Nigeria (CBN). Federal Office of Statistics, Nigerian Institute for Social and Economic Research. 2001. *A Study of Nigeria's Informal Sector, Volume 1: Statistics on Nigeria's Informal Sector* (Abuja: CBN).

Geneva Declaration. 2008. *Global Burden of Armed Conflict* (Geneva: Geneva Declaration Secretariat). (www.genevadeclaration.org/measurability /global-burden-of-armed-violence/global-burden-of-armed-violence -2008.html)

Ghani, E., and S. D. O'Connell. 2014. Can Service be a Growth Escalator in Low-Income Countries?" Working Paper 6971 (Washington, D.C.: World Bank).

Gutierrez, C., C. Orecchia, P. Paci, and P. Serneels. 2007. "Does Employment Generation Really Matter for Poverty Reduction?" Working Paper 4432 (Washington, D.C.: World Bank).

Hull, K. 2009. "Understanding the Relationship between Economic Growth, Employment, and Poverty Reduction," in *Promoting Pro-Poor Growth: Employment* (Paris: OECD).

Islam, I., and S. Nazara. 2000. "Estimating Employment Elasticity for the Indonesian Economy." Technical Note on the Indonesian Labor Market (Geneva: International Labor Organization).

Jerome, A. 2015. "Lessons from Columbia for Fighting Boko Haram Insurgency in Nigeria." *PRISM Journal of the Centre for Complex Operations,* 5(2), pp. 94–106.

Kale, Y., and S. I. Doguwa. 2015. *On the Compilation of Labour Force Statistics for Nigeria.* June. CBN Journal of Applied Statistics 6(1a), pp. 183–98.

Kessides, C. 1993. "The Contributions of Infrastructure to Economic Development: A Review of Experience and Policy Implications." Discussion Paper 213 (Washington D.C.: World Bank).

Khan, M. 2007. "Governance, Economic Growth and Development since the 1960s." Working Paper 54 ST/ESA/2007/DWP/54 (DESA) (http://eprints.soas.ac.uk/9921/1/DESA_Governance_Economic_Growth_and_Development_since_1960s.pdf).

Kormawa, P., and A. Jerome. 2015. "Renewing Industrialization Strategies in Africa," chapter 7 in *Beyond a Middle Income Africa: Transforming Africa Economies for Sustained Growth with Rising Employment and Income,* edited by O. Badiane and T. Makombe (Washington, D.C.: International Food Policy Research Institute).

Lehmann, H. 1995. Active Labor Market Policies in the OECD and in Selected Transition Countries. Economic Policy." Working Paper 1502 (Washington, D.C.: World Bank).

Loayza, N., and C. Raddatz. 2010. "The Composition of Growth Matters for Poverty Alleviation." *Journal of Development Economics,* 93, pp. 137–51.

Malunda, D. 2013. "Employment Intensity of Non-Agricultural Growth in Rwanda: Analyzing the Links between Growth, Employment, and Productivity in Rwanda." Research Paper (Institute of Policy Analysis and Research [IPAR]-Rwanda). (https://editorialexpress.com/cgi-bin/conference/download.cgi?db_name=CSAE2013&paper_id=814).

Mba, P. N., and C. Ekeopara. 2012. "Brain Drain: Implication for Economic Growth in Nigeria." *American Journal of Social Issues and Humanities,* 2(2).

National Bureau of Statistics (NBS). 2010a. "Nigeria Poverty Report 2010." (www.nigerianstat.gov.ng/pdfuploads/Nigeria%20Poverty%20Profile%202010.pdf).

———. 2010b. Report of the National Literacy Survey, June (www.nigerianstat.gov.ng/pdfuploads/National%20Literacy%20Survey,%202010.pdf).

———. 2010c. "National Manpower Stock and Employment Generation Survey for Household and Micro Enterprise (Informal Sector)."

———. 2014. "Report of National Stakeholders' Workshop on the Review of Definition and Methodology for Computing Unemployment Statistics in Nigeria."

———. 2015a. "Nigerian Gross Domestic Product Report (Expenditure Approach) Q1 2015."

———. 2015b. "Presentation of Labour Statistics Based on Revised Concepts and Methodology for Computing Labour Statistics in Nigeria."

National Population Commission (NPC) [Nigeria] and ICF International. 2014. *Nigeria Demographic and Health Survey 2013* (Abuja, Nigeria, and Rockville, Maryland, USA: NPC and ICF International). (https://dhsprogram.com/pubs/pdf/FR293/FR293.pdf).

Nigerian Institute of Social and Economic Research (NISER). 2015. *Estimated Employment (Trend in Gainful Employment) from 1970–2014 by Sectors* (Ibadan: Nigerian Institute of Social and Economic Research).

Nkurayija, J. C. 2011. "The Requirements for the African Continent's Development: Linking Peace, Governance, Economic Growth and Global Independence." (http://www.culturaldiplomacy.org/academy/content/pdf/participant-papers/africa/Jean-De-La-Croix-Nkurayija-The-Requirements-For-The-African-Continent's-Development-Linking-Economic-Growth.pdf).

Oduh, M., E. Eboh, H. Ichoku, and O. Ujah. 2008. "Measurement and Explanation of Informal Sector of the Nigerian Economy, African Institute for Applied Economics." Research Paper 3, August (Enugu: AIAE).

Okun, A. M. 1962. "Potential GNP: Its Measurement and Significance," in *Proceedings of the Business and Economic Statistics Section* (Washington, D.C.: American Statistical Association), pp. 98–104.

Olaniyan, O., A. Soyibo, and A. O. Lawanson. 2012. "Demographic Transition, Demographic Dividend and Economic Growth in Nigeria." *African Population Studies*, 26(2), pp. 159–76.

Olotu, A., R. Salami, and I. Akeremale. 2015. "Poverty and Rate of Unemployment in Nigeria." *International Journal of Management (IJM)*, 2(1).

Onaran, O. 2008. "Jobless Growth in the Central and East European Countries: A Country-Specific Panel Data Analysis of the Manufacturing Industry." *Eastern European Economics*, 46(4) pp. 90–115.

Ratha, D., S. Mohapatra, K. M. Vijayalakshmi, and X. Zhimei. 2007. "Remittance Trends 2007." (Washington, D.C.: World Bank). (https://openknowledge.worldbank.org/handle/10986/11024).

Rodrik, D. 2014. "Are Services the New Manufactures?" (Project Syndicate). (www.project-syndicate.org/commentary/are-services-the-new-manufactures-by-dani-rodrik-2014-10).

———. 2015. "Premature Industrialization in Developing World." (CEPR Policy Portal). (www.voxeu.org/article/premature-deindustrialiation-developing-world).

Sanusi, S. L. 2012. "The Role of Development Finance Institutions in Infrastructure Development: What Nigeria Can Learn from Bndes and the Indian Infrastructure Finance." Keynote address at the 3rd ICRC PPP Stakeholders Forum, Lagos, Nigeria, 18 July. (www.cenbank.org/out/speeches
/2012/gov_ppp%20stakeholder%20forum_160712.pdf).

Soares, R. R. 2006. "The Welfare Cost of Violence across Countries." *Journal
of Health Economics*, 25(5), pp. 821–846.

Treichel, V., ed. 2010. *Putting Nigeria to Work: A Strategy for Employment
and Growth* (Washington D.C.: World Bank).

United Nations Department of Economic and Social Affairs. 2015. (http://
esa.un.org/unpd/wpp).

United Nations Development Programme (UNDP). 2014. "Human
Development Report 2014 Makes a Case for Sustaining Human Progress by Reducing Vulnerabilities and Building Resilience." (UNDP).
(www.ng.undp.org/content/nigeria/en/home/presscenter/pressreleases
/2014/08/18/-human-development-report-2014-makes-a-case-for
-sustaining-human-progress-by-reducing-vulnerabilities-and-building
-resilience-.html).

Warimeh, O. A. 2007. "Contemporary Issues in Good Governance in Nigeria: A Proactive Approach." *Nigerian Journal of Economic and Social
Studies*, 49(1), pp. 276–94.

World Bank. 2005. *Pro-Poor Growth in the 1990s: Lessons and Insights from
14 Countries* (Washington, D.C.: World Bank). (http://siteresources.world
bank.org/INTPGI/Resources/342674-1119450037681/Pro-poor_growth
_in_the_1990s.pdf).

———. 2010. "Job Generation and Growth (JoGGs) Decomposition
Tool." (Washington, D.C.: World Bank). (http://go.worldbank.org
/E5PB0575Z0).

———. 2011. "World Development Report 2011: Conflict, Security, and
Development." (Washington, D.C.: World Bank). (https://openknowledge
.worldbank.org/handle/10986/4389).

——— 2012. "World Development Report 2013: Jobs." (Washington, D.C.:
World Bank). (https://openknowledge.worldbank.org/handle/10986/11843)
License: CC BY 3.0 IGO.

———. 2015a. "World Development Indicators 2015." (http://databank
.worldbank.org/data/reports.aspx?source=world-development-indicators).

———. 2015b. "Nigeria Economic Report, No 3, November." (Washington,
D.C.: World Bank).

——— 2016. "More, and More Productive, Jobs for Nigeria: A Profile of
Work and Workers." (Washington, D.C.: World Bank). (http://documents
.worldbank.org/curated/en/2016/03/26066141/more-more-productive
-jobs-nigeria-profile-work-workers).

World Bank Group. 2016. "Migration and Remittances Factbook 2016,"
    Third Edition. (Washington, D.C.: World Bank). (https://openknowledge
    .worldbank.org/handle/10986/23743) License: CC BY 3.0 IGO.
World Economic Forum (WEF). 2014. "Prospects for Reaping a Demo-
    graphic Dividend in Nigeria. A Case Study by the World Economic Fo-
    rum's Global Agenda Council on Population Growth." (www3.weforum
    .org/docs/GAC/2014/WEF_GAC_NigeriaCaseStudy_2014.pdf).

SEVEN

South Africa

Demographic, Employment, and Wage Trends

**Haroon Bhorat, Karmen Naidoo, Morné Oosthuizen,
and Kavisha Pillay**

Afer negative and slow growth in the late 1980s and early 1990s, South Africa's triumphant transition to a democratic and more inclusive society in 1994 saw the economy once again begin to grow steadily. This renewed growth was supported by strong macroeconomic management and effective institutions. Since then, the South African economy has grown at an annual real average of 3.19 percent. Accompanying this growth performance are significant welfare gains seen in the rise of access to social services, housing, and basic infrastructure, as well as a moderate reduction in extreme poverty (Bhorat and others 2015b). One of the factors preventing greater development and welfare improvements is that economic growth has come with considerable variation.

In the five years immediately after democracy, growth averaged 2.76 percent, rising to 3.17 percent in the following five years (table 7-1). The period of fastest economic growth was between 2004 and 2008, where real GDP expanded at an annualized average rate of almost

TABLE 7-1. *Real GDP and GDP per Capita Annual Average Growth Rates, South Africa*

Percent

	1994–98	1999–2003	2004–08	2009–13
GDP	2.76	3.17	4.92	1.91
	(1.40)	(0.73)	(0.84)	(2.03)
GDP per capita	0.50	1.09	3.55	0.56
	(1.43)	(0.78)	(0.83)	(2.00)

Source: World Bank, World Development Indicators (WDI) (2015); authors' calculations.
Note: Standard deviations shown in parenthesis.

5 percent. This period of relatively fast growth was then abruptly interrupted by the global financial crisis, which caused the South African economy to enter a brief recession in 2009.

National output subsequently rose to just over 3 percent in 2010, but has since weakened. Over the last five years, therefore, GDP per capita has grown at an annual average of merely 0.56 percent. This weakening of the South African economy can ultimately be attributed to a combination of factors, including slow global growth, industrial disputes, electricity shortages and concomitant price hikes, a lack of international competitiveness in manufacturing, and declining gold, platinum, and coal prices since 2012.

A brief analysis of the sectoral composition at two points in time shows that four sectors are expanding relatively faster than overall GDP: transport, storage, and communication; financial and business services; construction; and wholesale and retail trade.[1] Transport, storage, and communication is now one and a half times the size it was in 1994, financial and business services have expanded by 42 percent over the period, and construction by 47 percent. The remaining five sectors have all declined in their share of GDP.

The most marked change is that of the mining sector. From constituting up to 15.5 percent of GDP in 2014, it is now almost half that proportion, at 8.5 percent. In addition, agriculture and manufacturing have also declined considerably in their shares of GDP, by 22 percent and 10 percent, respectively. While the country has effectively transitioned away from its earlier reliance on the mining sector, mining remains an important contributor to economic activity. Most important, the sector generates more than half of the country's foreign exchange revenue and its firms account for a quarter of the national stock exchange market capitalization (Chamber of Mines 2015). Thus, exports are heavily concentrated in natural resources, where gold and other mining products make up 44 percent of exports, a proportion similar to that of manufacturing (Industrial Development Corporation 2013).

Based on the sectoral composition of GDP, then, it is evident that South Africa has become a service-driven economy since 1994. The share of output contributed by wholesale and retail trade, transport, and communication—and most visibly—financial and business services, shows increases over the first two decades of democracy in South Africa. The economy, it is fair to argue, has slipstreamed onto an economic development trajectory that is increasingly intensive in the provision of services. What is most starkly evident in this deepening output from services, however, is the stagnation in manufacturing. Hence, we find that the manufacturing sector's share of GDP has declined marginally since 1994 in South Africa. Since trade became more liberalized in the early 1990s, South Africa's manufacturing sector has failed to compete in global manufacturing export markets. Increased import competition and the level and volatility of the real exchange rate have been shown to be important drivers of South Africa's manufacturing decline (Rodrik 2006). No country to date has managed to transition out of a middle-income to a high-income country status without the dynamism of a vibrant, labor-intensive manufacturing industry. In the lexicon of post-apartheid South Africa, however, this notion of labor-intensive manufacturing as a driver of growth and jobs in the country is strikingly absent.

South Africa is classified as an upper middle-income country, with real GDP per capita currently at US$5,916, up from US$4,652 in 2000. The uneven and, at times, sluggish growth in average income levels, however, has meant a moderate decline in poverty, from 40 percent of the population in 1995, to 26 percent in 2013, using the World Bank's $2-a-day poverty line. With a current population of almost 53 million, this equates to about 13.7 million people living in poverty in South Africa. At perhaps the more appropriate national poverty line, the poverty headcount ratio has increased from 31 percent in 1995 to a current level of 53.8 percent.[2] This headcount ratio is calculated using the upper bound level of a newly rebased national poverty line, but even at the national lower bound headcount poverty rate of 37 percent, poverty has undoubtedly remained high.

Thus, while extreme poverty has declined, the trends on the national poverty line are more worrying. South Africa's inability to translate growth into reducing poverty is not surprising given the extremely unequal nature of the society. With a Gini coefficient of 0.59, the exceptionally high level of income inequality is arguably the most important factor hindering the poverty reducing power of economic growth.[3] The exclusivity of South Africa's growth path is further emphasized by an unemployment rate of 25 percent, and one that has averaged 23.7 percent over the last two decades, with its lowest level at 17 percent in 1995.[4] South Africa is clearly in a labor market crisis, which in a low growth environment serves only to reinforce further the unsustainably high level of income inequality.

Therefore, despite the optimistic outlook for the South African economy as the country transitioned to democracy in 1994, economic growth over the last two decades has been moderate. In addition, while the comprehensive social welfare system has succeeded in reducing inequalities in access to public services and housing, poverty has remained stagnant and inequality has remained exceptionally high— underpinned by one of the world's consistently highest unemployment rates. Given this all too brief background to the economy's growth record and the structure of this growth trajectory, the remainder of this paper focuses on demographic and labor market trends during the period to understand better some of the factor market underpinnings of South Africa's economic performance.

ESTIMATING SOUTH AFRICA'S DEMOGRAPHIC DIVIDEND

The South African labor market has undergone considerable changes since the end of apartheid and the elimination of various statutory restrictions on labor market access and participation. The key feature of the latter half of the 1990s and the early 2000s was the rapid growth in the size of the labor force, driven by increasing labor force participation rates—rather than a rapidly growing working-age population—particularly among rural African women (Casale and Posel 2002). For the 1995 to 2002 period, for example, growth in the working-age population averaged 2.1 percent per annum, which was less than half the rate of growth of the labor force (irrespective of the unemployment definition utilized) (Bhorat and Oosthuizen 2006, p. 145). As a result, although employment growth was able to keep pace with growth in the working-age population and, largely, with economic growth, it was unable to keep up with the growth in the labor force. Unemployment, thus, moved rapidly higher, both in absolute terms and as a proportion of the labor force.

This disconnect between employment growth and labor force growth points to the importance of understanding the longer-term challenges and opportunities associated with demographic change. Projections from the United Nations Population statistics suggest that the share of the working-age population (WAP) in the total population in South Africa will remain between 65 percent and 67 percent until the year 2030. Given slowing population growth rates, this means that the working-age population is expected to increase gradually, from the current 34.2 million to 36.5 million by 2030. South Africa is, therefore, quite some way along its demographic transition. In fact, the median age in South Africa has risen from eighteen years to twenty-five years over the last three decades, and is estimated to rise to thirty-one over the next three decades as the population continues to age (Oosthuizen 2014).

According to the National Transfer Accounts (NTA) framework, the shift from a high-fertility, high-mortality equilibrium to a low-fertility, low-mortality equilibrium—referred to as the demographic transition—is associated with two potential dividends that can contribute toward longer term economic growth and development (Mason and Lee 2007; NTA 2013). The first demographic dividend is triggered by falling fertility rates, having been preceded by falling mortality rates, particularly among children. This process helps to boost economic growth through lowering the extent of dependency on working-age adults.

Typically, dependency is measured in terms of dependency ratios, namely the ratio of economically inactive cohorts to economically active cohorts (for example, the total dependency ratio is the ratio of children under the age of fifteen and adults aged sixty-five years and older to the working-age population). This one–zero switch between dependence and nondependence, though, is not realistic, and is avoided within the NTA framework by calculating the support ratio. The support ratio measures the number of effective workers (a country's population-weighted per capita labor income profile) relative to the number of effective consumers (the population-weighted per capita consumption profile). A rise in the support ratio implies a relative increase in the number of effective workers and, therefore, a lower level of dependence.

Declining fertility leads to a reduction in the ratio of dependent children relative to nondependent (that is, earning) adults and is the underlying driver of the demographic dividend—defined as the rate of change of the support ratio—as it drives the support ratio higher. This raised support ratio implies an increase in the number of effective workers relative to effective consumers and, thus, income per effective consumer rises, *ceteris paribus*. This, in turn, implies higher standards of living and an improved scope for human capital investment. Upon this foundation, then, a second demographic dividend, achieved through capital deepening, can be realized if the benefits of the first dividend are invested in human, physical, and financial capital.

For South Africa, the average fertility rate has already declined significantly, from 6.4 births per woman in the 1950s to 2.4 births in 2005–10 (United Nations 2012). However, the high level of unemployment and the resulting low labor income—particularly for young workers—has significantly constrained the economy's ability to reap the potential benefits of this demographic dividend. In addition to demographic change, both labor income and consumption are important factors influencing the rate of change of the support ratio and, therefore, the magnitude of the demographic dividend.

Figure 7-1 shows that labor income begins to rise at a later age and is markedly lower among young people in South Africa than in a range of other developed and developed countries. The interquartile ranges (IQR) of normalized labor income and consumption profiles across a variety of other countries are plotted in the graph using NTA data.[5] In addition, per capita labor income is shown to fall significantly and more steeply for older working-age adults in South Africa compared to the group of thirty-three other countries.

FIGURE 7-1. *Per Capita Labor Income, Consumption and Lifecycle Deficit, 2005*

Relative to Mean Labor Income for 30- to 49-year-olds

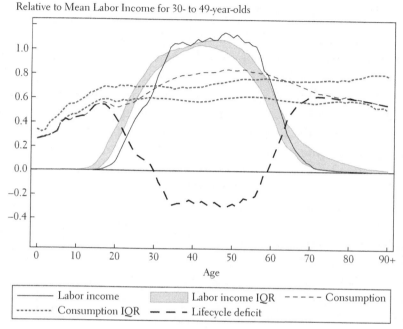

Labor income ——— | Labor income IQR ▓▓▓ | Consumption – – – – –
Consumption IQR ·········· | Lifecycle deficit — — —

Source: Oosthuizen (2014) using National Transfer Accounts (2013) data.
Note: Values are expressed as ratios to average per capita labor income at age 30–49. For a list of NTA member countries, see www.ntaccounts.org.

South Africa's consumption pattern also differs significantly from other countries. Consumption for children and young adults in South Africa is positioned within the first quartile of the IQR of the other countries, but rises to the top quartile for those between the ages of thirty and sixty years. For older individuals in South Africa, consumption declines quite strongly compared to other countries, where elderly consumption remains relatively stable. This decline in consumption among older cohorts in South Africa points to underlying weaknesses in the private and public institutions that should allocate resources to ensure that consumption among the elderly is maintained at a level that is comparable to that among prime working-age cohorts (Oosthuizen 2014). Finally, evaluating income and consumption together, South

Africa's lifecycle surplus period lasts thirty years, between the ages of thirty and fifty-nine years, which is broadly typical of NTA countries, albeit slightly delayed.

Estimates of the first demographic dividend for South Africa show that the country has passed through at least half of the period in which the first demographic dividend is expected to be positive, and is now in the stage during which the magnitude of the dividend is falling. The magnitude of South Africa's demographic dividend is in line with other middle-income countries. Over the 2005–10 period, the annual growth in the support ratio ranged between 0.15–0.40 percent, compared to an average of 0.40 percent for a group of twelve other upper middle-income countries for which there are NTA estimates (Mason and Lee 2012, as quoted in Oosthuizen 2014).

The continuing weaknesses within the South African labor market and the historical problems in the public provision of quality education to the broader population remain as two of the most significant challenges to realizing some benefit of the final phase of the positive demographic dividend over the next thirty years. While the low level of employment and labor income of young South Africans is critical to address, a greater positive impact on the demographic dividend would be achieved if South Africa's consumption profile were similar to that of the median NTA country. As figure 7-1 suggests, this would imply lowering the level of consumption of prime age adults relative to peak labor income to levels that are in line with international trends, while raising per capita consumption among the elderly. Underlying this finding is South Africa's relatively advanced point within the demographic transition. The youngest cohorts within the working-age population are expected to stabilize in size and begin to contract, while older working-age cohorts—which would comprise a relatively large proportion of effective consumers, given their high per capita consumption—are expected to grow rapidly. This suggests that weak sharing mechanisms within South African society may have a negative impact on per capita income growth over time (Oosthuizen 2014). In some sense, this provides support for the argument that inequality can act as a brake on economic growth.

STRUCTURE OF THE LABOR MARKET AND
GROWTH–EMPLOYMENT INTERACTIONS

The South African labor market has received considerable analytical and research attention over the past fifteen years and, as a result, there are a large number of labor market reviews covering the post-apartheid era (see, for example, Burger and Woolard 2005; Bhorat and Oosthuizen 2006; Branson 2006; Oosthuizen 2006; Yu 2008). Instead of a detailed review of the post-apartheid labor market, this paper seeks to explore the particular trends relating to skills-biased labor demand, as well as to highlight two new, more recent post-apartheid labor market trends. The latter is displayed in the rise, first, of temporary employment services as a form of alternative employment and, second, in the sharp increase in the level of public sector employment.

The number of the employed in South Africa is currently just under 15 million individuals, rising from 12.4 million in 2004. This increase of 2.6 million over the last decade is equivalent to an average annualized growth rate of 2.3 percent, with the most rapid growth occurring between 2004 and 2008, when the economy was growing at its fastest rate. Employment, thus, peaked at 14 million workers in the final quarter of 2008. The effects of the global economic recession, however, were felt heavily in South Africa, where the first three quarters of 2009 saw an estimated 900,000 jobs lost, and by the end of 2010, the number of employed equaled 13.2 million (Oosthuizen 2011). Employment creation has since remained weak.

The slow pace of job creation in South Africa over the last decade has meant the number of unemployed individuals has increased from 4.2 million in 2004 to a current level of 4.9 million by the narrow definition—an unemployment rate increase from 13 percent to 24 percent. Since 1994, the number of unemployed has doubled. When using an expanded definition of unemployment, the current unemployment figure stands at 8.1 million, a 35 percent unemployment rate.[6] The economic challenges then become clear: labor intensive sectors have failed to grow at a rapid enough pace to absorb the rising levels of labor force participation and the growing working-age population over time.

Simple elasticities of employment to GDP growth are provided in table 7-2. The estimates indicate that over the entire twenty-year period,

TABLE 7-2. *Employment–Growth Elasticities, South Africa, 1994–2013*

	Employment (thousands)	Real GDP (US$ millions)	Employment-growth elasticities		
			1994–2004	2004–13	1994–2013
1994	9,847	173,021.42	0.71	0.64	0.64
2004	12,342	234,667.86	. . .	. . .	. . .
2013	14,983	313,465.97	. . .	. . .	. . .

Source: DataFirst PALMS (1994, 2004); StatsSA Quarterly Labour Force Survey (QLFS) (2013); World Bank WDI (2015); authors' calculations.

employment increased on average by 0.64 percent for every 1 percent in GDP growth. The employment intensity of growth was clearly higher in the first decade after democracy than the second. Against other comparable economies, South Africa's simple output elasticity of total employment is by no means an outlier (Bhorat 2012). Following this, there is no immediate evidence here that South Africa's economy has a weak labor absorptive capacity (Bhorat 2012).

Furthermore, relative to a small subset of countries, Bhorat (2008) shows that South Africa's simple elasticity is relatively high. For example, fast growing economies (such as India and Malaysia) experienced a more moderate employment response to the high growth during the 2001–05 period; South Africa's estimate then was 0.60, while Malaysia and India were 0.47 and 0.25, respectively (Bhorat 2008). Of course, within South Africa's high unemployment environment, consumption levels are likely to be less than optimal and there may be lower incentive for investment, which would work together to dampen economic growth. The wide-scale provision of social grants would partly serve to offset these effects. Clearly, there is a nontrivial two-way relationship between growth and employment. Arguably, though, any development plan for South Africa needs to place economic growth at its core, with a focus on growth in labor-intensive sectors, for the benefits of growth and employment creation to be more equitably distributed.

Uneven Sectoral Shifts in Employment

Table 7-3 shows that the South African economy has created about 2.5 million jobs over the 2001–12 period, with significant job losses in the primary sector. It is evident in the sectoral breakdown that the over-

TABLE 7-3. *Employment Shifts by Industry, South Africa, 2001–12*

Percent share in total employment

| | Growth (2001–12) | | Employment shares | | Share of change $(\Delta E_i/\Delta E)^b$ |
	Absolute	Relative[a] $(\%\Delta E_i/\%\Delta E)$	2001	2012	(2001–12)
Primary	−719,232	−2.6	0.15	0.07	−0.28
Agriculture	−514,468	−2.7	0.1	0.04	−0.2
Mining	−204,764	−2.2	0.05	0.02	−0.08
Secondary	537,376	1.0	0.2	0.21	0.21
Manufacturing	112,149	0.3	0.14	0.12	0.04
Utilities	10,774	0.5	0.008	0.008	0.004
Construction	414,453	2.5	0.05	0.07	0.16
Tertiary	2,720,821	1.6	0.63	0.71	1.08
Trade	513,572	0.9	0.21	0.21	0.2
Transport	288,364	2.1	0.04	0.06	0.11
Financial	782,108	2.8	0.09	0.13	0.31
CSPS[c]	1,041,524	2.1	0.17	0.22	0.42
Private households	95,253	0.4	0.09	0.08	0.04
Total	2,497,763	1	1	1	1

Source: Bhorat and others (2014) using PALMS dataset (2012).

a. The ratio of the percentage change for each respective subsector and industry to the total overall percent change in employment over the period (relative sectoral employment growth).

b. The ratio of the percentage change in the share of employment to the overall change in employment over the period (share of change in employment). This measure shows, within each broad sector, where the sources of employment growth are. For example, employment in the tertiary sector is 1.08 times (or 108 percent of) the level of employment in 2001, which is the sum of the changes for all the industries within this subsector. CSPS, then, is the greatest contributor to employment growth in the tertiary sector.

c. CSPS (community, social, and personal services) is predominantly public sector employment.

whelming majority of jobs in the other two sectors (84 percent) have emanated from the tertiary sector. This is completely consistent, of course, with our output share analysis above.

Two additional sectoral shifts are crucial to note. First, job destruction in the primary sectors is very clear. Specifically, agriculture and mining together lost almost 72,000 jobs. One factor contributing to declines in agricultural employment over this period was the introduction of a minimum wage in March 2003 (Bhorat and others 2012). The poor performance of the mining sector can be attributed to a range of factors, including a strongly appreciating Rand in the mid-2000s, infrastructural constraints (such as rail transport), energy constraints, and the application of new mining laws in South Africa (Organization of Economic Cooperation and Development [OECD] 2008). The recent widespread strike action in the mining sector in 2010 and 2011 exacerbated the problems.

Second, consistent with the lack of dynamism in manufacturing, employment levels in the sector have stagnated. Hence, it is instructive that the South African manufacturing sector has generated just over 110,000 jobs over an eleven-year period, yielding a relative employment growth rate of only 0.3 percent per annum. In contrast, the relative employment growth rates of the transport, finance, and community, social, and personal (CSP) services sectors all exceed 2 percent per annum. Employment and growth generators in the South African economy since 2001 have been disproportionately located in the services sectors.

In terms of the share of this change in employment since 2001, the last column in table 7-3 provides a key insight into the scale of this economic and employment shift. In particular, then, we see that the CSP sector and the financial and business services accounted for 73 percent of the total employment shift in this period. As a result, the financial sector now accounts for 13.5 percent of employment, from 10 percent a decade ago. The CSP result suggests, in the first instance, that one of the biggest drivers of job creation since 2004 has been the expansion of employment in the public sector, which makes up the majority of community, social, and personal services. Hence, from contributing 17 percent of employment in 2001, the broader industry now accounts for 22.5 percent of employment, once again making it the largest industry by employment. Furthermore, public sector employment is the main driver of employment growth in the tertiary sector. This rising trend in public sector employment is an important focus of this paper, and is discussed in more detail later.

In essence, we observe important and new characteristics relative to the early post-apartheid years: job destruction in the primary sectors, a manufacturing sector that has been ineffective as a generator of large-scale jobs, and a tertiary sector that has stepped in to fill this vacuum. Employment has, thus, disproportionately emanated from the tradable and nontradable services sectors. We turn next to a relatively new phenomenon characterizing job creation in South Africa, the rise of temporary employment services.

Rise of Temporary Employment Services

In terms of the second largest sectoral contributor to the overall employment change, the financial and business services industry result is slightly more complex, given that this sector is not often a large generator of jobs. Disaggregating the sources of employment in the financial sector reveals an interesting pattern: employment growth in financial services is about growth in the business service colloquially known as "labor brokering" or, as it is known globally, temporary employment services (TES) provision. This statistical hidden identity of the TES sector arises because the labor force survey data does not list TES as a separate sector, but houses it within the financial and business services sector, classifying it as the subsector Business Services Not Elsewhere Classified (NEC). TES employment essentially involves the practice of companies providing, as a third-party employer, workers across various occupations (such as cleaning, accounting, secretarial, security services, and so on) to formal sector firms. The latter, then, do not directly hire these workers. TES employment as a percentage of the financial industry employment increased rapidly in the post-apartheid period in South Africa from 26.64 percent in 1995 to 47.36 percent in 2014. As a proportion of total employment, while remaining quite small, TES employment has nearly tripled, by increasing from 2.22 percent to 6.44 percent over the same period.[7]

To understand where employment is actually concentrated within the Business Activities Not Elsewhere Classified (NEC) sector for the period 1999 to 2014, our analysis shows that Protective Services Workers Not Elsewhere Classified[8] accounted for the relatively largest share of the employed, at between 43 percent and 47 percent.[9] The second largest share, at 15 percent, was accounted for by commercial helpers and cleaners (as opposed to residential cleaners), highlighting the increased use of contract cleaners over this time. By 2014, 6 percent of those employed in this subsector were categorized as farmhands and laborers, compared to an almost negligible category in 1999 (only 131 employed as farmhands and laborers). While this employment category remains relatively small, Bhorat and Mayet (2012) point out that the rapid growth in this type of employment classification is reflective of increased labor broker recruitment in this area of work.

There are two possible explanations here. One is that these results suggest that the rapid expansion of employment related to protective and crime-prevention services is a response to South Africa's high crime rate. At another level, these results provide some powerful evidence of the rise of labor-brokering agencies that have for some time been an important topic of public debate in the country. In this debate, it is the burden of South Africa's regulatory environment that is often thought to be a central factor in the rise of TES employment. This form of employment, while not always offering lower direct costs of employment, often allow firms to circumvent the indirect costs of employment thought to reside in the economy's labor regulatory environment (Bhorat and van der Westhuizen 2013).

To assess whether South Africa's scores on a set of normalized employment protection legislation measures are indicative of an over-regulated or rigid labor market, Bhorat and others (2015a) use the 2013 World Bank's Doing Business survey to provide a comparison of South Africa's measures of labor regulation against other regions of the world. As table 7-4 indicates, low-income and high-income OECD countries exhibit the highest average scores of labor market rigidity, nonwage labor costs, and firing costs. Countries that lie between these two extreme income categories exhibit two distinct patterns. First, there is declining rigidity and firing costs as income level rises; and second, nonwage labor costs rise with income level, as is expected.

South Africa's rankings for the firing costs and nonwage labor costs indices are both below its income category (upper middle-income) means, and the global means. While South Africa's difficulty of firing and rigidity of hours indices are above the respective income category and global means, it is the difficulty of hiring index that stands out as remarkably high. Therefore, as Bhorat and others (2015a) highlight, South Africa's labor legislation framework maintains a relatively flexible

TABLE 7-4. *Mean Measures of Labor Regulation by Income Level*[a] *in South Africa, 2006–2013*

Area of regulation	Low income	Lower-middle income	Upper-middle income	High-income: Non-OECD	High-income: OECD	South Africa	All countries
Difficulty of hiring[b]	50.89	35.28	30.40	17.79	27.72	55.67	33.13
Difficulty of firing[c]	36.88	33.96	25.60	16.25	22.26	30.00	27.95
Rigidity of hours[d]	19.38	18.33	14.00	16.67	24.52	20.00	18.16
Aggregate rigidity of employment index	35.71	29.19	23.33	16.90	24.83	35.22	26.41
Non-wage labor costs[e]	12.40	16.01	17.31	21.43	10.17	2.40	15.62
Firing costs[f]	65.32	50.91	44.63	31.32	54.64	24.00	51.34

Source: Bhorat and others (2015a) using World Bank (2013) data; Benjamin and others (2010).

a. Regarding the consistency of South Africa's ranking over time, the 2013 results show no change in South Africa's relative position (compared to each country income-category and the global averages) in the aggregate rigidity of employment index from 2006 to 2013.

b. The "difficulty of hiring" index measures restrictions on part-time and temporary contracts, together with the wages of trainees relative to worker value-added.

c. The "difficulty of firing" index assesses and ranks specific legislative provisions on dismissals.

d. The "rigidity of hours" index measures the various restrictions around weekend, Sunday, and public holiday work, limits on overtime, and so on.

e. "Labor costs" indicates results from the 2006 *Doing Business Report*, which focused on the jobs challenge and, thus, provided more detailed labor market indicators.

f. "Firing costs" measures the cost of terminating the employment of an individual in terms of legislated prior notice requirements, severance pay, and so on.

labor market in terms of hiring and firing costs; however, the legislated procedural requirements on hiring workers introduces a degree of regulatory inflexibility. Benjamin and others (2010) argue, however, that the World Bank's Doing Business survey does not measure the inefficiency of the labor courts system, which potentially adds a very high cost to the firing of workers. Thus, it is arguably these degrees of inflexibility that firms can overcome through employing workers through labor brokers or temporary employment service providers.

Human Capital and Skills-Biased Labor Demand

The rising shares of tertiary sector employment have implications for the underlying occupational shifts as they relate to skills levels. This section looks more closely at South Africa's educational profile and the economy's skills-biased growth trajectory to better understand the underlying implications for the labor market.

Weaknesses in South Africa's Educational System

One of the fundamentally destructive legacies of the apartheid government's reign was a highly unequal schooling system and a tertiary system that was not accessible to those with poor levels of schooling. While there have been enormous strides in the last twenty years to increase access to schooling, the poor quality of schooling in South Africa remains a critical challenge.

Enrollment in primary school in South Africa has reached almost 100 percent, supported by a no-fee policy for children from poor households, fulfilling the constitutionally enshrined right to basic education for all children. This is, no doubt, a positive development over time; however, the average quality of the schooling provided to all these children remains weak. Comparing the grade 6 standardized mathematics and reading scores from SACMEQ III (Southern and Eastern Africa Consortium for Monitoring Educational Quality) for a number of African countries, South Africa's average for both subjects fall below many other countries, such as Tanzania, Swaziland, Kenya, Botswana, and Zimbabwe, as well as below the African mean scores (Presidency 2014).[10] In addition, using TIMSS (2011) data for grade 8 students, we can compare the results of standardized mathematics and science tests. The results show that South Africa does not compare favorably to comparator countries such as Turkey, Thailand, Botswana, and Chile, and is actually one of the worst performing countries. More than 50 percent of grade 8 pupils in South Africa score below 400 for mathematics—the low international benchmark score—and a mere 6 percent score above 550 (the high international benchmark score).[11] South African pupils perform equally poorly on the standardized science test.

As such, South Africa's education system is comprised of a very high primary school enrollment rate, a very low dropout rate before grade 6, and low-level learning for those who do complete grade 6 (Spaull and Taylor 2015). High levels of between-school inequality in learning outcomes have also shown to be strongly dependent on the socioeconomic differentials, where clearly the South African schooling system—and poorer schools, in particular—has not been able to overcome inherited socioeconomic disadvantages (van der Berg 2006). Thus, for every 100 pupils who start school in South Africa, fifty make it to grade 12 (final year of high school), forty will pass, and only twelve will qualify for university (Spaull 2013). There is considerable education research to suggest that learning deficits are acquired early on, during primary school, and grow each year until they become insurmountable, leading to failure (and thus grade repetition), and eventual dropout during grades 10 to 12. Research using two waves of the National Income Dynamics Survey panel data confirms the notion that grade repetition—a signal of learning deficits—is a key determinant of school dropout even after controlling for school quality and socioeconomic status (Branson and others 2013). Given the significantly positive returns to higher education in the South African labor market, it is not surprising that the extremely high levels of income inequality have persisted.

Clearly, the South African government has found it difficult to influence the quality of education over time, which is evident in the numerous changes to the national curriculum. The outcomes-based curriculum was introduced in 2005 and, due to implementation problems, was replaced by various revisions between 2011 and 2014 (Presidency

2014). Some of the important supply-side challenges to educational outcomes over the last two decades have been related to the delivery of basic school materials (particularly textbooks), as well as the lack of establishing minimum standards for school infrastructure and teacher quality.

The country's education crisis has had important implications for the levels of human capital available in the workforce. There has been notable improvement. The proportions of those in the workforce with no education, incomplete primary school education, or completed primary education as their highest educational attainment, have all declined substantially since 1994.[12] However, the current educational profile of the employed shows that only 20 percent have post-secondary education and 32 percent have a high school completion. Of the remaining half of the workforce, 70 percent have an incomplete secondary education as their highest level of education. The South Africa workforce is, at best, a semi-skilled workforce.

More worrying, then, is that one-third of the unemployed also have a complete high school qualification, a proportion that has risen from 17.5 percent in 1994. These are individuals who, though having a basic level of education, do not possess the skills in demand in the workplace or are otherwise ill prepared for the work force. A further 48 percent of unemployed are those who have dropped out of high school, most likely due to accumulated learning deficits as a result of being educated in poorly resourced schools, with poor teacher quality and an inability to provide remedial classes to those pupils who most need it. The returns to these lower levels of education in the South African labor market remain low, which has wide-reaching consequences for future generations of these unemployed individuals. This, in turn, will likely serve to perpetuate high levels of inequality as these individuals are excluded from the benefits of economic and employment growth, and perhaps also from accessing opportunities for self-employment.

Skills-Biased Labor Demand

Table 7-5 explores the interaction between occupational skills and sectoral changes for the 2001–12 period. A few key observations emerge. First, the primary sector lost more than half a million medium-skilled

TABLE 7-5. *Changes in Skills Shares by Sector, South Africa, 2001–12*

Percent unless otherwise specified

	Within sector shares					Change over 2001–12	
	2001	*2004*	*2007*	*2010*	*2012*	*Percent*	*Number of jobs in category*
Primary							
High skilled	2.9	5.4	4.8	7.2	7.6	4.8	27,602
Medium skilled	54.5	52.5	53.1	35.2	36.8	−17.7	−571,229*
Unskilled	42.6	42.1	42.1	57.6	55.5	12.9	−175,392*
Total	100	100	100	100	100		−719,232*
Secondary							
High skilled	14.2	15.3	16.6	19	18.1	3.9	188,518*
Medium skilled	69.8	64.7	63.6	64.2	61.5	−8.3	136,140
Unskilled	16	19.9	19.8	16.8	20.4	4.4	214,002*
Total	100	100	100	100	100		537,376*
Tertiary							
High skilled	27.4	27.1	31.8	28.3	29.3	1.9	931,498*
Medium skilled	41.8	41.5	39.8	42.6	42.6	0.8	1,214,349*
Unskilled	30.8	31.4	28.4	29.1	28.1	−2.7	576,288*
Total	100	100	100	100	100		2,720,821*

Source: Bhorat and others (2014) based on StatsSA LFS (2001–07) and PALMS (DataFirst 2014) data.

The primary sector includes agriculture and mining; the secondary sector includes manufacturing, utilities, and construction; and the tertiary sector includes trade, transport, financial services, community services, and private households.

High-skilled workers include managers and professionals; medium-skilled workers include clerks, service and sales workers, skilled agricultural and fishery workers, craft and trade workers, and operators and assemblers; and unskilled workers include elementary workers and domestic workers.

* denotes a significant change at the 5 percent level based on a simple t-test in STATA.

jobs and 175,000 unskilled jobs over the period, with no significant change in the number of high-skilled jobs. Over the period, there was positive output growth in both agriculture and mining, which suggests, then, that an increase in the capital intensity of production resulted in the reduction of medium-skilled and unskilled labor.

Second, the secondary sector saw an increase of about half a million jobs over the period, predominantly in high-skilled and unskilled employment. Therefore, while the proportion of unskilled workers in the sector rose significantly, it remains low at 20 percent of employment. Medium-skilled workers continue to make up the large majority of employment in the secondary sector. Growth in employment was driven primarily by the construction sector, which was boosted by investment in infrastructure for the 2010 Football World Cup.

Finally, then, it is clear that the tertiary sector was the largest creator of jobs between 2001 and 2012, growing by 2.7 million workers. While employment grew significantly across the skills spectrum, more than 70 percent of the increase in jobs was associated with high- and medium-skilled employment. As a result, both the proportions of high-skilled and medium-skilled workers in the sector rose, while the proportion of unskilled workers marginally declined. By 2012, high-skilled workers accounted for just under 30 percent of tertiary sector workers, while medium-skilled and unskilled workers accounted for 42.6 percent—adding up to approximately three-quarters of the sector's workforce. Interestingly, the major occupational group within the TES subsector is service and sales workers—medium-skilled employees—which account for slightly less than half of overall TES employment. Therefore, TES employment growth has also been an important contributor to the shifting skills shares seen in the table.

Overall, both the secondary and tertiary sectors witnessed a rise in the proportion of high-skilled employment, along with a rise in the proportion of medium-skilled employment in the tertiary sector. At the same time, the primary and tertiary sectors saw declining proportions of unskilled labor. It has earlier been shown that employment losses between 1994 and 2003 were likely due to skills-biased technological changes, though trade liberalization accounts for some of the change (Bhorat and Hodge 1999; Bhorat 2001; Dunne and Edwards 2006; Bhorat and others 2014). This trend seems to have continued over the last decade. In the context of a growing economy, it would suggest that firms are investing in capital and skills, causing the shift away from unskilled labor. The results show that while unskilled employment rose in both secondary and tertiary sectors, the proportion of unskilled workers rose only in the secondary sector. Both the primary and secondary sectors of the economy witnessed dramatically declining proportions of medium-skilled workers.

To have employment disproportionately favoring the skilled is a huge long-run concern for an economy like South Africa's, which has an excess supply of labor that is greater than most other emerging markets in the world as well as serious challenges in improving access to and quality of secondary and higher education. It is clear that the tradable sectors have adopted production techniques that are increasingly capital-intensive. Essentially, the mismatch between labor demand and labor supply goes to the heart of what is wrong with the structure of South Africa's growth pattern.

ROLE OF THE PUBLIC SECTOR IN EMPLOYMENT

While the growth in TES employment is novel and involves regulatory avoidance, the rise of public sector employment has a much greater potential import for the future trajectory of the economy's employment path. This is the focus of the rest of the chapter. Table 7-6 shows that the total number of public sector employment has increased from 2.16 million in 2008 to 2.69 million at the end of 2014—an increase of more than half a million jobs in a six-year period. We further disaggregate public sector employment here into government (national, provincial, and local) and state-owned enterprises (SOEs). Public sector employment is largely dominated by national, provincial, and local government, which has accounted for about 88 percent of public sector employment over the period.

Therefore, from constituting 14.5 percent of total employment at the beginning of 2008, the share of public sector employment has risen to 17.5 percent by the end of 2014—which is 1.2 times the 2008 share. The data also makes it clear that the growth in public sector employment is driven by employment in national, provincial, and local government structures, as opposed to employment in state-owned enterprises. The latter has maintained a stable share in overall employment since 2008. Evident in table 7-6, the fastest period of public sector employment

TABLE 7-6. *Employment in the Public Sector, 2008–14, South Africa*

Year	Government[a]	SOEs	Total	Year-to-year change in share of public sector total employment	Share in employment index
2008 Q4	1,903,027	254,920	2,157,947	n.a.	1.00
2009 Q4	1,912,965	265,561	2,178,526	6.79	1.07
2010 Q4	1,960,613	292,007	2,252,620	3.92	1.11
2011 Q4	2,104,959	281,393	2,386,352	2.72	1.14
2012 Q4	2,215,565	318,064	2,533,629	4.81	1.20
2013 Q4	2,328,769	319,749	2,648,518	0.00	1.20
2014 Q4	2,365,131	322,960	2,688,091	0.46	1.21

Source: StatsSA QLFS (2008–2014), authors' calculations.
a. "Government" comprises national, provincial, and local governments.

growth was during 2009, immediately following the global financial crises, during which South Africa experienced significant job losses. This suggests that the state possibly acted as an unintended creator of jobs during a period of extreme labor market distress. Public sector employment growth was also high in 2012, after which employment stabilized.

For the more than half a million jobs created in the public sector over the 2008–14 period, figure 7-2 plots the contribution of each occupation toward this change. Many of the occupations that are large contributors to public sector job growth fall under the category of elementary occupations (unskilled workers): sweepers and related laborers, farmhands and laborers, helpers and cleaners, construction and maintenance laborers, and garbage collectors. The other major contributors to public sector jobs creation are primarily within the service and related workers category (medium-skilled workers): police and traffic officers, institution- and home-based care workers, other protective services, prison guards, technikon teacher training, cooks, and childcare workers.[13] Apart from jobs in these two broad occupations, higher skilled jobs such as primary and secondary school teachers, finance and administrative managers, and legislators have also contributed to public sector job growth.

From this brief analysis, it would seem that the government's Expanded Public Works Program (EPWP) is an important driver of

FIGURE 7-2. *Share of Change in Public Sector Jobs by Detailed Occupation, 2008 Q1–2014 Q4*

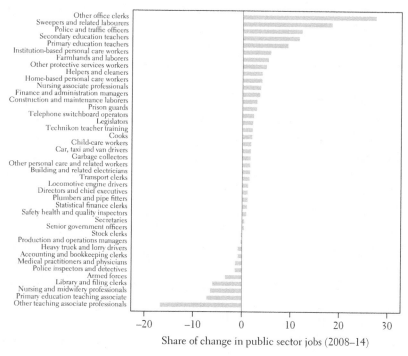

Share of change in public sector jobs (2008–14)

Source: StatsSA QLFS 2008Q1, StatsSA QLFS 2014Q4, authors' calculations.
Note: These occupations are the largest 42 public sector occupations, making up 80 percent of total employment in the public sector in 2014, and 97 percent of the change in the number of public sector jobs over the 2008–14 period.

public sector job creation. The EPWP was launched in 2004, and focuses on providing income relief through creating jobs for the unemployed and unskilled that involve socially useful activities. The EPWP creates jobs through government-funded infrastructure projects, through its nonprofit organization and community work program, as well as through its public environment and culture programs. As such, much of the public sector job growth shown in figure 7-2 relates to the construction industry, the protection and safety sector, public sanitation, and personal care industries. Apart from EPWP, this data provides some evidence of the South African government's attempts to address the education crisis through increasing the number of primary and secondary school teachers within the public schooling system.

Table 7-7 clearly shows that there are significant differences between the average profile of employees in the public and private sectors, across all the demographic indicators and occupational categories, and for both time periods. The average age of public sector workers is forty-one years old, compared to thirty-eight in the private sector. Public sector workers have a significantly higher average educational level in both time periods, with this average rising faster in the public sector than the private. Females have greater representation in the public sector, making up 52 percent of the respective workforce, compared to 44 percent in the private sector. From making up 72 percent and 66 percent of public and private sector employees in 2008, respectively, Africans now make up 77 percent of public sector employment, with little change in this proportion in the private sector. There have been no changes in the proportion of Indian and Coloured[14] workers in either sector, and white workers make up a smaller proportion of workers in both sectors now than they did in 2008. The public sector has clearly been able to transform its labor force at a faster pace than the private sector, given the higher proportion of both women and African workers in the sector—groups that have faced historical discrimination in the South African labor market.

In terms of the skills profile of each sector, the data shows that the public sector is more skills-intensive. Almost 45 percent of all public sector employees fall into the top three occupational categories, compared to 26 percent of workers in the private sector. Both sectors, however, have a similar proportion of unskilled (elementary) workers, which indicates that private sector workers are concentrated in the medium-skilled occupations. Interestingly, the proportion of the two most skills-intensive occupations have not changed in the public sector between 2008 and 2013, but the proportion of professionals in the private sector has increased by 25 percent—consistent with the skills-biased labor demand shifts discussed earlier. As shown in figure 7-2, growth in public sector jobs was driven by the medium-skilled occupation of service workers, as well as in elementary occupations, where these shares grew by 31 percent and 23 percent, respectively. Again, this may point to the

TABLE 7-7. *Mean Characteristics of Public and Private Sector Workers, 2008 and 2013,*[a] *South Africa*

	2008	2013	2008–13	
	Ratio of means (public / private)	Ratio of means (public / private)	Percent Δ Public	Percent Δ Private
Demographics				
Age	1.10*	1.07*	0.51	2.63
Male	0.84*	0.86*	−2.04	−3.45
Race				
African	1.09*	1.15*	6.94	1.52
Colored	0.91	0.91*	0	0
Indian/Asian	0.50*	0.50*	0	0
White	0.83*	0.65*	−26.67	−5.56
Years of school	1.07*	1.10*	4.12	1.04
Married[b]	1.15*	1.09*	−4.92	0
Union[c]	2.27*	3.18*	2.34	−26.91
Occupation:				
Legislators, senior officials, and managers	0.60*	0.60*	0	0
Professionals	1.83*	1.57*	0	25
Technical and associate professionals	4.13*	3.00*	−18.18	10.48
Clerks	1.25*	1.25*	0	0
Service, shop, and market workers	1.18*	1.31*	30.77	18.18
Craft and related trades workers	0.36*	0.33*	−20	−14.29
Plant and machine operators, and assemblers	0.30*	0.30*	0	0
Elementary occupation	0.76	0.94*	23.08	0

Source: StatsSA QLFS (2008, Quarter 4), StatsSA LMDS (2013), authors' calculations.

a. Public sector includes all levels of government and state-owned enterprises (SOEs). Non-public sector excludes those working in agriculture or the informal sector.

b. Married includes individuals who are married or have partners and live together.

c. Union data is from the 2007 QLFS: Q4.

* Indicates that the mean for the public and private sectors for each characteristic is significantly different at a 5 percent significance level.

state being able to absorb excess unskilled and medium-skilled labor at times of economic and labor market distress.

Therefore, public sector workers are more educated, older, more skilled, and mostly African in comparison with the formal private sector. Furthermore, the data shows that the public sector is more gender equitable than the private sector.

Bargaining Power and the Wage Premium

Another feature of the public sector labor market is the relatively higher rates of unionization, which is often associated with a wage premium. Bhorat and others (2015a) show that the proportion of the public sector's formal workforce who are union members—or the public sector's union density—rose from 55 percent in 1997 (834,000 workers) to almost 70 percent in 2013 (1.4 million workers). The private sector union density displays the opposite overall trend, declining from 36 percent in 1997 (1.8 million workers) to 24 percent in 2013 (1.9 million workers), while the absolute number of private sector unionized workers has remained fairly constant.

Interestingly, as employment in the public sector has risen, so has membership of public sector trade unions, to the extent that they now dominate union membership in South Africa. Not only, then, do we witness a rise in public sector employment, but this data also makes it clear that this employment rise has been commensurate with the rise of public sector trade unions in South Africa.

Powerful labor unions are often associated with creating a wage premium for their members, given their ability to mobilize industrial action and negotiate in favor of their members during times of wage negotiations. There is extensive literature on the union wage gap in South Africa, but slightly fewer studies on the bargaining council premium.[15] Taking account of this, Bhorat and others (2012) use the 2005 South African Labor Force Survey data to investigate the union and bargaining council wage premiums and correct for the endogeneity of union status through a two-stage selection model, controlling for firm-level and job characteristics. In their most richly specified estimation,[16] it is found that union members outside of the bargaining council system earned a premium of 7.04 percent and those members of private and public bargaining councils not belonging to unions earned an 8.97 percent and 10.5 percent premium over nonunion workers outside of the bargaining council system, respectively.[17] The total estimated premium to union workers within the public bargaining council stands at 22 percent.[18] Therefore, there is evidence that belonging to either unions or bargaining councils is associated with statistically significant wage premiums, and, furthermore, that unions may negotiate at the plant level for additional gains for their members within the bargaining council system.

When comparing wage levels between the public and private sectors, the data shows that both median and mean wages of the public sector are significantly higher than that of the private sector (which is confirmed by simple t-tests). The real monthly wage of an average public sector employee is R11,668 (US$1,209) compared to R7,822 (US$811) for an average private sector worker.[19]

Disaggregating the wage distributions by unionization reveals a slightly different picture (figure 7-3). For nonunionized workers, the average real monthly wage in the private sector is statistically significantly larger than that of the public sector, by a margin of R952 (US$99). While small, this suggests that the public sector premium is negative, or at the least disappears, for workers who do not belong to a union. Therefore, this provides some initial evidence that the public sector premium may be very closely tied to a public sector union membership premium.

Our analysis confirms that the 30 percent of public sector workers who are not union members are, on average, distinctly (and statistically) different from those who are unionized on a number of characteristics. Unionized public sector workers are slightly older, more likely to be male, and have a higher average level of education than nonunionized public sector employees. African employees make up almost 80 percent of nonunion public sector employees, and Coloured workers a further 10 percent. Most important, though, nonunionized public sector workers are concentrated in elementary occupations (30 percent), service and sales occupations (16 percent), and technical and associate professional occupations (16 percent). While it remains uncertain, the nonunionized workers in the first two occupational groups are likely to be those employed under the EPWP.

FIGURE 7-3. *Wage Distributions for Public and Private (Non-Public) Formal Sector Employees, by Union Status, 2013*

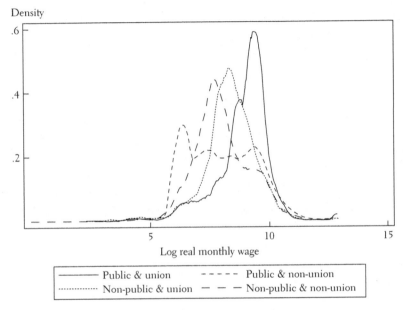

Source: StatsSA LMDS (2013), authors' graph.
Note: Non-public sector excludes agriculture and the informal sector. A two-sample Kolmogorov-Smirnov test of the equality of distributions confirms that the distributions of unionized workers' wages by sector are significantly different from each other, as are the distributions of wages for non-unionized workers by each sector. Within the public sector, the wage distributions of unionized workers are significantly different from nonunionized workers, and similarly for the private sector.

Ultimately though, these wage distributions suggest that, at least in terms of earnings, a dual labor market may, indeed, be prevalent in the South African labor market. Previous models of segmentation in the South African labor market have commonly referred to the distinction between the employed and the unemployed, or more recently, the formal and informal sector (Hofmeyr 1998; Bhorat and Leibbrandt 1999; Fields 2000; Devey and others 2006; Valodia 2007) as the key identifying markers of this segmentation. We suggest a nuance to South Africa's segmented labor market here. In particular, and on the initial evidence of these bimodal wage distributions, it would appear that the distinction between public and private sector, in terms of earnings and employment, would seem to be a new form of segmentation that has evolved in the South African labor market.

An Econometric Estimation

To investigate the public sector wage premium more rigorously, we estimate a two-stage Heckman employment model correcting for selection into the labor market. In this respect, then, the standard earnings function of the following form is run:

$$y_i = \propto + \beta_1 X_i + \delta PS_i + \mu U_i + \eta(PS_i \times U_i) + \gamma TES_i + \varepsilon_i$$

Equation (1)

where y_i represents each individual's, i, log monthly real earnings, X_i is a vector of individual characteristics, PS_i indicates whether an individual is employed in the public sector or not, U_i indicates whether an individual is a union member or not, TES_i is a dummy variable for whether the individual is employed in the TES sector or not, and ε_i is a normally distributed error term. δ shows the wage premium for public sector workers who do not belong to a union, and coefficient μ provides the wage premium for union members who are not employed in the public or TES sectors. The sum of coefficients $(\delta + \eta)$ yields the conditional estimate for the public sector premium of unionized workers. In our richest estimation, we split the public sector dummy variable into two separate dummies for government employment and SOE employment:

$$y_i = \propto + \beta_1 X_i + \delta Gov_i + \tau SOE_i + \mu U_i + z(Gov_i \times U_i)$$
$$+ y(SOE_i \times U_i) + \gamma TES_i + \varepsilon_i$$

Equation (2)

The results of the OLS earnings function are shown in table 7-8. In specifications 1 and 3, we model the public sector as a whole, while in 2 and 4, we disaggregate it into government employment and SOE employment. Specification 3 is differentiated from specification 1 by interacting the public sector dummy with the union dummy, and similarly for specification 4, government and SOE are interacted with the union dummy.

In the first two specifications, which merely control for union membership, we find no significant wage premium for workers in the

TABLE 7-8. *Estimated Earnings Function, Corrected for Selection Bias,*[c,f] *South Africa, 2013*

Log of real monthly wages[a]	Specifications			
	(1)	(2)	(3)	(4)
Government level				
Public sector[d]	0.0109	. . .	−0.205***	. . .
	(0.0162)	. . .	(0.0223)	. . .
Government[e]	. . .	0.0194	. . .	−0.233***
	. . .	(0.0165)	. . .	(0.0230)
SOE	. . .	−0.0392	. . .	−0.0287
	. . .	(0.0393)	. . .	(0.0619)
Interaction with union				
Public*Union	. . .	. . .	0.393***	. . .
	. . .	. . .	(0.0285)	. . .
Government*Union	. . .	. . .	. . .	0.444***
	. . .	. . .	. . .	(0.0294)
SOE*Union	. . .	. . .	. . .	0.0558
	. . .	. . .	. . .	(0.0785)
Union	0.318***	0.317***	0.207***	0.207***
	(0.0139)	(0.0139)	(0.0162)	(0.0162)
TES	−0.108***	−0.108***	−0.111***	−0.110***
	(0.0209)	(0.0209)	(0.0209)	(0.0209)
Lambda	−0.180***	−0.179***	−0.165***	−0.162***
	(0.0353)	(0.0354)	(0.0352)	(0.0352)
Observations[b]	52,475	52,475	52,475	52,475
R-squared	0.402	0.402	0.406	0.406

Source: StatsSA LMDS (2013), authors' calculations.

a. Dependent variable is log of real monthly wages.

b. We exclude the agricultural sector and informal workers. Therefore, we only considered those employed in the formal non-agricultural sectors, who are within the 15–65 age category.

c. We include the following controls: gender, age, race, education splines, province dummies, whether the person lives in an urban or rural location, occupation dummies, and firm size.

d. The public sector is made up of both government and state-owned enterprises (SOEs), which are interrogated separately in specifications (2) and (4).

e. "Government" is comprised of national, provincial, and local governments.

f. Robust standard errors in parentheses.

*** $p < 0.01$, ** $p < 0.05$, * $p < 0.1$.

public sector. The union membership premium, however, is large and significant at 37 percent.[20] Given our earlier analysis, however, it seems likely that the interaction between union membership and public sector employment would reveal a more interesting picture. The results of the interacted specifications show that, for nonunionized members, there is a wage penalty for working in the public sector, relative to the private sector, of 18.5 percent. In addition, there is also a wage penalty associated with TES employment for nonunionized workers. For unionized workers, however, the public sector wage premium is 20.7 percent.[21] In particular, for government workers, the wage premium within the group of workers belonging to a union is 23.5 percent, whereas there is no significant wage premium for employees of SOEs.

Therefore, these initial results show that, when also controlling for TES employment, there is no public sector wage premium. However, as a member of a union, the premium is significant and large. This result is certainly novel. Earlier estimates of the public sector wage premium are provided by Woolard (2002), who finds a premium of 18 percent for public sector workers. Her results also show that the premium is higher for women (21 percent) than for men, and particularly for African women, who were associated with a 36 percent premium. While these results control for union membership, there is no interaction of union membership with public sector employment.

Given the rising membership of public sector unions already shown, together with the growing political influence of these unions, these results possibly allude to the role played by unions in driving higher returns for their members in the post-2000 period. This pattern of wage returns potentially suggests segmentation between unionized public sector workers versus all other formal, nonagricultural workers.

A more nuanced analysis of the public sector wage premium can be performed using quantile regressions, presented in table 7-9. This analysis is conducted to investigate whether the results shown in table 7-8 are purely mean effects (for example, driven only by a few specific occupations that, then, influence the mean wage premium), or whether the premium exists across the income distribution. Recall that quantile regressions refer to the generalized case of the least absolute deviations estimator. While through ordinary least squared estimation, as per the above estimations, we derive a sample mean by minimizing the sum of squared residuals, the sample median can be derived through minimizing the sum of absolute residuals (Koenker and Bassett 1978; Koenker and Hallock 2001).

We estimate the returns to government and SOE employment using interacted variables, presented in table 7-9. The coefficients of interest are plotted in figure 7-4. The results show that for South African workers

TABLE 7-9. *Estimated Quantile Earnings Function with Interactions, Corrected for Selection Bias,*[c,d] *South Africa, 2013*

Log of real monthly wages[a]	Specifications				
	(1) 10th	(2) 25th	(3) 50th	(4) 75th	(5) 90th
Government (non-union)	-0.239***	-0.447***	-0.316***	-0.0966***	-0.0237
	(0.0292)	(0.0146)	(0.0272)	(0.031)	(0.0240)
SOE (non-union)	-0.0792	-0.0783**	-0.0336	0.128***	0.0307
	(0.122)	(0.0324)	(0.0593)	(0.0352)	(0.0218)
Union (non-public sector)	0.225***	0.227***	0.229***	0.221***	0.186***
	(0.0289)	(0.0188)	(0.0128)	(0.0142)	(0.0206)
Government*Union	0.334***	0.680***	0.636***	0.374***	0.164***
	(0.0562)	(0.0316)	(0.0319)	(0.0361)	(0.0293)
SOE*Union	-0.111	0.0699	0.103	0.104*	0.137**
	(0.153)	(0.104)	(0.0791)	(0.0537)	(0.0542)
TES	0.126***	0.00510	-0.126***	-0.224***	-0.284***
	(0.0331)	(0.0183)	(0.0148)	(0.0178)	(0.0322)
Lambda	0.00453	-0.105***	-0.218***	-0.238***	-0.280***
	(0.0544)	(0.0371)	(0.0300)	(0.0346)	(0.0407)
Observations[b]	52,475	52,475	52,475	52,475	52,475

Source: StatsSA LMDS (2013), authors' calculations.

a. The dependent variable is log of real monthly wages.

b. We exclude the agricultural sector and informal workers. Therefore, we only considered those employed in the formal non-agricultural sectors, who are within the 15–65 age category.

c. We include the following controls: gender, age, race, education splines, province dummies, whether the person lives in an urban or rural location, occupation dummies, and firm size.

d. Robust standard errors in parentheses.

*** $p < 0.01$, ** $p < 0.05$, * $p < 0.1$.

FIGURE 7-4. *Estimated Public Sector Wage Premia across the Wage Distribution, 2013*

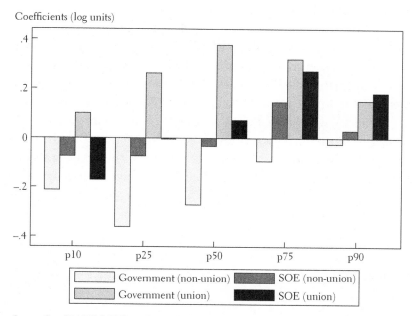

Source: StatsSA LMDS (2013), authors' calculations.

who do not belong to a union, there are significant wage penalties associated with government employment, across the wage distribution. This penalty is highest at the 25th percentile and decreases toward the highest wage levels. The wage returns for nonunionized workers to SOE employment has a different pattern. There are small wage penalties below the median wage; however, this becomes positive and high at the 75th percentile.

For unionized workers in the labor market, there are high and positive returns to government employment relative to those unionized workers in the non-TES private sector. The median wage premium is 37 percent, which declines to 15 percent at the 90th percentile. Unionized employees at SOEs only experience positive wage premiums in the top quartile of the distribution, relative to non-TES private sector unionized workers in this same quartile.

In summary, our results do not show any significant average public sector premium using the latest data available. Instead, we find average wage penalties to government employment at lower wage levels, and positive wage premiums at higher levels, while controlling for union membership that is associated with positive wage premiums across the distribution. When isolating unionized workers, we find that there are significantly large wage premiums associated with government employment relative to unionized workers in non-TES private sectors.

Therefore, we find that a key new facet of the South African labor market is an estimated wage wedge between unionized public sector workers and other formal nonagricultural workers in the labor market. In one conception, we could argue that the post-2000 period has generated a new labor elite in the labor market, namely the unionized public sector employee.

FINAL REFLECTIONS ON THE CURRENT MARKET TRENDS

South Africa's economic growth over the past two decades has been driven primarily by the services sector; namely the financial and business services sector, construction, and to some extent wholesale and retail trade. Employment growth has been driven by services sectors and, in particular, higher-skilled occupations. This is against a backdrop of stark human capital deficits that are a result of elevated rates of high-school dropouts and low levels of learning for those who do complete high school. In combination, these two factors are arguably central to the persistently high levels of unemployment and inequality.

The growth of the TES sector was shown to be a relatively new labor market trend. Part of the growth in services employment has been the rise in labor brokers that source workers for the TES sector. On the surface, it seems to be related to South Africa's stringent labor market regulations, however, this needs deeper investigation.

This chapter has also shown that an important trend in the South African labor market has been the rising share of workers in the public sector, and in government in particular. Job creation in government over the last six years is concentrated in unskilled and medium-skilled occupations, and the data suggests that it may be linked to a government-led program to create jobs for the unemployed and the unskilled in activities relating to infrastructure building, public safety, and other community-based public service jobs.

Overall, though, we see higher average wages in the public sector relative to the private sector. Estimations of the wage premiums for public sector workers show that much of the difference in public–private wages has to do with union membership. For unionized workers in the South African labor market, employment in government is associated with significantly higher returns than private sector employment. We show, then, a key new form of segmentation in the South African labor market, namely between the higher earning unionized public sector worker and the rest of the labor market.

Ordinarily such segmentation would be of general curiosity and academic interest. However, coupled with a sclerotic economy that is unable to generate large numbers of jobs in the private sector (most notably in manufacturing), or where its firms are actively engaged in avoiding direct employment, this result is particularly worrying. A long-run employment trajectory built on the public sector requires critical reassessment as part of a broader revitalizing of the economy's growth and development strategy.

NOTES

1. Data from the South African Reserve Bank (2015).

2. The South African National Poverty Line is measured at the lower bound at US$3.50 a day and at the upper bound at US$5.43 a day (StatsSA 2015). These poverty lines were recently rebased by StatsSA so that they are reflective of a current average basket of food and nonfood consumption items. The 2011 poverty headcount rate at the lower bound is 37 percent.

3. There is a rich literature on the linkages between growth, poverty, and inequality, which includes Kanbur (2005); Kanbur and Squire (1999); Kakwani (1993); Datt and Ravallion (1992); Ravallion (1997, 2001). While this is an important area in the macroeconomics of growth and development, it is not the focus of this chapter.

4. World Development Indicators (World Bank 2015), using national estimates.

5. The IQR is the spread between the upper and lower quartiles of income and consumption for all the NTA countries, at each age.

6. This definition includes those who are unemployed and willing to work but have stopped searching for jobs, commonly referred to as discouraged workers.

7. These are calculated using data from StatsSA October Household Survey (OHS) 1996–99; StatsSA LFS September 2001–07; StatsSA QLFS Quarter 4 2008–13; and StatsSA QLFS Quarter 1 2014.

8. The category specifically includes security guards, security patrolmen, security patrolwomen, bodyguards, coastguards, beach guards, lifeguards, beach patrolmen, beach patrolwomen, traffic wardens, game wardens, bird sanctuary wardens, wildlife wardens, taxi-guards, and traffic coordinators.

9. StatsSA OHS 1999; StatsSA QLFS Quarter 1, 2014.

10. SACMEQ III was undertaken from 2005 to 2010, targeted all pupils in grade 6 level (at the first week of the eighth month of the school year) who were attending registered mainstream primary school. The desired target population definition for the project was based on a grade-based description and not age-based description of pupils.

11. According to the TIMMS methodology, four points in the overall subject scales are identified as international benchmarks: 400 is the low international benchmark, 475 is the intermediate international benchmark, 550 is the high international benchmark, and 625 is the advanced international benchmark.

12. Data analysis is based on StatsSA LFS (1994 and 2004) and StatsSA QLFS (2013), but is not shown here.

13. This relates to skill level 5 out of nine national skill level categories, where 9 is the least skilled category. See notes to table 7-5 for an explanation of how occupations map into skill levels.

14. Racial analysis in this chapter uses the country's four main race groups as defined by South African authorities and in the literature on South African society: African, Coloured (mixed-race), Indian, and white.

15. "Bargaining councils can be established by one or more registered trade unions and by one or more registered employer organizations for a specific sector and area. Worker interests are, therefore, represented at bargaining councils by the relevant trade unions. Participation by unions and employer organizations in the system is voluntary, and the issues to be negotiated are left to the discretion of the parties. Wage formation within the bargaining council system is, thus, a voluntary exercise ongoing annually between employer organizations and employees (represented by trade unions). In many cases, these councils have a long history of regularized

bargaining and engagement around worker issues" (Bhorat and others 2012, p. 402).

16. Including dummy variables for union status, private and public bargaining council status, type of work, firm characteristics, and nonwage benefits.

17. With significance at the 5 percent level.

18. This research suggests that institutional wage premiums in South Africa may be smaller than previously estimated, with most of the previous studies reporting a premium in excess of 20 percent—possibly overstated by not accounting for bargaining council coverage (Butcher and Rouse 2001; Armstrong and Steenkamp 2008; Miliea and others 2013).

19. All Rand figures are converted to US$, using an average 2013 exchange rate of ZAR/US$: 9.65.

20. Calculated as $e^{0.317}-1$.

21. Calculated as $\exp^{(-0.205+0.393)}-1$. The remaining wage premiums are calculated similarly.

REFERENCES

Armstrong, P., and J. Steenkamp. 2008. "South African Trade Unions: An Overview for 1995 to 2005." Working Papers 15/2009 (Stellenbosch University).

Benjamin, P., H. Bhorat, and H. Cheadle. 2010. "The Cost of 'Doing Business' and Labour Regulation: The Case of South Africa." *International Labour Review* 149, no. 1, pp. 73–91.

Bhorat, H. 2001. "Employment Trends in South Africa." Occasional Paper 2 (Bonn, Germany: FES).

———. 2008. "Unemployment in South Africa: Descriptors and Determinants." Unpublished.

———. 2012. "A Nation in Search of Jobs: Six Possible Policy Suggestions for Employment Creation in South Africa." Working Paper 12/150. Development Policy Research Unit (DPRU) (University of Cape Town).

Bhorat, H., S. Goga, and B. Stanwix. 2014. "Skills-Biased Labour Demand and the Pursuit of Inclusive Growth in South Africa." Working Paper 2014/130 (Helsinki: UNU-WIDER).

Bhorat, H., and J. Hodge. 1999. "Decomposing Shifts in Labour Demand in South Africa." *South African Journal of Economics* 67, no. 3, pp. 155–68.

Bhorat, H., R. Kanbur, and B. Stanwix. 2012. "Estimating the Impact of Minimum Wages on Employment, Wages, and Non-Wage Benefits: The Case of Agriculture in South Africa." Working Paper 12/149. Development Policy Research Unit (DPRU) (University of Cape Town).

Bhorat, H., and M. Leibbrandt. 1999. "Modelling Vulnerability and Low Earnings in the South African Labour Market." Working Paper 99/32. Development Policy Research Unit (DPRU) (University of Cape Town).

Bhorat, H., and N. Mayet. 2012. "Employment Outcomes and Returns to Earnings in Post-Apartheid South Africa. Working Paper 12/152. Development Policy Research Unit (DPRU) (University of Cape Town).

Bhorat, H., K. Naidoo, and D. Yu. 2015a. "Trade Unions in an Emerging Economy: The Case of South Africa," in *The Oxford Handbook of Africa and Economics: Policies and Practices*, edited by C. Monga and J. Yifu Lin (Oxford University Press).

Bhorat, H., and M. Oosthuizen. 2006. "Evolution of the Labour Market: 1995–2002" in *Poverty and Policy in Post-Apartheid South Africa*, edited by H. Bhorat and R. Kanbur (Cape Town: HSRC Press).

Bhorat, H., B. Stanwix, and D. Yu. 2015b. "Nonincome Welfare and Inclusive Growth in South Africa." Africa Growth Initiative Working Paper 18 (Brookings).

Bhorat, H., and C. van der Westhuizen. 2013. "Temporary Employment Services in South Africa: A Brief Note." *World Development Report* (Washington D.C.: World Bank). (http://siteresources.worldbank.org/EXTNWDR2013/Resources/8258024-1320950747192/8260293-1320956712276/8261091-1348683883703/WDR2013_bp_Temporary_Employment_Services_in_SA.pdf).

Branson, N. 2006. "The South African Labour Market 1995–2004: A Cohort Analysis." Paper presented at DPRU/TIPS conference on "Accelerated and Shared Growth in South Africa: Determinants, Constraints and Opportunities." Johannesburg, 18–20 October. (www.commerce.uct.ac.za/Research_Units/DPRU/DPRUConference2006/List_of_Papers.htm).

Branson, N., C. Hofmeyr, and D. Lam. 2013. "Progress through School and the Determinants of School Dropout in South Africa." Working Paper 100. Southern Africa Labour and Development Research Unit (SALDRU) (University of Cape Town).

Burger, R., and I. Woolard. 2005. "The State of the Labour Market in South Africa after the First Decade of Democracy." Working Paper 133. Centre for Social Science Research (CSSR) (University of Cape Town) (www.cssr.uct.ac.za/pubs_cssr.html).

Butcher, K. F., and C. E. Rouse. 2001. "Wage Effects of Union and Industrial Councils in South Africa." *Industrial and Labor Relations Review* 54, no. 2, pp. 349–74.

Casale, D., and D. Posel. 2002. "The Continued Feminisation of the Labour Force in South Africa: An Analysis of Recent Data and Trends." *South African Journal of Economics* 70, no. 1, pp. 156–84.

Chamber of Mines of South Africa. 2015. "The Mining Industry in South Africa." South Africa: Chamber of Mines. (www.chamberofmines.org.za /mining-industry/comsa-members).

DataFirst. 2014. "South Africa—Post Apartheid Labour Market Series, 1994–2012 (PALMS)." (South Africa: DataFirst). (www.datafirst.uct.ac.za /dataportal/index.php/catalog/434).

Datt, G., and M. Ravallion. 1992. "Growth and Redistribution Components of Changes in Poverty Measures." *Journal of Development Economics* 38, pp. 275–95.

Devey, R., C. Skinner, and I. Valodia. 2006. "The State of the Informal Economy," in *State of the Nation: South Africa 2005–2006*, edited by S. Buhlungu and others (South Africa: HSRC). (www.hsrcpress.ac.za/).

Dunne, J. P., and L. Edwards. 2006. "Trade Technology and Employment: A Case Study of South Africa." Working Paper 0602 (University of West England).

Fields, G. 2000. "The Employment Problem in South Africa." *Trade and Industry Monitor* 16, no. 3–6. (http://digitalcommons.ilr.cornell.edu/cgi /viewcontent.cgi?article=1458&context=articles).

Hofmeyr J. F. 1998. "Segmentation in the South African Labour Market." Working Paper 15 (Potchefstroom: South African Network for Economic Research).

Industrial Development Corporation (IDC). 2013. *South African Economy: An Overview of Key Trends since 1994* (South Africa: IDC Department of Research and Information).

Kakwani, N. 1993. "Poverty and Economic Growth with Application to Côte D'Ivoire." *Review of Income and Wealth* 39, no. 2 (June 1993).

Kanbur, R. 2005. "Growth, Inequality, and Poverty: Some Hard Questions." *Journal of International Affairs* (Spring).

Kanbur, R., and L. Squire. 1999. "The Evolution of Thinking about Poverty: Exploring the Interactions," in *Frontiers of Development Economics: The Future in Perspective*, edited by G. Meier and J. Stiglitz (Oxford University Press).

Koenker, R., and G. Bassett. 1978. "Regression Quantiles." *Econometrica* 46, no. 1, pp. 33–50.

Koenker, R., and K. F. Hallock. 2001. "Quantile Regression." *Journal of Economic Perspectives* 15, no. 4, pp. 143–56.

Mason, A., and R. Lee. 2007. "Transfers, Capital, and Consumption over the Demographic Transition," in *Population Aging, Intergenerational Transfers, and the Macroeconomy*, edited by R. Clark, N. Ogawa, and A. Mason (Cheltenham, UK: Edward Elgar).

———. 2012. Demographic dividends and aging in lower-income countries. National Transfer Accounts Working Paper No. 12-01 (http://www .ntaccounts.org).

Miliea, M. J., J. P. Rezek, and J. Pitts. 2013. "Minimum Wages in a Segmented Labor Market: Evidence from South Africa." (Bloemfontein, South Africa: Economic Society of South Africa). (www.essa2013.org.za /fullpaper/essa2013_2735.pdf).

National Transfer Accounts. 2013. "NTA Database." (Berkeley, CA: UCB). (www.ntaccounts.org).

Organization of Economic Cooperation and Development (OECD). 2008. *African Economic Outlook—South Africa* (Paris: AfDB/OECD).

Oosthuizen, M. 2006. "The Post-Apartheid Labour Market: 1995–2004." Working Paper 06/103. Development Policy Research Unit (DPRU) (University of Cape Town). (www.commerce.uct.ac.za/Research_Units /DPRU/WorkingPapers/wpapers.asp).

———. 2011. "Assessing the Employment Impact of the State." Research Paper. Development Policy Research Unit (DPRU) (University of Cape Town)

———. 2014. "Bonus or Mirage? South Africa's Demographic Dividend." *Journal of the Economics of Ageing*. DOI: 10.1016/j.jeoa.2014.08.007.

Presidency, The. 2014. "Twenty Year Review, South Africa 1994–2014." (Pretoria: Government of South Africa).

Ravallion, M. M. 1997. "Can High-Inequality Developing Countries Escape Absolute Poverty?" *Economics Letters* 56, pp. 51–57.

———. 2001. "Growth, Inequality and Poverty: Looking beyond Averages." *World Development* 29, no. 11, pp. 1803–15.

Rodrik, D. 2006. "Understanding South Africa's Economic Puzzles." Working Paper 130 (Boston, Mass.: Centre for International Development at Harvard University).

Spaull, N. 2013. "South Africa's Education Crisis: The Quality of Education in South Africa 1994–2011." Report Commissioned by the Centre for Development and Enterprise. (University of Johannesburg). (www.uj.ac .za/EN/Faculties/edu/CentresandInstitutes/ELI/Documents/ELI%20 SMT%20Capacity%20building%20South%20Africas%20Education%20 Crisis%20N%20Spaull%202013%2018%20Oct%202014.pdf).

Spaull, N., and S. Taylor. 2015. "Access to What? Creating a Composite Measure of Educational Quantity and Educational Quality for 11 African Countries." *Comparative Education Review* 59, no. 1, pp. 133–65.

Statistics South Africa. 1996, 1997, 1998, 1999, 2001, 2002, 2003, 2004, 2005, 2006, 2007. "October Household Survey." (Pretoria, South Africa: Statistics South Africa). (www.statssa.gov.za).

———. 2008, 2009, 2010, 2011, 2012, 2013, 2014. "Quarterly Labour Force Survey." (Pretoria, South Africa: Statistics South Africa). (www.statssa.gov.za/).

———. 2013. "Labour Market Dynamics Survey." (Pretoria, South Africa: Statistics South Africa). (www.statssa.gov.za/).

———. 2015. "Methodological Report on Rebasing of National Poverty Lines and Development on Pilot Provincial Poverty Lines." (Pretoria, South Africa: Statistics South Africa). (www.statssa.gov.za/).

South African Reserve Bank. (SARB). 2015. "Time Series Database." (Pretoria, South Africa: South African Reserve Bank). (www.resbank.co.za/Research/Statistics/Pages/OnlineDownloadFacility.aspx).

TIMMS. 2011. "International Database." (http://timssandpirls.bc.edu/timsspirls2011/international-database.html#database)

United Nations. 2012. "World Population Prospects: The 2012 Revision." (New York: United Nations). (http://esa.un.org/wpp/Excel-Data/population.htm).

Valodia, I. 2007. "Informal Employment in South Africa." Employment Growth and Development Initiative. HSRC report (Pretoria, South Africa: HSRC).

Van der Berg, S. 2006. "How Effective Are Poor Schools? Poverty and Educational Outcomes in South Africa." Working Paper 06/06 (Stellenbosch University).

Woolard, I. 2002. "A Comparison of Wage Levels and Wage Inequality in the Public and Private Sectors, 1995 and 2000." Working Paper 02/62. Development Policy Research Unit (DPRU) (University of Cape Town).

World Bank. (2013). 'Employing Workers Database'. Washington DC: The World Bank. Available at: http://www.doingbusiness.org/data/exploretopics/employing-workers (accessed 15 October 2013).

World Bank. 2015. "World Development Indicators." (Washington D.C.: World Bank). (http://data.worldbank.org/data-catalog/world-development-indicators).

Yu, D. 2008. "The South African Labour Market: 1995–2006." Working Paper 05/08 (Stellenbosch University). (www.ekon.sun.ac.za/wpapers/2008/wp052008/wp-05-2008.pdf).

Contributors

Olu Ajakaiye is currently executive chairman, African Centre for Shared Development Capacity Building, Ibadan. He was president of the Nigeria Economic Society, honorary special adviser to the Nigerian president on the economy, and a member of the National Economic Management Team, director of research at the African Economic Research Consortium, Nairobi, and director-general, Nigerian Institute of Social and Economic Research.

Olufunke Alaba is a senior lecturer in the Health Economics Unit, School of Public Health and Family Medicine, at the University of Cape Town. She is an applied econometrician with research interest in social determinants of health, poverty, health, and development economics.

Seid Nuru Ali is a senior fellow and head of the Macroeconomic Division at the Ethiopian Economics Association/Ethiopian Economic Policy Research Institute (EEA-EEPRI). He is a visiting lecturer at Bahir Dar University, Arba Minch University, Dire Dawa University, and Addis Ababa University, teaching advanced econometrics, advanced macroeconomics, and macroeconomic policy. Previously, he was a senior researcher at the Center for Development Research (ZEF) at the University of Bonn, a researcher at the National Bank of Ethiopia (Central Bank), and a researcher in the Economic and Social Research Team of the Federal Parliament of Ethiopia.

Ernest Aryeetey is the vice-chancellor of the University of Ghana and also the university's chief executive officer of the University. Before this he was director of the Institute Social and Economic Research at the university. Aryeetey is a nonresident senior fellow of the Brookings Institution and was the director of the Africa Growth Initiative, 2009–10. He is a member of the American Economics Association, the United Nations University World Institute for Development Economics Research, and the Global Development Network.

William Baah-Boateng is a senior lecturer in economics at the University of Ghana where he works in the area of employment and labor market, quantitative analysis, and relevant issues related to development. He is also a senior research fellow of African Centre for Economic Transformation and a fellow of the International Institute for Advanced Studies.

Afeikhena Jerome is currently consulting for the FAO Subregional Office for Eastern Africa, Addis Ababa, on policy. He is also visiting professor of economics at Igbinedion University, Okada, Nigeria. He previously served with the UNDP and NEPAD Secretariat as coordinator for economic governance and management, APRM Secretariat, South Africa. Jerome has held distinguished positions at the International Monetary Fund, the World Bank, Saint Anthony's College (Oxford), and the Research Group on African Development Perspectives, University of Bremen, Germany.

Sam Jones is associate professor in the Department of Economics at the University of Copenhagen. He is a development economist with interests in applied economic and policy analysis in developing countries, focusing on sub-Saharan Africa and Lusophone Africa, in particular. Jones works extensively with macro- and microeconomic data from developing countries, applying a range of empirical tools.

Mwangi Kimenyi was a senior fellow and former director of the Africa Growth Initiative (AGI) at the Brookings Institution. Through his leadership, AGI established partnerships with six African think tanks, launched the Africa Policy Dialogue on the Hill, and developed AGI's annual publication, *Foresight Africa*, which takes a look ahead at the most critical issues facing the continent. He was also the first executive director of the Kenya Institute for Public Policy Research and Analysis, a government think tank. Mwangi Kimenyi sadly passed away on June 6, 2015, while this book was nearing its final stages.

Francis Mwega is a professor of economics at the University of Nairobi, where he has been teaching since the mid-1980s. He was director of the School of Economics from 2007 to 2011. He has edited several books and published many journal articles and book chapters.

David Nabena is an economist with the Nigeria Governors' Forum (NGF), Abuja, Nigeria. He is a research analyst on fiscal policy and also coordinates NGF's policy activities with development partners including the World Bank, the United Nations System in Nigeria, and the U.K. Department for International Development.

Karmen Naidoo is currently pursuing a PhD in economics at the University of Massachusetts–Amherst. She was a senior researcher at the Development Policy Research Unit at the University of Cape Town and has worked extensively in profiling, through the use of micro-datasets, to study poverty, inequality, and labor markets in selected African economies.

Njuguna Ndung'u is a Kenyan economist, researcher, and immediate former governor of the Central Bank of Kenya. He is currently on a leave of absence from the School of Economics, University of Nairobi. Ndung'u has held senior positions at the African Economic Research Consortium, the International Development Research Centre, and at the Kenya Institute for Public Policy Research and Analysis.

Morné Oosthuizen is deputy director of the Development Policy Research Unit at the University of Cape Town. Oosthuizen's research interests include labor markets, poverty and social inequality, inflation, wage inequality, economic demography, and microeconomics.

Kavisha Pillay was previously a junior researcher at the Development Policy Research Unit at the University of Cape Town (UCT). She is currently an associate consultant at IQ Business in Johannesburg. Pillay also tutored in UCT's Economics Department and lectured at the Cape Peninsula University of Technology. Her research interests include growth, development, and labor economics.

Yared Seid is currently working for the International Growth Centre (IGC) as a country economist for the Ethiopia Country Program. His research interests are applied microeconomics, development economics, and applied econometrics, with a specific concentration on topics in human capital investment in children in developing countries. Before joining the IGC, Seid held teaching and research assistant positions at Georgia State University.

Alemayehu Seyoum Taffesse is currently a senior research fellow at the International Food Policy Research Institute (IFPRI). His most recent research covered impact evaluation of safety-net programs, intersectoral growth linkages, performance of cooperatives, crop productivity, aspirations and well-being, and rainfall indexed insurance. Taffesse is also the current president of the Ethiopian Economics Association.

Index

Adeyinka, A., 188
African Development Bank, 28, 125
Afrobarometer surveys, 155–57
Agricultural sector: employment in, 14, 16;
    in Ethiopia, 45, 59, 68; in Ghana, 78, 81,
    83, 85, 93, 103; in Kenya, 118, 131–32,
    138; in Mozambique, 21, 151, 158, 163,
    172–73; in Nigeria, 185, 187, 189, 192,
    204, 205; in South Africa, 230, 239, 247;
    in Sub-Saharan Africa, 16; trends in, 7
Ajakaiye, Olu, 7, 181
Ajaokuta Steel Company, 185
Alaba, Olufunke A., 181
Al-Shaabab, 138
Ancharaz, V., 195
Angola: economic growth in, 1; export
    growth linked to economic growth in,
    195
Annan, Kofi, 113
Arndt, Channing, 10
Aryeetey, Ernest, 77
Atlas of Economic Complexity, 23

Baah-Boateng, William, 77, 86, 89, 95, 96
Bank of Ghana, 80

Barriers to economic growth, 16–31;
    capital accumulation lacking, 22–24;
    in Ghana, 98–102; governance, 24–28;
    informalization of labor, 28–31;
    infrastructure, 24–28; in Kenya, 136–39;
    manufacturing sector issues, 19–28; in
    Mozambique, 168–71; in Nigeria, 213–16;
    resource-led growth, 17–19
Barro, R. J., 132
Bbaale, E., 195
Benin, informal sector employment in,
    28–29
Benjamin, Nancy, 28, 244
Bhorat, Haroon, 1, 14, 17, 229, 238, 242, 254
BHP Billiton, 153
Bigsten, A., 128
Blinder–Oaxaca wage decomposition, 61, 65
Bloom, D. E., 123, 124, 212
Boateng, K., 100
Boeri, T., 194
Boko Haram, 183, 215
Botswana, education sector in, 244, 245
Bravo-Ortega, Claudio, 19
Burkina Faso, informal sector employment
    in, 28–29

Burundi: middle class in, 125; and transport
	networks, 26
Byiers, B., 196

Canning, D., 123
Capital accumulation: in Ethiopia, 42, 45;
	in Kenya, 30, 119, 134, 140–41; in Nigeria,
	22; in South Africa, 22
Ceglowski, Janet, 26
Central Bank of Nigeria (CBN), 183
Central Statistical Agency (Ethiopia), 47
Chad, economic growth in, 1
Chile, education sector in, 245
Collective bargaining, 254–62
Colleges and universities: in Ethiopia,
	50–51; in Ghana, 87, 100–01; in Kenya,
	132; in Nigeria, 193
Collier, P., 114
Commodity prices, 17–18, 117, 183
Common Market for Eastern
	and Southern Africa (COMESA), 137
Conditional resource curse, 19
Construction sector: in Ethiopia, 59, 69; in
	Ghana, 81; in South Africa, 230
Côte d'Ivoire, labor migration from, 101
Country Policy and Institutional Assessment
	(CPIA), 113, 124
Current account deficits, 3–4, 115

Deindustrialization, 7, 187
Demographic dividend: effects of, 3; in
	Ethiopia, 46–48; in Kenya, 118, 119–26,
	140; in Nigeria, 212–13, 218; in South
	Africa, 232–36
Dependency ratio: in Ethiopia, 47; in
	Kenya, 121, 123; in Mozambique, 168; in
	Nigeria, 196; in South Africa, 233–34; in
	Sub-Saharan Africa, 47
Devolution, 137
Domestic workers, 29–30
Drivers of economic growth: in Africa, 6; in
	Ghana, 79–83; in Kenya, 110, 139; in
	Mozambique, 166

Ease of Doing Business index (World Bank),
	24–25, 242, 244
East African Community (EAC), 109, 137
Economic growth: in Africa, 1–36; barriers
	to, 16–31; inclusive, 5–16; and inequality,
	10–16; and labor market, 13–16;
	macroeconomic overview, 3–5; and

poverty, 10–16; structural economic
	transformation for, 5–16. *See also specific
	countries*
Economic Recovery Strategy (ERS), 113
Economist on economic growth in Africa, 1
Education: in Ethiopia, 48–54; in Ghana,
	103; in Nigeria, 184–93, 217–18; in South
	Africa, 236, 244–46. *See also* Colleges
	and universities
Educational attainment: in Ghana, 99–100;
	in Mozambique, 168–69; in Nigeria, 193,
	213; of women, 133–34
Education Sector Development Programs
	(ESDPs, Ethiopia), 48
Egypt, unit labor costs in, 28
Eifert, Ben, 24
Employment elasticity: in Kenya, 134–36; in
	Nigeria, 210–11
ERS (Economic Recovery Strategy),
	113
ESDPs (Education Sector Development
	Programs, Ethiopia), 48
Ethiopia, 37–76; agricultural sector in,
	45, 59, 68; capital accumulation in,
	42, 45; construction sector in, 59, 69;
	demographic dividend in, 46–48;
	dependency ratio in, 47; economic
	growth trends in, 1, 39–40; education in,
	48–54; education sector reforms in,
	48–54; employment-to-population ratio
	in, 56–57; extractives industry in, 59;
	fertility rate in, 46–47, 67; financial
	services sector in, 59; formal sector
	employment in, 61; human capital
	development in, 46–54; industrial sector
	in, 45; informal sector in, 61;
	infrastructure in, 40, 60; investment
	financing in, 60; labor force participation
	in, 46, 56; labor market in, 55–67;
	manufacturing sector in, 22, 45, 59, 69;
	mortality rate in, 46; population growth
	in, 46–48; public sector employment in,
	65–66; sectoral employment shift in,
	57–61; services sector in, 60; skilled
	workers in, 38, 49–51, 61, 65; social
	protection programs in, 66–67; sources
	of growth in, 40–42; structural economic
	transformation in, 42–46; structural
	transformation in, 42–46; total factor
	productivity (TFP) in, 41–42; and transport
	networks, 26; unemployment rate in,

50–51, 61; unskilled workers in, 38, 61, 65; wage differentials in, 38; youth in, 50–51
Ethnic violence, 138
Expanded Public Works Program (South Africa), 250–51, 255
Exports: and economic growth, 3, 195; from Ghana, 80, 81; from Kenya, 3, 109, 112, 114–15; and manufacturing sector, 20–21, 22, 28; from Mozambique, 174; from Nigeria, 195; and resource-led growth, 17–18, 19; from South Africa, 231
Extractives industry: in Ethiopia, 59; in Ghana, 80–81, 83, 102; in Kenya, 109; in Mozambique, 151, 158, 163, 164; in Nigeria, 183, 187; and resource-led growth, 17–19; in South Africa, 230–31, 239–40, 247; trends in, 7. *See also* Oil and gas industry

Fertility rate: in Ethiopia, 46–47, 67; in Kenya, 122, 125; in Nigeria, 217; in South Africa, 234
Financial services sector: in Ethiopia, 59; in Ghana, 81; in South Africa, 230, 231
Food and Agriculture Organization (FAO), 149
Food security, 149
Foreign aid, 150–51
Foreign direct investment (FDI), 109, 112, 151
Formal sector employment: in Ethiopia, 61; in Ghana, 85, 89–90; in Kenya, 126–28, 140
Free Compulsory Universal Basic Education (Ghana), 100
Frente de Libertação de Moçambique (FRELIMO), 148, 149

Gabon, export growth linked to economic growth in, 195
Garibaldi, P., 194
Gas industry. *See* Oil and gas industry
Gelb, Alan, 24, 29
GGDC (Groningen Growth and Development Centre), 55, 57
Ghana, 77–108; agricultural sector in, 78, 81, 83, 85, 93, 103; barriers to economic growth in, 98–102; construction sector in, 81; drivers of economic growth in, 79–83; earnings differentials by employment in, 89–92; economic growth in, 79–83,

98–102; education in, 87, 101, 103; exports from, 80, 81; extractives industry in, 80–81, 83, 102; financial services sector in, 81; formal sector employment in, 85, 89–90; growth-employment-poverty linkage in, 95–97; human capital development in, 78; industrial sector in, 94–95; inequality in, 88; informal sector in, 30, 78, 85, 89, 100, 102; job creation in, 78, 96, 98–102; labor market in, 83–87, 98–100; labor productivity in, 92–95; manufacturing sector in, 81, 83, 102, 103; policy recommendations, 102–03; population growth in, 98–99; poverty in, 88; services sector in, 95, 102; skilled workers in, 100–02; structural economic transformation in, 5, 85; unemployment rate in, 86–87; unskilled workers in, 100–02; women in, 86–87; youth in, 86
Ghani, E., 187
Gilligan, D. O., 67
Gini coefficients: in Africa, 10, 12; in Ghana, 88; in South Africa, 232
Girma, S., 53
Global Infrastructure Nigeria Ltd (GINL), 186
Global Peace Index, 215
Governance: and economic growth, 2, 24–28, 31; in Kenya, 110, 113, 118, 138; in Mozambique, 145; in Nigeria, 196, 214–15
Grand Ethiopian Renaissance Dam, 59
Gregorio, José, 19
Groningen Growth and Development Centre (GGDC), 55, 57
Growth and Transformation Plan (GTP, Ethiopia), 37, 38, 43–44
Gutierrez, C., 194, 197

Harmonized National Living Standard Survey (HNLSS), 182
Hausmann, Ricardo, 23
Health Policy Project (USAID), 125
Higher education. *See* Colleges and universities
Hong Kong, demographic dividend in, 212
Hull, K., 194
Human capital development: in Ethiopia, 46–54; in Ghana, 78; in Kenya, 131–34; and labor market, 2; in Mozambique,

Human capital development (cont.)
  168–69; in Nigeria, 182, 217–18; in South
  Africa, 244–49

Import substitution strategy, 213–14
Inclusive growth: and inequality, 10–16; and
  poverty, 10–16; and structural economic
  transformation, 5–16
India, labor market in, 238
Industrial sector: in Ethiopia, 45; in Ghana,
  94–95; growth in, 7; in Nigeria, 185,
  213–14
Inequality: in Ghana, 88; in Kenya, 138–39;
  and labor market, 13–16; trends in, 2–3
Informal sector: in Benin, 28–29; in
  Burkina Faso, 28–29; in Ethiopia, 61; in
  Ghana, 30, 78, 85, 89, 100, 102; in Kenya,
  29, 30, 126–28, 140; in Mozambique, 29,
  158; in Nigeria, 187, 190; in Senegal, 29;
  in South Africa, 30; in Sub-Saharan
  Africa, 16; unskilled workers in, 30–31
Information and communications technology
  (ICT), 187
Infrastructure: in Ethiopia, 40, 60; in
  Mozambique, 171, 173, 176; in Nigeria, 214
Institutional capacity: in Kenya, 114; in
  Nigeria, 214–15
International Court of Arbitration, 186
International Labor Organization (ILO), 29,
  129, 134
International Monetary Fund (IMF), 1, 149,
  173
Inter-sectoral labor shifts, 206–10
Investment financing: domestic vs. external
  sources for, 5; in Ethiopia, 60; in Kenya,
  116
Islam, I., 210

Japan, economic complexity in, 23
Jerome, Afeikhena T., 181, 188
Job creation: in Ghana, 78, 96, 98–102;
  in Nigeria, 202–05; in Rwanda, 195; in
  South Africa, 237, 249–50, 262–63; in
  Uganda, 195
Job Generation and Growth (JoGGs)
  decomposition tool, 195–96
Jones, Sam, 145

Kedir, A., 53
Kenya, 109–44; agricultural sector in, 118,
  131–32, 138; barriers to economic growth

in, 136–39; capital accumulation in, 30,
  119, 134, 140–41; demographic dividend
  in, 118, 119–26, 140; dependency ratio in,
  121, 123; drivers of economic growth in,
  110, 139; economic complexity in, 24;
  economic growth in, 111–18; education
  sector in, 244; employment elasticity in,
  134–36; exports from, 3, 109, 112, 114–15;
  extractives industry in, 109; fertility rate
  in, 122, 125; formal sector employment
  in, 126–28, 140; governance in, 110, 113,
  118, 138; human capital development
  in, 131–34; inequality in, 138–39;
  informal sector in, 29, 30, 126–28, 140;
  institutional capacity in, 114; investment
  financing in, 116; labor market in,
  126–36; labor productivity in, 131–34;
  manufacturing sector in, 21, 114–15;
  markets' role in growth process, 117–18;
  middle class in, 125–26, 138, 141;
  mortality rate in, 122; National Youth
  Policy, 120; political economy of growth
  process in, 112–14; population growth in,
  119–26; ports in, 26; poverty in, 113,
  138–39; public sector employment in,
  124, 129; and transport networks, 26;
  urbanization in, 118, 119–20, 139; Vision
  2030 Plan, 116, 118, 136; women in,
  133–34; youth in, 118, 120, 137–38
Kenya African National Union (KANU),
  113
Kenya Institute for Public Policy Research
  and Analysis (KIPPRA), 130
Kenya National Union of Teachers (KNUT),
  130
Kenya Post and Telecommunications
  Company, 117
Kibaki, Mwai, 113
Kimenyi, Mwangi S., 3, 109, 132, 133
Kormawa, P., 187

Labor brokering, 241, 242
Labor force participation: in Ethiopia, 46,
  56; in Ghana, 87; in South Africa, 232–33
Labor market: as barrier to economic
  growth, 28–31; between- and within-
  sector employment shifts, 57–61; earnings
  differentials, 89–92; employment-to-
  population ratio, 56–57; in Ethiopia,
  55–67; in Ghana, 83–87, 98–100; and
  inequality, 13–16; informalization of,

28–31; inter-sectoral labor shifts, 206–10; in Kenya, 126–36; in Mozambique, 157–67; in Nigeria, 184–93, 196–210; in South Africa, 237–49
Labor mobility, 30, 206–10
Labor productivity: in Ghana, 92–95; in Kenya, 131–34; in Mozambique, 163–64, 166, 175; in Nigeria, 188, 202–05, 217
Labor unions, 254–62
Lam, David, 14
Lederman, Daniel, 19
Lee, J. W., 132
Lee, R., 124
Lehmann, H., 195
Leibbrandt, Murray, 14
Livelihood Empowerment Against Poverty (LEAP, Ghana), 88
Loayza, N., 194

Malaysia, labor market in, 238
Maloney, William F., 19
Malunda, D., 195
Manufacturing sector: as barrier to economic growth, 19–28; capital accumulation lacking in, 22–24; decline of, 2; in Ethiopia, 22, 45, 59, 69; in Ghana, 81, 83, 102, 103; governance issues, 24–28; infrastructure issues, 24–28; in Kenya, 21, 114–15; in Mozambique, 21, 151, 158, 163, 167; in Nigeria, 7, 187, 189, 204, 209; and skilled workers, 21; in South Africa, 21, 230, 231, 240; trends in, 7; unit labor costs, 24–28; in West Africa, 21
Mason, A., 124
Mauritius, unit labor costs in, 28
Mayet, N., 242
Mbaye, Ahmadou Aly, 28
McMillan, Margaret, 7
Mehlum, Halvor, 18–19
Middle class, 125–26, 138, 141
Millennium Development Goals (MDGs), 88
Minimum wage, 91, 174, 239
Minimum Wage-Fixing Machinery Convention (1928), 91
Mining. *See* Extractives industry
Moene, Karl, 18–19
Mortality rate: in Ethiopia, 46; in Kenya, 122
Mozambique, 145–80; agricultural sector in, 21, 151, 158, 163, 172–73; barriers to economic growth in, 168–71; dependency

ratio in, 168; drivers of economic growth in, 166; economic growth in, 1, 149–57; education in, 168–69; exports from, 174; extractives industry in, 151, 158, 163, 164; governance in, 145; human capital development in, 168–69; informal sector in, 29, 158; infrastructure in, 171, 173, 176; labor market in, 157–67; labor productivity in, 163–64, 166, 175; macroeconomic trends in, 149–53; manufacturing sector in, 21, 151, 158, 163, 167; microeconomic growth in, 153–57; policy recommendations for, 171–74; population growth in, 168; poverty in, 10, 153–55; services sector in, 151, 158, 164, 167, 175; skilled workers in, 174; structural economic transformation in, 5, 146; study methodology in, 159–61; total factor productivity (TFP) in, 42; wage differentials in, 174
Mozambique Liberation Front (Frente de Libertação de Moçambique, FRELIMO), 148, 149
Mwega, Francis M., 109, 139

Nabena, David, 181
Naidoo, Karmen, 229
National Bureau of Statistics (Nigeria), 181, 182, 192, 196
National Daily Minimum Wage (NDMW, Ghana), 91–92
National Emergency Management Agency (Nigeria), 215
National Rainbow Coalition (NARC, Kenya), 113
National Transfer Accounts (South Africa), 233–34
Natural gas industry. *See* Oil and gas industry
Natural resources. *See* Extractives industry
Ndung'u, Njuguna S., 109, 139
Newman, Carol, 20, 25
Nigeria, 181–227; agricultural sector in, 185, 187, 189, 192, 204, 205; barriers to economic growth in, 213–16; capital accumulation in, 22; demographic dividend in, 212–13, 218; dependency ratio in, 196; economic complexity in, 24; economic growth in, 1, 181–84; education in, 184–93, 213, 217–18; employment elasticity in, 210–11; exports from, 195;

Nigeria (cont.)
  extractives industry in, 183, 187; fertility rate in, 217; governance in, 196, 214–15; growth per capita in, 201–02; human capital development in, 182, 217–18; industrial sector in, 185, 213–14; informal sector in, 187, 190; infrastructure in, 214; institutional capacity in, 214–15; inter-sectoral labor shifts, 206–10; job creation in, 202–05; labor market in, 184–93, 196–210; labor migration from, 101; labor productivity in, 188, 202–05, 217; literature review, 193–96; manufacturing sector in, 7, 187, 189, 204, 209; policy recommendations, 216–18; political economy of growth process in, 215; population growth in, 188–89, 209, 217; sectoral employment changes in, 205; security challenges in, 215–16; services sector in, 30, 187, 189, 196; structural economic transformation in, 190; study methodology in, 197–99; unemployment rate in, 188, 191–93; urbanization in, 214, 217; Vision 20:2020 plan, 214; women in, 213; youth in, 14, 192, 218

Nigeria Investment Promotion Commission, 218
Nigerian Institute for Social and Economic Research (NISER), 196
Nigeria Poverty Profile Report, 182

Occupational certification, 50
O'Connell, S. D., 187
Odinga, Raila, 113
Ofori-Sarpong, E., 100
Oil and gas industry: in Ghana, 79–81, 101; in Nigeria, 187. *See also* Extractives industry
Okun, A. M., 193, 210
Olotu, A., 195
Oosthuizen, Morné, 229

Page, John, 19
Pillay, Kavisha, 229
Plan for Accelerated and Sustained Development to End Poverty (PASDEP, Ethiopia), 43–44
Political economy of growth process, 111; in Kenya, 112–14; in Nigeria, 215
Population growth: in Ethiopia, 46–48; in Ghana, 98–99; in Kenya, 119–26; in

Mozambique, 168; in Nigeria, 188–89, 209, 217
Ports, 26, 110, 148
Portugal, colonial administration by, 148
Poverty: in Ghana, 88; growth elasticity of, 11; in Kenya, 113, 138–39; in Mozambique, 10, 153–55; in South Africa, 231–32; in Sub-Saharan Africa, 16; in Vietnam, 10
Prebisch, Raúl, 17
Premature deindustrialization, 187
Price controls, 117, 151
Primary education: in Ethiopia, 52–53; in Ghana, 99–100; in Kenya, 132, 133–34; in South Africa, 244, 245, 252
Privatization, 117
Productive Safety Net Programme (PSNP, Ethiopia), 66–67
Productivity. *See* Labor productivity
Public sector employment: in Ethiopia, 65–66; in Kenya, 124, 129; in South Africa, 240, 249–63

Raddatz, C., 194
Rail infrastructure, 26, 110
Ramachandran, Vijaya, 24
Remittances, 218
RENAMO (Resistência Nacional Moçambicana), 149
Resource curse, 18–19
Resource-led growth. *See* Extractives industry
Retail sector in South Africa, 230, 231
Returns to education, 52–54, 245–46
Riversdale (company), 151
Road networks, 25–26, 110
Robertson, C., 118
Rodrik, Dani, 6, 187
Rooney, Christopher, 17
Rule of law, 24, 114, 138
Rural-urban migration, 120
Rwanda: economic growth in, 1; job creation in, 195; middle class in, 125; and transport networks, 26

Sachs, Jeffrey D., 17, 18
Safaricom, 117
Salaries and Remuneration Commission (SRC, Kenya), 130
Sanusi, S. L., 214
SASOL (company), 151

Secondary education: in Ethiopia, 52–53; in Kenya, 132, 133–34; in Nigeria, 193; in South Africa, 245, 246, 252

Sectoral employment changes: in Nigeria, 205; in South Africa, 238–41. *See also specific sectors*

Security challenges in Nigeria, 215–16

Seid, Yard, 37

Self-employment, 14, 126

Senegal, informal sector employment in, 29

Services sector: in Ethiopia, 60; exports by, 3; in Ghana, 95, 102; in Mozambique, 151, 158, 164, 167, 175; in Nigeria, 30, 187, 189, 196; in South Africa, 240

Shapley decomposition method, 197

Singapore, demographic dividend in, 212

Single Spine Pay Structure (SSPS, Ghana), 92

Skilled workers: in Ethiopia, 38, 49–51, 61, 65; in Ghana, 100–02; and manufacturing sector, 21; in Mozambique, 174; shift toward, 13–14; in South Africa, 14, 246–49

Social protection programs: in Ethiopia, 66–67; and informal sector, 30

Söderbom, M., 45

SOEs (state-owned enterprises), 249, 261

Solow, R., 40

South Africa, 229–69; agricultural sector in, 230, 239, 247; capital accumulation in, 22; construction sector in, 230; demographic dividend in, 232–36; dependency ratio in, 233–34; economic complexity in, 24; education in, 236, 244–46; exports from, 231; extractives industry in, 230–31, 239–40, 247; fertility rate in, 234; financial services sector in, 230, 231; human capital development in, 244–49; informal sector in, 30; job creation in, 237, 249–50, 262–63; labor market in, 232–33, 237–49; manufacturing sector in, 21, 230, 231, 240; poverty in, 231–32; public sector employment in, 240, 249–63; sectoral employment changes in, 238–41; services sector in, 240; skilled workers in, 14, 246–49; structural economic transformation in, 5; temporary employment services in, 241–44; total factor productivity (TFP) in, 42; and transport networks, 148; transport sector in, 230, 231; unemployment rate in, 233,

234, 237; union bargaining power in, 254–62; unit labor costs in, 28; unskilled workers in, 14, 246–49; welfare gains in, 5; women in, 233, 252, 259

South Africa Development Community, 137

South Korea, demographic dividend in, 212

South Sudan: oil exports, 109; and transport networks, 26

SRC (Salaries and Remuneration Commission, Kenya), 130

SSPS (Single Spine Pay Structure, Ghana), 92

State-owned enterprises (SOEs), 249, 261

Steenkamp, Francois, 17

Structural economic transformation: for economic growth, 2, 5–16; in Ethiopia, 42–46; in Ghana, 5, 85; in Mozambique, 5, 146; in Nigeria, 190; in South Africa, 5

Sub-Saharan Africa (SSA): agricultural sector in, 16; dependency ratio in, 47; economic complexity in, 24; economic growth in, 79; growth elasticity of poverty, 11–12; informal sector employment in, 16, 28; labor markets in, 14, 83; poverty in, 16; structural economic transformation in, 146; unit labor costs in, 28; wage differentials in, 29. *See also specific countries*

Swaziland, education in, 244

Switzerland, economic complexity in, 23

Taffesse, Alemayehu Seyoum, 37

Tanzania: education in, 244; middle class in, 125

Tarp, Finn, 1, 145

Technical and Vocational Education and Training (TVET), 49–50

Temporary employment services, 241–44

Tertiary education. *See* Colleges and universities

Thailand, education in, 245

Torvik, Ragnar, 18–19

Total factor productivity (TFP): in Ethiopia, 41–42; in Mozambique, 42; in South Africa, 42

Trade liberalization, 28

Transfer of Knowledge through Expatriate Networks (TOKTEN) program, 218

Transport sector: ports, 26, 110, 148; rail infrastructure, 26, 110; road networks, 25–26, 110; in South Africa, 230, 231; transport costs, 26
Treichel, V., 184
Tunisia, unit labor costs in, 28
Turkey, education in, 245

Uganda: job creation in, 195; middle class in, 125; oil exports, 109; and transport networks, 26
Underemployment, 217
Unemployment rate: in Ethiopia, 50–51, 61; in Ghana, 86–87; in Nigeria, 188, 191–93; in South Africa, 233, 234, 237
Unions, 254–62
United Nations, 120
United Nations Development Programme (UNDP), 182, 218
Unit labor costs, 26, 28. *See also* Labor productivity
Universities. *See* Colleges and universities
Unskilled workers: in Ethiopia, 38, 61, 65; in Ghana, 100–02; in informal sector, 30–31; in South Africa, 14, 246–49
Urbanization: and economic growth, 2; in Kenya, 118, 119–20, 139; in Nigeria, 214, 217
USAID, 125

Vale (company), 151
Vietnam, poverty in, 10
Vision 20:2020 plan (Nigeria), 214

Wage differentials: and economic growth, 3; in Ethiopia, 38; in Mozambique, 174; in Sub-Saharan Africa, 29
Wambugu, A., 128
Warimeh, O. A., 215
Warner, Andrew M., 17, 18
Welfare Monitoring Survey (WMS), 132
West Africa, manufacturing sector in, 21. *See also specific countries*
Women: educational attainment of, 133–34; in Ghana, 86–87; in Kenya, 133–34; labor force participation by, 46, 56, 60–61, 233; in Nigeria, 213; in South Africa, 233, 252, 259
Woolard, I., 259
World Bank: Country Policy and Institutional Assessment, 113; Ease of Doing Business index, 24–25, 242, 244; economic development programs in Mozambique, 149; on economic growth in Nigeria, 194, 217; on population growth in Kenya, 119; on poverty reduction in Nigeria, 184; on price controls in Mozambique, 151; Structural Adjustment Program, 65
World Economic Forum, 194

Youth: in Ethiopia, 50–51; in Ghana, 86; in Kenya, 118, 120, 137–38; and labor market, 14; in Nigeria, 14, 192, 218

Zimbabwe: education sector in, 244; and transport networks, 148